The Poet's Guide
to
Food, Drink, & Desire

The Poet's Guide

to

Food, Drink, & Desire

•

A COOKBOOK-MEMOIR, OF SORTS

GAYLORD BREWER

Illustrations by James Dankert

For more information:
Stephen F. Austin State University Press
P.O. Box 13007 SFA Station
Nacogdoches, Texas 75962
sfapress@sfasu.edu
www.sfasu.edu/sfapress

Cover Artwork: *A Florentine Fruit Stall*, c. 1777, Johan Zoffany (1733-1810)
Photo Credit: @ Tate, London 2015
Back Cover Photo: Trevor Amery
Book design: Teri Klauser

Distributed by Texas A&M Consortium
www.tamupress.com

LIBRARY OF CONGRESS CATALOGING-IN-PUBLICATION DATA

Brewer, Gaylord
The Poet's Guide to Food, Drink, & Desire / Gaylord Brewer

p.cm.

ISBN: 978-1-62288-065-2

In memory of
King Henry I
1068/69-1135
who died from eating "a surfeit of lampreys"
(as recorded by Henry of Huntingdon).

Across cobblestones,
stalls high with summer's first
temptings—cherries, peas in shell,
strawberries, lettuce, stalks of scallion,

small, dark potatoes—their cost
writ large. What appetite you had
in your time . . .

> —*from* "Ghost Visits the Quay
> in Tampere, Eats Blood Sausage"

They are grateful, though,
alive and blessed, and know it
and speak it. Sausages in an iron pot
sweet with honey and curry;
onions roasted whole, black skin
sticky on fingers; bread;
a copa of wine.

> —*from* "Found Map of Spain"

All day we couldn't help ourselves:
Battle of Brussels Sprouts,
Cranberry Crusade, the Great
Eggnog Debacle. Over and again . . .

> —*from* "Apologia for a Thanksgiving
> Pissed Away"

The sad etiquette of solitude, however,
what conversation may follow,
these require an artistry not considered here
so remain your own concern. *Bon appetit.*

> —*from* "Why Eating Alone Is Fortunate"

CONTENTS

"The Secret Project"; or, Dinner *à Deux*

And now, places determined,
candles lit, your song low and luminous. Perhaps love's
on wing, perhaps October breezes blow just right.
Perhaps in any case the world's yours, time's now—
to extend a chair to your partner in life, to sit at last . . .

—*from* "Apologia for Cooking"

I recently enjoyed a shameful moment of decadence that I can't wait to confess to you. I was wrapping small squares of foie gras into pairs for the freezer and there was—I swear—an errant piece. I cut off an edge to nibble, which induced a full-blown flashback of a small restaurant (Cabanoix et Châtaigne) in Domme, in the Périgord Region of France, that we stumbled upon years ago that specialized in foie gras, including serving it raw. This latter idea was new to me, and I've not seen it served raw since. Suddenly, moving of their own volition as if in a Peter Lorre horror film, my hands sliced the cube of liver into six slivers, arranged them on a small plate, dusted them with truffle salt, placed two water crackers above the thin slices, and retrieved a round-edged spread knife. I ate the slices out on the front porch. Each was luxurious—a dizzying, heavenly guilt. Luckily no one was there to witness except my dog, a beautiful American Eskimo, and Lucy tells no tales as long as she's included in the culinary action. I can virtually guarantee it was her first experience of foie gras in any form, and she concurred with my review. (Apropos of the term foie gras throughout this book, I decided not to italicize, as it's a phrase common to the author's vocabulary, close to his heart, and not foreign in the least.)

What was the genesis of this quirky volume? Several forces and events aligned in ways I didn't foresee. I was between books of poetry, meaning my eighth collection, *Give Over, Graymalkin*, had been released early in 2011 and so was still a reasonably new release. I had another full-length collection, or at least a plausible version of such, completed, and therefore several months— "between the heaves of storm," as Emily Dickinson might have it—susceptible to undertaking something different. I quit writing academic criticism many happy years ago, but on scattered occasions have undertaken less stuffy, more congenial prose (viz., a foreword to Michael Gray Baughan's biography of Charles Bukowski, more recently several long interviews in promotion of the aforementioned book of poems) that I enjoyed, and I was intrigued by the notion of something more sustained. But what? At the same time, I noticed I was cooking more often and more elaborately, increasingly brushing up against various (famous and infamous) foodies (inter alia: the Southern Foodways Alliance at Ole Miss; the lovely and lively literary journal *Alimentum*, which had surreptitiously relocated its editorial towers from New York to down the street in Nashville; meeting a few chefs I admired; an on-going subscription to *Saveur*; et cetera).

For a long time, food had been increasingly creeping into my poetry, and cooking and excessiveness constituted themes in my 2008 comic novella *Octavius the 1ˢᵗ*. Sometime in mid-2011 I was asked to submit a sort of anecdotal recipe to what would be a compilation of like-minded entries, all by poets. (The journal *River Styx* produced something similar in their double issue numbers 76/77, "A Readable Feast." I contributed a poem to the issue as well as a recipe in prose—an abbreviated version of rabbit salmorejo, *vide* Chapter 7.) I was attracted to the idea, and the peculiar crossing of genres—poems and recipes?—no longer seemed especially odd to me, but I got busy and missed the deadline, then also missed the editor's kindly offered extension. I speculate now whether I did so with unconscious intent, that perhaps something bigger was brewing and had been for a long while.

Shortly after the second deadline for the poetry/recipe anthology passed, somewhere out of the events above, out of the air (and, curiously, the day after Thanksgiving, when I'd prepared multiple—too many—dishes for two), I started writing this book—writing it rather furiously, largely at the cost of other commitments, and top secret to everyone except my wife. (I realized early on that she'd need some explanations—e.g., why I had baked four cakes in succession, or why we were eating quail night after night [after night].) A journal editor would e-mail requesting a submission of poetry. "Thanks, sorry, no poems at the moment," would be my cryptic response, not, "Impossible, I'm 'braising' this week!" because a) I wasn't at all certain that the "secret project" would get finished or would gel if it did, and b) I have accrued over 25 years at least a modicum of "street cred" in the literary community. I could hear the head-shaking recriminations: "Brewer's writing a *cookbook*?! I *told* you he was losing hold."

The opening chapters, with their obsessive emphasis on duck, seemed the natural place to begin—one working title for the book, which I had to be talked out of with some tough love, was *Duck, Duck, Muse*—and, as I wrote, other ideas and approaches announced themselves until the rough shape of the whole animal was in place. (*Vide* Afterword for a brief résumé of what didn't make the menu.) From the beginning, elements of romance and sensuality seemed a good and necessary fit, and the complementary emphasis on dinner *à deux* fell into place early. One curious detour was a brief flirtation with concocting the book as a novel (somewhere south of *Chocolat* in tone, perhaps, although not as wickedly dark as John Lanchester's *The Debt to Pleasure*). I liked the idea in a vague way, both aesthetically as a genre bender and also as a practical way to sell some books, but after a few pages of notes the conceit sounded more and more strained, and I gave it up. Ironically, the book you hold resulted not only in not being fiction, but indeed became to my mind possibly the most personal book I've written, a memoir of sorts, albeit a fragmented one with a preoccupation with freshly ground black pepper. (All citations of poetry in these chapters, excepting a handful of clearly cited in-text references, are cribbed from various books of mine and remain solely the blame of the self-cannibalizing author. *Vide* Food & Literary Sources for specifics and a few more far-reaching culinary/literary suggestions.)

As I elaborate throughout the following text, I've always considered recipes as "good suggestions to consider," happily adapting someone's tour de force according to whim, taste, and what was in the pantry. What surprised me a bit, however, was the challenge of working back in the other direction: cf., a daunting, and sometimes frustrating, chasm between "mucking around in the kitchen to amuse oneself" and actually fixing a recipe to tested, precise specifics that produce a consistent result. Like me, you've probably been repeatedly duped by others' recipes that simply didn't work, recipes that are far too often astoundingly wrong, and have felt manipulated, lied to, and just generally perplexed by the carelessness.

I was also struck again by the amazing unreliability of even the most assured memory: I would write out the specifics and quantities, et cetera, of a recipe I "knew by heart" and had prepared many times, then sit back and begin to eye it skeptically. Finally, damn it, I'd have to stop faking, tie on my lucky Three Stooges apron—bearing the famous still of the boys stuffing a turkey—and start cooking like I knew I should (*vide supra*, feckless recipes that don't bloody work). Inevitably, an ingredient would be missing or out of proportion, some included step pointless or even harmful, and my previous suspicions were justified. The dish, if prepared as written, would have fallen flat. Sometimes, everything was just about right but I lucked upon an improvement.

Not quite Eliot's "Between the idea / And the reality / . . . Falls the Shadow," but sufficiently humbling to the upstart cookbook author. No surprise either, I'm sure, to anyone who's tried to conscientiously, accurately, and clearly write recipes, but it was an intriguing learning curve for this aspirant.

·

> Where we collected like hungry magpies
> chèvre, niçoise and lemon olives,
> saucisson, bread and cherries and wine.
>
> —*from* "Ode to a Paring Knife"

So I worked on this book in Tennessee—both in the kitchen and at the writing table—through the late fall of 2011, then on through the holidays and winter and the spring as it unfolded and the days again slowly lengthened. As I write this foreword, I finish a complete draft of the book—a rough-edged one—just days before I leave for France for a month's writing residency at the Camac Centre d'Art 30 miles outside Paris. It's May, so strawberries and asparagus will be in season, then later in the month the cherries will darken. *Fraise, asperge, cerise.* Lovely syllables in the mouth, and I look forward to eating every day what's fresh and local. (Plus, I'm having dinner cooked for me for a full month. Delightful. I hope the cook goes to a lot of unnecessary trouble.) I haven't been to France, a country I adore (and the pages that follow testify to that affection) for four years. After a month of trying my luck at writing poems, interacting with a new group of artists and oddballs, and perhaps seeking out friends, I'll head south to meet my wife for two weeks of hiking and r & r in the Périgord (first the hiking, then the r & r).

On the latter agenda? The fat, luscious prunes of Agen. The famous Sarlat foie gras market and a fresh and crusty croissant *amande* to whet the buying appetite as one strolls the stands. A *degustation*, or two, of Armagnac from some small producer whose battered and poorly marked *vente directe* signs we have followed far too long down a tortuously twisting road. *Santé* to d'Artagnan and Dumas, to the bastides, to the glowing light, to the rolling fields of vines and, now and then, perhaps sunflowers. Cheers to us and our good fortune. And, oh yes, perhaps a sojourn to Domme in hope of finding Cabanoix et Châtaigne, with the chalked menu of the day's offerings and the lovely young women scurrying from table to table with the toasters for your bread.

(Postscript: We found the restaurant, and although the chalkboard has been replaced by a slick printed menu, the toasters are now largely ceremonial—an homage to the past by the excellent new management—and the décor is generally upgraded, the meal and surfeit were absurdly sublime. My tile of slate, as those around watched on, contained 4 thick slabs of foie gras: a) *grillé* with spices and sea salt; b) *cru en carpaccio* with salts of the world; c) *poché* with a caramel of spices and Bergerac wine; and d) *torchon*, macerated in Armagnac with *mélange du trappeur* [maple syrup evaporated to grains of sugar, I believe, blended with garlic, pepper, coriander, et cetera]. Lovely excess.)

Don't worry. I'll be back in Tennessee, at our log house in the postage-stamp patch of woods yet unspoiled, in late June—in time to admire and count the last of our Virginia Peck daylilies—and for the duration of summer. Murfreesboro's new farmers market on the city square will be in full force on Saturdays, and we'll brace ourselves for small, black watermelons and heirloom tomatoes; for sweet corn, green onions, peas, and purple hull beans; for the organic golden beets I'm addicted to and honey from bees feasted on what few cotton fields remain; for the prize-winning country ham ("Grand Champion," Tennessee State Fair) cured down the street at the Hamery for the past forty years; for the grilling season of fresh trout and wild salmon finally running again; as summer cedes to autumn for squashes and apples and fresh-pressed cider; and for a few surprises.

Drinks and appetizers at 5:00 are our sacrament. Dinner, in the summer, around 7:30, out on the deck with candles if it's not too hot, then coffee, maybe Cognac or port, and into the yard to call in the screech owls and their young—if they haven't already called to us—at just that ripe moment of twilight. Come early, if you like. We'll use those shallots if they're firm, and someone needs to chop that chiffonade of basil and thyme from the garden. Show me how it's done. Just promise to arrive hungry, thirsty, and desirous.

Then come on in.

CHAPTER 1

.

Duck Part I: A Beak-to-Feathered-Tail Feast

A duck is love. No part of it should be wasted or unappreciated. Here's a festive multi-course meal for a birthday or anniversary. Like all other recipes in this book, unless otherwise specified, it feeds two. (Or one or three—you'll get the hang of our modus operandi.) Cumulatively, it's a bit of work, but you can parse out the steps: Cut up the duck, make the pâté, and do most of the prep earlier in the day or the day before, then appear impressively confident and at ease during cooking and assembly. Sure. Ready?

Butchering the Duck. Get out two medium-sized bowls—one for the good parts and one for the nasty bits (i.e., still tasty trim). On the cutting board, with a mid-size knife and a sharp set of cooking shears, take your time. This part's important. First, of course, empty the cavity of the bird of the neck, liver, gizzard, and heart. The neck is trim. The rest is good stuff. If your duck has been violated by a plastic pouch of gelatinous substance advertised as "orange glaze," discard said pouch with disdain. Cut away any large flaps of skin and fat—around the neck, for instance—and, of course, retain.

Clip off the wings, then cut each into three parts: wing tip (discard), mid-joint, and drumette. Next, remove each leg, being careful to keep the thigh as whole as possible and cutting minimally into the flesh. Use the knife. Use your fingers. It takes some patience to find the joints on a nice fat duck. Again, take your time. Leave the legs whole. Do not separate thighs from drumsticks. Scissor off any excessive fat around the edges, but don't go crazy. Of course, keep all trimmed fat.

The easiest next step is just to go ahead and cut off the entire back with the shears and add to trim. Place the double breast flat down on the board and, using your large butcher knife and your best eye and judgment, slice into equal halves. One half at a time, feel your way along, clipping off all bone and any remaining slivers of cartilage while being gentle with the flesh. Trim off any obvious excesses of fat, but again, don't get puritanical.

Wrap and secure your lovely, boneless breasts appropriately and freeze for later use, either to grill or to cure in the garage (*vide* Chapter 2).

Finally, take the choicest selections of fatty skin (meaning, nearly all of it) and slice or scissor these into ¼" strips. They needn't be exact or pretty, just a lovely handful of white goo. Add these to the good parts.

Baking the Trim. You could attempt to make a stock with the bits and pieces, but I wouldn't bother. Anyway, with the trim of just one duck, the effort's probably not worth the result even if you're a stock fanatic. Instead, simply toss the back, neck, odd bits of bone and fat, gizzard and heart, lightly salted, into a baking dish and cook at 350° F until the kitchen smells good and everything looks cooked, maybe an hour. Allow to partly cool. Retain the gizzard and heart for the salad.

When the bits have cooled just enough to handle, clean the bones, eating some of the crispy skin as reward for your fortitude and chopping up the striations of back and neck meat for the dog, who will be quivering and making an odd moaning sound somewhere close beside or behind you. (Alternately, you could toss bits of chopped meat into the pâté, suggesting rillettes.)

> The older man approaches, one hand protecting
> a prime piece of the animal, the center of ham,
> the tip of loin, the heart or liver of bird. The son
> bends forward, takes the offering into his mouth.
>
> He tastes briefly the other's fingers, greasy with fat,
> then leans away eating, let's say, the heart.
> The young man chews, slowly, the salty vital
> as the older man returns to his carving.
> They relish this, the rare part, while they can.
>
> —*from* "Before the Welcoming Dinner"

Pâté

1 plump duck liver

1 large shallot

3-4 sprigs fresh thyme

4 Tbs. unsalted butter, softened

2 Tbs. brandy

coarse sea salt & freshly ground black pepper

Sauté the diced shallot in 1 Tbs. of butter (and, if inclined, a splash of olive oil) over medium heat. Try not to brown the shallot as it softens. Add the liver, a generous pinch of salt, and several grinds of pepper. (Resist adding the blood that will have accumulated in your bowl, however tempting. It will make your pâté too thin. You might sauté, salt, and eat the curdled blood separately, hot, with your fingers, while you wait for the liver to cook.) Cook the liver over low-medium heat until just pink inside. Don't overcook it. Remove liver. Add the brandy and roughly chopped thyme to the skillet and cook until most of the liquid is reduced. Add liver and skillet ingredients to a mini-chopper. Add half of the chunked, softened butter. Purée. Add the rest of the butter, salt and ground pepper to taste. Purée for several seconds. Don't worry if the consistency is a little rough. Taste is what matters. Transfer to a ramekin and refrigerate until firm.

Again, don't despair if the chilled pâté is a bit softer than you'd hoped. Redemption's in that first spread cracker. (It's fine to serve this with simple water crackers and not fuss over fresh bread. In fact, water crackers are better. They give a nice crunch and fit more easily and attractively on your assembled platter.)

N.b.: Regarding the butter, stay calm. It's a special occasion, remember? The more butter you add the better the pâté gets, and if your duck's liver is a goodly size, you might add up to an entire stick. Why not? You're going to lie about it later, anyway, if your companion inquires.

Bonus Alternative Recipe:
Deviled Duck Liver on Sautéed Rounds of Apple

The pâté is one of my favorite elements of this multi-course duck meal: It adds texture, is luxurious, and can and should be made a day ahead. If for whatever reason, however, you can't be bothered, or if the thought of all that butter truly daunts you (in which case, you may find this book a tough read), here's another option for the bird's liver, not as good but interesting. I rather liked the spiciness and curious mix of tastes here, and I believe if you're attracted to the ingredients you will too. It's also an oddly attractive dish. My taster was less enthusiastic, but who asked her? Well . . .

1 plump duck liver

1 tsp. ketchup

1 tsp. Worcestershire sauce

½ tsp. dry mustard

3-4 shakes Tabasco sauce

pinch cayenne powder

pinch sea salt & 3-4 grinds black pepper

1 Granny Smith apple

½ tsp. confit oil*, olive oil, unsalted butter, or duck fat

Prepare the sauce by mixing the ketchup, Worcestershire, dry mustard, Tabasco, cayenne powder, and salt and pepper in a small bowl. You'll want it with a fair kick of heat. Set aside.

Slice 2 ¼" rings from near the middle of the apple, peel with a paring knife, and core sufficiently to remove seeds and any tough membrane. In a small skillet, heat ¼ tsp. of the fat, oil, or butter (**vide* Chapter 2 re. the confit oil), and brown the apple slices until softened but not mushy, about 3 minutes on each side. Place on a plate in a 190° F oven to keep warm. Add the additional ¼ tsp. of oil, fat, or unsalted butter to the medium skillet and sauté the liver, divided into 2 equal pieces, for 2 minutes on each side. Pour the "devil" sauce over the liver, turning the liver with a spatula to coat, and continue cooking for 1 minute more on each side. Serve the liver over the browned apple wafers.

Roasted Duck Legs with Honey & Balsamic Vinegar

2 duck legs

2 Tbs. honey

2 Tbs. balsamic vinegar

1½ Tbs. soy sauce

2 scallions, chopped

2 cloves garlic, diced

coarse sea salt & generous grind black pepper

Mix all ingredients together and pour half into a small dish or Tupperware. Add the legs, skin side down, cover with the rest of the marinade and refrigerate for 2 hours, turning once. (I'd be wary of leaving them overnight, with all that sodium in the soy). Once you've assembled this easy glaze and the legs have marinated, the rest—the actual cooking—is simple. Just don't forget to time this in conjunction with the other courses.

Place the duck legs, skin side up, on a wire rack over a baking dish containing an inch of water (otherwise, the dripping marinade will burn on the dish and make a royal mess and nearly impossible cleanup). Reserve the remaining marinade. Bake legs at 350° F for 90 minutes, turning once and brushing with marinade midway through, then turning skin side up again for the last 10 minutes and brushing with whatever marinade remains.

Duck Cracklings and Rendered Fat. Once the legs are in the oven, spread out the strips of fatty skin in a small-medium baking dish. Broil these on high in the top oven. (You do have a double oven, right? You need one.) Keep an eye on them, and once or twice pour off the fat (to be preserved) in a bowl and turn the strips with a fork. After about 15-20 minutes (but for god's sake don't burn them!), when crispy and brown, drain the cracklings on a towel and salt them. Sample one to make sure it's right. Sample a second while they're hot and you've time to reflect on the proper order of the world.

Seal the fat in glass and chill. White and beautiful, this will last for several weeks in the fridge or forever in the freezer and is ideal for sautéing, basting a chicken, or just generally as a replacement or complement—when no one's looking—to cooking with butter.

Mustard-Breaded Duck Wings

2 duck wings divided at the joint (tips discarded)

Dijon mustard

seasoned breadcrumbs

Brush the drumettes and mid-joints with Dijon mustard then roll them in seasoned breadcrumbs. These cook quickly, about 30 minutes at 400° F, so plan accordingly to bake in the small oven and finish at approximately the same time as the thighs. No need to turn them. You want them crispy on top.

Gizzard Crackling Salad

How can these words, uttered together, not melt the heart of even the most dyspeptic Francophobe and force a secret smile? (One summer, in the quack-crazed region of Quercy-Périgord, I indulged in my famous "duck diet," eating the fowl for 35 consecutive days in its myriad forms and presentations—albeit "merely" a mousse or local slice of foie gras for a couple of those days. The experiment constituted a breakthrough in the science of health and nutrition. I never felt better, although walking several miles each morning is recommended. Any irregular heart palpitations merely indicated the body's appreciation.)

For an easy and tasty corruption of the regionally popular Quercynoise salad, take a mix of fresh greens, preferably containing some frisée, and mix it with a touch of dressing, something light with a bit of sweetness (pears? citrus?). (No olive oil, please. We're loaded for bear already.) Top with the warmed, diced gizzard and heart and with the cracklings, *vide ante. Voilà!*

Assembly and Presentation. Light the candles. Open another bottle of whatever robust and fruity red you're drinking. Turn on, at a subdued volume, Tony Bennett (or if you can't help yourself, fine, Madeleine Peyroux/Norah Jones). On a large and decorative serving platter—I like one that's powder-blue and reminiscent of the sky—attractively and symmetrically arrange your salad, legs, wings, and pâté and crackers (and a few cornichons if you have them).

Summon your companion and pull out the chair with a flourish. Once seated, pause a moment, staring modestly into your glass, to allow the *oohs* and *aahs* of tribute. A romantic toast is optional, but remember that the bird's getting cold.

Tuck in. Thank me later.

CHAPTER 2

•

Duck Part II: Fowl Holidays

The connective tissue, method to the madness, listen:
By day three we had carved the holiday carcass to bone,
shred and tendon. No one moved from the table.

—*from* "Apologia for a Frozen Surplus"

   I encourage you to eat duck year round, but, admittedly, there is something festive during the holiday season about lifting a steaming and beautifully browned whole duck from the oven or wrestling its parts into any of their many transcendent configurations. In other words, duck and the holidays go together like Tiny and Tim. Here are two fun courses that use the whole bird and also make sense to prepare in the winter. The leg confit is filling and comforting; the cured breasts require a cool, dry place to hang.

4:11 a.m. I can assure you is no time for indulgence,
for silliness, to rethink life's bargain.
It is the moment, instead, glasses askew,
to lift each thigh from overnight caress
of garlic, fresh bay leaf, home-harvested thyme,
to massage flesh under cold water
with priestly certainty, free all excess of salt,
lay each upon its pallet of skin and fat.

. . . four cups of green virgin, first press,
sampled from drowsy fingertips to drowsy lips.

14 hours remain between toil and ascendance.

—*from* "Duck Confit"

Duck Confit

4 whole duck legs

8 sprigs fresh thyme

12 cloves garlic

4 bay leaves

black peppercorns

coarse sea salt & freshly ground black pepper

1 qt. extra virgin olive oil

Buy two ducks. You're already going to the expense and bother, and preparing two birds takes little more effort than one. Your beloved will be grateful if you do, resentful if you don't. Thaw thoroughly. (Dissecting a half-frozen bird is ice-burn torture for the hands.) As detailed in Chapter 1, carefully remove the entire legs and remove, split, and thoroughly debone the breasts. Wrap the breasts and set aside to cure, *vide infra*. Set aside or freeze the giblets and a handful of fatty skin for some other purpose (*vide* Chapter 1 —Quercynoise salad, or just broiling, salting, and noshing for research). For this recipe, I'd recommend you don't discard anything except perhaps excessive additional fat.

Place all of the trim and odd bits of fat and bone (there'll be some more meat there, on the wings and on the back and neck, so why waste any?) in a large dish. Place 2 legs, skin side down, on top of everything and sprinkle with 1 Tbs. of coarse salt and several grinds of pepper. (A note on numbers 1-10: for ease of reading, I've gone against custom and—perhaps unwisely—used numerals in the following situations: lists of ingredients, ingredients in the text, and food cooking and preparation times. In other instances, I've opted for the standard use of the word—i.e., "one" vs. "1." Many judgment calls were required, causing in more than one instance an eccentric result. There *was* an attempted method to the madness, I promise, and I beg the reader's forbearance.) Nestle the garlic cloves into the flesh, then cover with the thyme and bay leaves. (If you're doing this recipe as late in the year as November, depending on the season's weather and where you live, the thyme in your garden is probably well past its prime. I stubbornly persisted for years in using my anemic, thin, largely tasteless homegrown sprigs and have only recently given up. Buy thyme at the store that is dark green, thickly leaved, and smells heavenly, just like, um . . . thyme. It's a hell of a lot easier to clean, too. Next spring, you can re-pledge fealty to your own patch.) Place the remaining 2 legs flesh down over the others and sprinkle everything with ½ tsp. of coarse salt. Cover or wrap tightly in plastic wrap and refrigerate for 12 hours.

With your hands, brush the legs free of thyme, bay leaves, and garlic cloves (retaining everything), then rinse the legs just a bit under cool water. Let them dry on paper towels for a few minutes as you transfer everything—trim of neck, back, and wings; thyme, cloves, bay leaves—into a large ovenware dish. (I use an unusually deep steel pan—designed for an enormous lasagna, I believe—with convenient handles. Whatever your choice, the vessel needs to be deep and broad enough for everything to be immersed in the olive oil but, obviously, small enough to fit in the oven.) Add the legs, skin side down, and cover all with the olive oil. (I've seen it recommended that extra virgin oil is not only unnecessary but inappropriate for this recipe and cooking in general, but don't you believe it, gentle reader. You're buying the least expensive quart of oil you can get, anyway, so the cost is about the same. Go for the dark, sexy extra virgin.)

Cook for 12 hours at 200° F. (In the spirit of full disclosure I feel compelled to confess that the first several times I made confit, I set my alarm clock and got out of bed at 4:00 a.m. in order to have the dish in the oven and ready for that evening's dinner. Bleary-eyed in the middle of the night, handling fat and animal parts, is not particularly a spiritual or secular pleasure. At some point, as I was telling this tale of woe and sacrifice, someone asked—a student of mine, to add to my chagrin, and one who knew nothing about cooking—"Why don't you just put it in the oven *before you go to bed?*" [Italics mine.] Long pause from the professor. Huh. Well, I suppose the novice *could* go that way . . .)

Put in the oven before you go to bed and cook for 12 hours. In the morning, after the pan has cooled, remove the legs from the oil and place them in a stoneware dish with a lid. I like to debone the legs first, leaving large chunks of confit. A full leg makes a nice entrée, if that's your preference, but you'll find it goes further deboned. Pick the bits of meat from the trim and add these to the crock. Strain the oil/fat and pour over the meat until completely covered. (If you choose to save some of the additional oil/fat—and of course you will—it's an indulgent delight for vegetable sautés, smeared on warm bread, or wherever imagination leads.) Cover confit with the stoneware lid and congratulate yourself for your care, diligence, and discipline in pleasure deferred.

Eating/Serving Confit. I've been told the confit will last one month or longer in the refrigerator, although in my house we've never come even close to testing that expiration date. My estimation is that approximately 50% of your confit, tops, will ever make it onto the plate, and 50% will mysteriously vanish on non-existent forks and fingers—"the devil's portion." (Re. this mysterious vanishing, the "eating standing up, so zero calories" rule is definitely in play, especially late at night, in the exposing glow of the open fridge door, recovering from a particularly harsh and unforgiving dream.) Otherwise, does anyone really need to be instructed in how to eat duck confit? It's exquisite as an entrée or shred over a salad or pappardelle, heated, room temperature, or cold.

One dish I like is (very) loosely based on something served to me in Portugal years ago. We might as well call it *arroz con pato*. Cover the bottom of a circular *cazuela* with shredded confit. (*Cazuelas* are the common clay baking dishes from Spain—you'll recognize the large variety, earth-hued, steaming with shrimp and shellfish and saffron rice, used to serve paella. They're inexpensive, attractive, adaptable to cooking styles, and come in many sizes. The Portuguese equivalent, fired terra cotta, auburn and without adornment, is also common. Caveat: These dishes are prone to chipping, which you'll just have to get over. Consider the chips well-earned, the dings and medals of service. Anyway, use what you have that's similar.) Cover with a smoothed layer of prepared rice with some body, preferably white. Basmati works. Heat in the oven. Everything's already cooked, so oven time is only a few minutes. Before serving, cover the rice with a handful of shredded, pungent, hard cheese. Whatever Reggiano you keep on hand is good enough. Broil for 2-3 minutes, until cheese is melted and the top of the rice is beginning to crisp. Serve hot with a Tempranillo or something from Portugal's overlooked Alentejo region (or if you're feeling whimsical, sure, a Vinho Verde—who's going to stop you?), a green salad if conscience demands, and a warm loaf of fresh bread for sopping. You'll want every drop on the bottom. Ideally, serve in individual *cazuelas*, to eliminate any irritating notion of sharing.

You'll go to bed a bit dizzy and confused, but happy.

The ribbon
of fat thick and white, brined flesh
an indulgent perfection. I lick fingers
clean of this wildly expensive grease
then ruin them for another bite,

teeth cutting easily the encasing crust,
rending meat delicately into strips.

—*from* "The Black Pigs"

Cured Duck Breast Prosciutto

2 duck breasts, deboned & trimmed

1 tsp. coriander seeds

20 juniper berries

20 whole black (or mixed) peppercorns

3 cloves garlic

2 bay leaves, dried from your garden

2 Tbs. coarse salt

The Great Breast Debate. You've heard the arguments of former kith and estranged kin, the angry reproaches across the table: Only the breast of the Moulard (e.g., mullard) duck (the cross, I believe, of a Muscovy drake and a Pekin hen, if you want to impress/torment/disgust your friends) is large enough to cure properly in this recipe or any other. Granted, the Moulard breast is enormous and lovely and would cure ideally (and also, grilled, is ample for two) if you can find one and afford it, but the humble Pekin breasts that you cleaned and trimmed prior to making confit or froze during prep for your multi-course duck feast (*vide* Chapter 1) will work, although perhaps with a result marginally not quite as splendid (meaty and tender). Everyone's going to be impressed, anyway, and eat every slice you're gullible and tipsy enough to put on the table. Buy the largest duck you can get at the grocer. (This is just common sense, anyway—the larger the bird, the more of everything you love.)

Crush the coriander, juniper, and peppercorns in a mortar and pestle (or in a pinch, under a heavy pan or skillet—but you need to invest in a serviceable mortar and pestle; mine's marble). Crush the garlic cloves. (The edge of a broad knife will suffice.) Chop the bay leaves. Combine all with the salt. Massage half the mixture into the flesh side of the breasts, place both flesh down in a shallow dish just large enough to hold them side by side, and massage the remainder of the rub into the skin. Cover tightly with plastic wrap and refrigerate overnight, preferably 24 hours. Pat each breast dry with a paper towel and roll snugly in a clean dish towel. Tie just above and below each breast with string, leaving the top string one foot long on each side. Tie these loose ends into another knot and carry your cool packages—both firm and yielding in your trembling hands—to the garage and the two nails you've earlier hammered into a prominent position approximately 7'-8' above the floor (explained below) and out of direct sunlight. (If you're using heavy staples instead, leave the top strings untied until you loop an end through the staple.) Hang your two plump beauties by the top-string knots. Stand back and beam like a deluded father or deranged gastro-scientist.

A cool, detached garage is ideal, and within a day or two the breasts will "gift" you with an intoxicating savory-salty-bacony-duck smell—an aroma such as to supply excellent karma for the day ahead while also teasing of future reward—each time you approach the car. I suppose a shed or other outbuilding would work as well, assuming it's critter-free, although you'll sacrifice the smell. (I don't know for certain that a squirrel or possum or raccoon or mouse or other furry and devious et cetera would help herself, but I'm betting yes. It's a tragic possibility we've no intention of tempting or testing.) A cellar would work, of course, or a basement or attached garage if kept cool. Better, though, to build a detached garage, *vide infra*.

Let hang—undisturbed except for an occasional and perfectly acceptable fondling—for two weeks. For Pekin breasts, you might shorten the time by a couple of days, based on their size and your instinct.

"Harvesting" and Serving the Prosciutto. The evening you're to serve your prosciutto, remember to conveniently "forget" to collect the breasts until after friends have arrived and drinks are poured. (The fact that an empty serving platter or chopping block is conspicuously situated on the table between a bowl of crackers, jars of coarse mustard and cornichons and olives, plates and napkins and hors d'oeuvres forks, is irrelevant. In fact, the transparency of the charade is an integral component of its personal reward.) After profuse apologies, and caught up in the celebratory and spontaneous emotion of the moment, insist with minimal explanation that everyone accompany you out into the cold, dim evening. As your guests shiver in the light of the garage's raised door, the winter night cruel at their backs, nonchalantly raise a supplicant hand to each breast (the 7'-high nails are solely for "heightened" dramatic effect) and sever the strings with a violent flash of the paring knife just sprung from your jacket pocket. Apologize again, this time for the suddenly silly impetuosity of coercing folks into the cold, and follow the initiates as they stumble back through the dark with their drinks. To serve, cut the knots and unwrap one breast (hide the other in the back of the fridge to guard against impulsive "over hosting"), wipe/scrape free all errant flakes of the rub, rinse briefly under cold water, dry with paper towels, and slice thinly crosswise. (Whether to leave the skin and its strip of fat on the slices is a judgment call, based on its relative tenderness/toughness and the pervading ethos of the crowd. Probably, not.) Spread the slices across the platter or block to optimize an illusion of generosity. Set on the table with a flourish.

CHAPTER 3

·

Duck Part III: Of Bondage & Blow Dryers

Sliced breasts one container,
torn dark another. Late bright
morning. Plate and goblet
stored and no print left of war.

—*from* "Another Friday Morning After,
More Silence from Adjoining Rooms"

You enter the kitchen to a sight unnatural and unnerving, a drama grotesque and, frankly, just plain wrong. The plucked carcass of a bird, legs obscenely spread, sways perilously at eye level above the sink by some Gordian snarl of crisscrossed string looped and levied through the joints and hinges of the adjacent cabinets. An eight-quart stockpot of water gurgles like a witch's cauldron. And in the middle of this carnage, your beloved—sweaty, sinister, nearly unrecognizable—is blow-drying a duck's ass.

Approach from behind and take him or her gently but firmly in your arms. Slowly, move your hand toward the hair dryer, loosen the grip, and still the infernal roar. Whisper that everything will be alright. Hold this lost soul, hold tightly until the shaking stops and pray, pray the intervention is in time. How did you look away so long that it came to this?

Peking Duck

1 6-lb. Pekin duck

½ cup honey

3 Tbs. sherry vinegar

3 Tbs. fresh ginger (grated)

1 tsp. five-spice or garam masala

sea salt & freshly ground black pepper

¼ cup sherry, port, or brandy

Mandarin pancakes or Chinese crêpes (recipes below)

2 batches scallions

1 cucumber (optional but recommended)

plum sauce (the good stuff, from an Asian market)

chili garlic sauce (also from your preferred Asian market)

Roasting the Duck. Consider this, *vide supra*: Submerge duck in rapidly boiling water for 1 minute. Hang to dry for 1 hour or, to speed process, blow-dry for 5 minutes. Repeat process 3 times more. Prepare glaze and let cool. Brush duck with glaze and let hang for 1 hour or, to speed process, blow-dry for 5 minutes. Repeat process 3 times more. Now you're *nearly* ready to roast!

Or this timeless classic: Insert air compressor, bicycle pump, or, if you can locate one, traditional bamboo tube between the skin and flesh of the duck. Slowly and carefully, begin to inflate . . . et cetera. *Hel*-lo.

Alternately: Discover the "simplicity" of steam-roasting . . .

Perhaps you might merely, in the morning, prick the duck all over with a fork, rub inside and out with coarse salt and let sit, uncovered, in the refrigerator until evening. Brush with (ridiculously elaborate and esoteric) marinade and leave, still uncovered, in the refrigerator overnight. When roasting, turn the duck every 15 minutes (each time pouring off the fat, smelling to gage whether said fat is "burned," and adding more broth to the roasting pan) to a succession of orchestrated temperatures. When time to baste . . .

Ad infinitum.

Obviously, if you have a Chinese restaurant nearby, one hygienic, friendly, competent in cooking, and conscientious in filling orders, the above techniques make take-out look extremely attractive. The "problem," of course, that all this madness attempts to address is the fatty nature of the commercial duck and how to render that fat during roasting to yield a moist flesh and, most importantly, the crispy skin that's the signature, the sine qua non, of Peking duck.

But allow me to let you in on a dirty little secret: Unless the Emperor is coming to dinner, a well-roasted duck, properly scored and cooked, the skin browned under a broiler at the end, free from the complexities of whips, chains, and industrial tools, will serve perfectly well for a more than serviceable home version of this perennial crowd-pleaser-*cum*-headache. Let's try the following deception/experiment and see if anyone at the table complains or whether fingers get licked clean.

Cut diagonal slashes across the skin of the breasts, thighs, and legs of the duck, then cross these perpendicularly with more slashes. Be careful not to cut too deeply and into the flesh. The whole idea here is to facilitate the rendering of fat during cooking.

In a saucepan, heat together the honey, sherry vinegar, ginger, spice, and sherry or port and reduce slightly. Let cool.

Salt and pepper duck inside and out, place breast up on a rack in a roasting pan, pour a cup of water into the pan, and slide into a cold oven. Set oven for 300° F and cook for 1 hour. Turn duck breast down, paint with honey marinade, and cook for 1 hour. Turn duck again, brush breasts with marinade, raise oven temperature to 350° F, and cook for another 1½ hours, brushing with marinade 2-3 more times. Test for doneness: The thigh meat should be tender and the leg easily separable. The skin should already be golden and shiny, but you might crisp it up under the broiler for 2 minutes or so. (Pay attention!) Set duck on carving board, tent with aluminum foil, and let it rest for 20 minutes as you prepare the serving condiments. Easy.

Keep an eye on the duck, the time, and the temperatures, and use your common sense. Depending on the size of the bird, the eccentricities of your oven, or the phase of the moon, the duck might, obviously, take more or less time at a slightly adjusted temperature. Accordingly, you may also adapt your technique according to your patience and how much time you want to devote, as the schemes sketched above clearly indicate. If the honey marinade feels like too much work, just use maple syrup (although you'll especially miss the ginger); if you don't care to undertake the bother/danger of (twice) turning a steaming-hot 6-lb. bird, then cook it breast up the whole time. It will turn out alright. If, on the other hand, the arcane chicanery of some of the above techniques appeals to you, I grant you permission to try a simplified version of our opening scenario: Slowly pour 4-6 quarts of boiling water in a thin stream over the duck until the skin is pearlescent. Pat the duck dry, rub inside and out with salt, pepper, and sherry, let sit uncovered in the refrigerator for several hours or overnight, then for Li Po's sake get *on* with it!

Postscript: I finally succumbed and contributed a few more shekels to the Ronco fortune (*vide* Chapter 12). Their 5000 Platinum Series Rotisserie— slightly larger than the traditional model—requires a monstrous amount of unimpeded counter space, but early reviews here are good. Bought primarily for ducks and rib roast, the machine cooks quickly, is mesmerizing to watch, and cleans up with moderate ease. The initial ducks have been attractively browned, tender, and moist. So far, it's a fun toy.

Preparing the Pancakes/Crêpes. Two options here. The more traditional and thicker pancakes are a bit more work and slightly trickier. They're also sturdier when rolled up, but be careful to make them sufficiently wide and not too thick (you don't want them coming out like heavy tortillas). After the first couple season the skillet, they'll start cooking/browning better.

Making the pancakes isn't overly arduous, but, when the time comes, bird warm on the counter, if you're suddenly impatient and salivating like a Pavlovian hound dog, you might opt for the crêpes, which are faster, easier, and nearly foolproof (well, you know . . .). They're more fragile than the pancakes during assembly, but Peking duck is a meal you devour mostly with your hands, so who minds if everything gets a little messy? Indeed, to the contrary.

Mandarin Pancakes

1½ cups all-purpose flour

½ cup boiling water

¼ tsp. salt

2 Tbs. cold spring water

sesame oil

In a bowl, mix together the flour, salt, and boiling water. Add the cold water. Shape the dough into a ball and knead until smooth. Roll dough into a 10" log, cover with a damp cloth or paper towel, and let rest 20 minutes if time allows. Divide log into 10 equal slices. On a lightly floured surface, roll the slices into 3" circles. Brush the tops of the circles with sesame oil, place them on top of each other into 5 pairs, oiled sides together. Roll each of the pairs into a 7"-8" circle, turning once or twice to assure both sides are rolled evenly.

In a dry skillet over medium heat, cook the circles 2-3 minutes on each side, until lightly browned and beginning to blister. Remove each to a plate and with your hands carefully separate the pancakes and stack them browned side up. Wrap in foil and, if not ready to serve immediately, place in a warm oven (190° F).

Chinese Crêpes

1 cup all-purpose flour

1½ cups spring water

2 large farm eggs

¼ tsp. salt

2 tsp. sesame oil

In a bowl, whisk together the flour, salt, eggs, and, slowly, the water. Add the sesame oil and whisk until relatively lump-free. Spray an 8" nonstick or cast-iron skillet with vegetable oil. Over medium heat, spoon in enough batter so that, as you tilt the skillet, it nearly covers the bottom at 6"-7". A bit less than ¼ cup of batter should be about right. Cook for 2-3 minutes until the crêpe begins to brown and curl, then with both hands lift it from the edge opposite you, flip, and cook for 1 more minute. As each comes out of the skillet, place in a warm oven on a cookie sheet covered with parchment paper. Don't stack them, as they will stick together. This recipe should make 14-16 crêpes, give or take; halve the recipe if you like, but bear in mind that a few may tear or stick. (For serving, loosely stack/arrange the crêpes on a plate or in a bread basket, wrapped in a cloth napkin. Just treat them tenderly.)

Preparing the Condiments and Carving the Duck. While the duck is roasting, clean and trim your scallions, leaving each about 7"-8" long (the diameter of a pancake). Preferably, use firm, small onions and leave them whole. If they're large and thick, slice each in half length-wise. If you're also including cucumber, peel and slice it into similarly sized spears, approximately ¼" x 7"-8." Place the scallions and cucumber sticks on a platter with bowls of plum sauce and chili garlic sauce.

Re. the duck: As close to the bone as you can, pull and cut around the carcass, removing the meat of the breasts and thighs. Debone legs and wings. Slice the meat into portions approximately 1" wide and 3"-4" long. Don't overly worry about exactness and don't bother separating the skin first (more folderol from the pedants). Serve the succulent flesh—perhaps accompanied by a few crispy broiled strips of additional skin/fat—warm on a platter with a little greenery.

Serving and Assembly (Viz., the Fun Part—Eating). Serve your platters of duck and condiments and your plate of pancakes/crêpes, along with chopsticks and a bowl of white or fried rice. (A cold bottle of plum wine is kitschy but fun, if you can handle the sweetness. Otherwise, a pot of hot tea, please sir.) To get the meal rolling, you'll probably have to demonstrate how it's done by the pros. Spoon up a perfunctory dollop of rice, then get to the business of the evening: Place a pancake or crêpe on your plate, smooth a ribbon of plum sauce down the middle, a thinner ribbon of chili garlic sauce beside this, then top with a scallion, a few sticks of thin cucumber, and 2-3 slices of meat (making sure you get your opening share of that glorious skin). Forget the elaborate origami folds. Roll everything snugly, pick up with your hands, and get after it. The time for gestures and errant talk has passed. Everybody's on his or her own, and the meek again inherit nothing.

One 6-lb. duck with the trimmings serves two, no more, without rancor and with negligible leftovers, and I'm not kidding. Don't let anyone tell you differently.

CHAPTER 4

·

Don't Try This at Home

The cotton of bread
weighted with thin slices of my hosts,
striated, beautiful, darker than the wine,
trimmed neatly but not excessively
by the Saturday porkmonger who wishes
for me always a good week.

—*from* "The Black Pigs"

Now, some random ruminations on foodstuffs—either through their rarity, expense, dubious quality, eccentricity, or the general tedium of their preparation—I advise you to leave in the hands of the professionals.

Snails

Even in the vastly improved and varied grocery counters of today, live snails are hard to come by to those of us land-locked and, worse, rural. In my experience, canned snails are not one of the joys of life. Viz.: I recently tried to replicate the Catalonian *cargols & conill i romesco* (snails and rabbit in romesco sauce), a dish I'd been cheated out of the opportunity of trying in Barcelona (don't ask). The first direction of your recipe will instruct something like, "Buy snails live and fast them for one week." Meanwhile, my little can was "all natural" (does anyone know what that was ever supposed to mean?) and "imported" (if, unfortunately, from Indonesia), so with the faith of the fool I proceeded to fail not-so-grandly with my black, rubbery, and oddly tasting little fellows, mutilating an evening and a nice big rabbit in the process. (Of course, I picked a night in the laboratory when I was home alone—"cooking for one"—so that, a] no one had to suffer my hubris, or b] would be allowed to witness my shame and ridicule my folly.) I'll spare you the unsavory details, but, ultimately, a garbage bag played significantly in the drama. Rabbit and snails also often feature prominently in paella Valenciana, so let's trash that, too, as a home possibility. Ah, Bartleby!

If you're fortunate enough to live where your seafood market is sufficiently superb to carry fresh, meaty snails, properly detoxed, then have at it, brothers and sisters, with my blessing and envy. Otherwise, order them on the odd occasion when they show up on a US menu—usually disguised in some puff pastry or whatnot—and wait until you get to Burgundy to indulge. There are two good, unassuming restaurants in Vézelay (you'll be obliged to go there anyway for the Basilique Sainte Marie-Madeleine) to savor a dozen—huge, tender, steaming in garlic butter in those charming, specially indented plates. (Try not to let the sudden flood of emotions interfere with your enjoyment.) They won't be cheap, but they're the best in the world.

(In high-end grocers, becoming more common are little aluminum foil trays of snails frozen in shell in butter sauce. You've seen them and wondered. I've tried two brands, one French and the other, as I recall, domestic, and both were surprisingly not bad. The snails were small but flavorful, and with a crusty roll and a tiny two-tined fork, the game was afoot and nothing went to waste. If you're really "snail jonesing," a cute little trayful, hot in 12-14 minutes, might offer some relief. Otherwise, don't bring'm to the door unless they can slither through on their own.)

Beef Carpaccio

Carpaccio is reported to have been invented at Harry's Bar in Venice in 1950—at the request of a countess instructed by her doctor to eat only raw meat—and named, due to its vivid crimson hues, after the painter Vittore Carpaccio. I offer this possibly spurious history as lagniappe. The fact that matters is that you and I love the stuff, which is easy to prepare and allows the home cook the theoretical chance for a splashy presentation. Carpaccio requires a sharp knife and a steady hand. Otherwise, it's a dish all about exquisite ingredients: absolutely fresh and top-quality beef tenderloin, Reggiano for shaving, the best olive oil or truffle oil (my preference) you can find. Toss on some arugula, coarse salt and freshly ground pepper, a few capers and a splash of lemon juice as you will, and layer/assemble artfully.

What could be better or simpler, right? Well, preparing carpaccio at home presents a few niggling—and related—problems. First, you obviously need a skillful and patient butcher, which I assume you have if you're serious about your kitchen. Even so, how much are you willing to test his good will? Will you have the temerity/audacity to request the dinky 8-oz. portion of tenderloin required, or, like me, are you more likely to leave the shop with an emptied wallet and a butcher-paper bundle of a pound or so? Similarly, what size wedge of Parmesan is practical and available, what size bottle of oil? (Granted, these last two items have many uses and aren't "on the clock" like the beef—which will last how long in the top grade and shape essential to the dish after being cut? Two days, maybe?) Such lovely ingredients are expensive— they're supposed to be—and costs will further escalate as you indulge that grandiose vision of carpaccio of elk, of buffalo, of venison, of Komodo dragon, of et cetera.

None of the expense matters (and perversely is even part of the enjoyment) *if* you can find someone to share your enthusiasm for a plate of raw red flesh, which in my home experience has been a challenge. (Suggestion: Ask on the Pre-Relationship Questionnaire.) Carpaccio is also, paradoxically, a rather delicate dish. You don't want too much, and then do you really want another platter tomorrow? (Tick-tick, tick-tock on the beef.) It's too dainty and absurd to prepare for yourself and, anyway—like sushi—no fun to eat alone. The less stressful and grudge-free approach—sigh—is to order carpaccio at restaurants when it too rarely appears, hope the ingredients are stellar and the preparation pure and unfussy (and good god, not seared—ask your server if you've *any* doubt).

Hey, I warned that my reservations were niggling. If you disagree with the trivial carping above, go ahead: Put all the good stuff on your Am Ex card, start slicing that organic buffalo tenderloin (don't partially freeze it first unless you just feel compelled to), and raise the carnivore's lonely bellow as you start plating. I'll be right over. Happy to oblige and doctor's orders. For the heart.

Sweetbreads

Unfortunately, the home cook may have even more trouble finding an enthusiastic companion for these creamy, tender delicacies than he or she did for the carpaccio. Add to this the rarity of seeing them for sale—it will probably take a special order to indulge this particular wrongheadedness— and you've another discouragement. The greatest hesitation, however, is the necessary removal of the membrane. I'm generally opposed—on grounds of philosophy and sanity—to ingredients that require double preparation. In the case of sweetbreads, moreover, the initial prep has the added benefit of being especially distasteful: Boil the sweetbreads until just cooked, then with fingers and edge of knife remove from the glands as much as possible of the membrane, gristle, bits of throat tubing, and miscellaneous raunchy animal bits. It's not difficult, per se, and sweetbreads are hard to overcook or ruin (don't worry if they come apart into good-sized pieces), but all the while you will be imagining the grimacing and dismissive face of your partner. And, ditto the carpaccio, do you really want to undertake this ordeal just for one?

Relatedly, let's extend the chapter's moratorium on home preparation to all odd and stray offal you might come across at the grocer (or along the roadside). That hunk of kidney may look dark and shiny, maddening with possibilities and seductive in its clinging wrap, but once home you'll commit yet more of your passing life and depleted emotional energy to an aching back, likely to end up with something edible only to the determined zealot or the simply bull-headed. Your Significant Other, meanwhile, pitying but less devoted to The Dream, is stirring up a bowl of tuna fish and noodles that really does smell pretty damned good.

Returning to the theme of our chapter: Order sweetbreads the once or twice each year they show up on a menu as an appetizer, hope they are lightly breaded and nicely pan-crisped, complemented with a restrained lemon-caper sauce rather than smothered and covered beyond recognition in some overbearing blah-blah-chile-*diablo* reduction or similar pretension, and try to enjoy the moment. It's all we have.

Otherwise, if you've an entrail-lovin' man or woman hungry in the next room, you lucky mutt, by all means boil those glands and start cleaning! In fact, while you're at it and inspiration hovers in the steamy air, the sweetbreads will pair obscenely well—oh mah *gawd!*—with that sultry sack of farm-fresh fava beans, which require of course a double shelling (from the pod, and then, either after parboiling or steaming, from the waxy shell on each individual bean) before cooking. Thus they constitute the rare triple preparation—the third being however you finish the dish—require a religious conviction, and are ideal for both your sweetbreads and your fervor. It'll be an afternoon of kitchen prep for the ages, but a scrumptious appetizer, I'm sure. Then you can begin the entrée.

> They are, of course, of infamous
> double preparation, that's their first
> advantage for you.
>
> Each thick pod torn at the seam
> between thumbs, each fat, bright bean
>
> a prize born of the hands' honest work.
>
> —*from* "More Honored in the Breach: Fava Beans"

Oysters on the Half Shell

If you're fortunate to live on a coast with a regular and reliable availability of fresh bivalve mollusks, then you may, I suppose, skip this section, although it would still behoove you to read on. If you're land-locked, with oysters an unpredictable arrival—season located somewhere between "now and then" and "whenever"—the attempt to enjoy these on the half-shell at home limits the inevitable failure to an impulsively purchased SLAGIATT ("seemed like a good idea at the time"). Out of the store you go, Styrofoam tray of iced bounty cradled purposefully under arm and afternoon sun. How impetuous you are, how adventuresome. Here's the sea's briny and ineluctable essence, the perfect, juvenating start to that heavy Thanksgiving menu or a cooling balm, complemented by a glass of champagne, to evening's warm spring sunset on the patio. Whatever. (For clarification: What the landlubber balances before him or her are not Bluepoints, Wellfleets, or Belons, Totten Inlets, Fanny Bays, or Kumamotos. This is Tennessee [or fill in the blank], and these are "oysters," identity unknown and unneeded, plain and simple and good enough. "An erster's an erster.")

Of course, you still don't own that oyster knife you vowed to buy last time this happened, but somehow, empowered by the right slant of light and the elation of your desire, *this* year that rusty dime-store paring knife (I mean, you're not going to use the Henckels) will pop those hinges with an easy insertion and amiable but sure twist of wrist. (Full disclosure: I briefly was a greeter/shucker at an experimental/prototype Red Lobster raw bar. Both bar and job were short-lived.)

The over-under in Vegas is that you might get *one* of the sandy little bastards open before you give up, wounded and cursing, but I wouldn't bet on it: the dull blade splintering repeatedly off the rock-hard surface, the vise-tight hinge unfazed in a craggy, mocking grin. Take my advice and throw in the proverbial (bloody) dish towel quickly: No need to prove a point, adding injury to mollusk insult, and hurt yourself sufficiently that ointments and elaborate bandaging are required. This will not make you look heroic, just even stupider. The spineless, brainless little sons of bitches have effortlessly defeated you again, without surrendering a drop of that precious fluid. Replace the twelve on fresh ice and return the leaky tray to where it again takes up half of the refrigerator. (You can grill the unholy dozen—*vide* Chapter 10—and try to salvage some pride tomorrow. Not today.) Announce that the champagne's cancelled. Nothing less than a perfectly constructed Martini is required (*vide* Chapter 22) to salve your throbbing, perforated hands and fill the hole where once your joy and confidence had been.

So, as per our pragmatic approach in this chapter, pay the king's ransom demanded at your local designer raw bar for a few of those Fanny Bays or whatnot the next time you absolutely have to have a fix, while, like any junkie, knowing full well that three or six will only jack your need. Then next Spring Break, forego the strip mall hells of Daytona and Panama City and drive straight for the quiet oysterly paradise of Apalachicola, check into a balcony room at the River Inn, and head directly to adjacent Boss Oyster. Sit outside in the heat, request a couple of dozen beauties from the bay, and watch the pelicans watching you. (And while you're waiting for your order, reflect on *next* time—top-line Williams-Sonoma stainless steel sharp-tipped patented oyster knife in one fist, first victim firm in the gloved other—and, well, you just wait and see.)

CHAPTER 5

·

The Deep Fryer: Five+ Happy Hour Happinesses

The first time stepping into your host's home, head immediately—without greeting or gesture—to the kitchen deep fryer. If you can smell the insides as soon as you pop the lid, this signals your worst fear realized: a turgid, viscous miasma the color of discarded motor oil, surest sign of a deranged, careless, and unsettled mind. *Horrible, most horrible.* Back away slowly, slowly toward the threshold, hands raised in vague warning, and bolt for the street.

The well-maintained deep fryer, on the other hand, nicely polished, its oil clear and clean, indicates a dedicated cook and entertainer, a fine citizen of the world with a balanced disposition and a pure heart. Granted, changing the "grease" isn't terribly pleasant, but you'll habituate to doing it efficiently. And, anyway, personal feelings don't enter into the situation: You need a deep fryer if your goal is to be considered a serious gourmand and a sensualist of any significance.

Choosing a Deep Fryer. You'll use the fryer primarily for appetizers, so a medium size is fine. You don't need a big, stainless steel industrial monster unless you intend to really commit to disaster, but conversely don't buy a dinky toy from the drugstore that clips your frying wings before you've even begun to fly. Those small and cheap models also tend to be so stripped down in design, with their temperature uncontrollable, as to be close to useless. Buy a quality, mid-sized fryer with, say, an 8" basket. A two-quart size should suffice. Both an adjustable thermostat and a timer are essential. Corn oil only, please; it doesn't matter which among the reputable brands.

Now, my friend, you're ready. Below are five easy appetizers and one bonus entrée—the only fried oyster recipe you'll ever need. Enough teaser. Let's fry.

Fried Chickpeas

1 15-oz. can chickpeas

sea salt

This is probably the easiest recipe in the book, embarrassingly so (and unapologetically appropriated from Gabrielle Hamilton's Prune in New York City shortly after it opened), and a quirky party snack that always pleases. Drain a can of chickpeas, empty into a colander, and rinse under cold water. Turn onto paper towels and dry thoroughly. No breading, no dips, no nonsense. Add chickpeas to raised basket (to avoid splattering), lower basket, and fry for 1 minute at 350° F.

Turn chickpeas onto a plate lined with paper towels (if your oil is clean, this is sufficient to drain them), salt liberally, transfer to a bowl, and serve hot. (These are best and most naturally eaten with the fingers, so just present with a serving spoon for hygienic appearances. You may as well forget the cute cocktail forks for now.) You might want to keep the fryer hot and a second can of chickpeas in close reserve, just in case of escalating tensions over the last pea.

Fried Olives

1 3-oz. can anchovy-stuffed olives

¼ cup milk

1 farm egg

⅓ cup all-purpose flour

⅓-½ cup seasoned breadcrumbs

I discovered these at the remote bed & breakfast Casa Guilla, dramatically perched (and precariously approached) in the Spanish Pyrenees, and now, recipe stolen and freely offered, you can enjoy them at home without risk to life or property. "Fried olives" sound inherently decadent, and these pungent, savory little bombs, also best eaten by hand, bring an inordinate happiness for their small size. They've become a staple snack, nearly an independent group in the food pyramid, in my house.

The original recipe, which I assume to be Spanish in origin, was passed on by word-of-mouth and involved stuffing each individual olive with cured ham, but—*vita brevis*—I wholly endorse the compromise suggested to me. Drain a 3-oz. can of anchovy-stuffed green olives. (These small cans are ubiquitous throughout Spain, and cheap. They'll cost you alarmingly more in the States, so I recommend buying online by the case.) Pat them partially dry with a paper towel, then, in three bowls—don't forget the "dry hand, wet hand" rule—1) roll in flour, 2) coat in a mix of the egg and milk beaten together, and

3) roll in seasoned breadcrumbs. No additional seasoning (including salt; they're salty enough thanks to the anchovies) or dips required. Over the sink—as you should with all dry-battered foods, to minimize crumbs in your oil—place them in the basket, shake gently, and fry at 350° F for 60-90 seconds. Turn onto a paper towel and eat immediately. A 3-oz. can contains around 25 olives (the cook gets the odd one), perfect as an appetizer for two. Or one.

Like the chickpeas, these are ideal with a glass of wine or a Martini (what isn't?) while you read by the window in your favorite chair and the sun arcs, tired yet implacably determined, westward.

Fried Asparagus

11 fat spears in-season asparagus

1 farm egg

1 cup plain panko breadcrumbs

½+ cup all-purpose flour

sea salt & freshly ground black pepper

dipping sauce of mayonnaise, Dijon mustard, and Tabasco

This recipe is purportedly Austrian in origin, although that hardly explains the Japanese panko breadcrumbs. A deep-frying pioneer of any nationality would have discovered it eventually. Anyway, these are a third fun finger food—the battered spears are also delightfully funky and artfully attractive—either as a happy hour snack/appetizer or, with some microgreens and a little vinaigrette, a salad.

Rinse 11 (again, the cook deserves an extra for luck) thick asparagus spears and crack at 6"-7", just short enough that they fit comfortably into your frying basket. Pat asparagus dry, then roll in flour except for the tips. In separate wide bowls, have 1 beaten egg and 1 cup of pulsed or crushed plain panko crumbs seasoned with salt and pepper. Continuing to keep the tips of the spears clean (this creates the painterly effect after frying), coat the asparagus in egg and then roll in the panko. Over the sink—I want you to remember this—space spears in the basket. Fry at 375° F for 2-3 minutes, until brown and crisp and lovely. As they're frying, whip up a quick dip of mayonnaise, Dijon mustard, and Tabasco, always a winner. Turn spears gently onto a paper towel and salt lightly or not. Immediately start playing with the odd spear and weaving it toward your mouth. (Again, fingers only please, unless as a salad.)

Serves two. Divide up the booty, top off your glass, return to your book, and enjoy. The night is young and its possibilities enticing.

Fried Calamari

5-6 oz. raw calamari

½ cup milk (optional but recommended)

½ cup all-purpose flour

½ cup semolina flour

sea salt & freshly ground black pepper

cayenne powder

grated Parmesan

lemon wedges

marinara or cocktail sauce

Clean and rinse calamari, separate legs from bodies, and slice bodies into rings ⅓" thick. 6-8 oz. of raw calamari make a generous happy hour snack for two, so a 1-lb. bag will make 2 large or 3 more modest portions. Let's say we dole it out to 3 and not be pigs. With your kitchen scale, divide prepared calamari equally into three one-pint freezer bags. Freeze two for future use (possibly tomorrow).

In the third bag, pour in the milk, seal, and place in refrigerator for 1 hour to tenderize. (If you don't have the time or patience for this, that's okay; it doesn't necessarily mean you're a bad person.) Drain calamari and dredge a few pieces at a time in a bowl containing a mixture of the all-purpose flour, the semolina flour, and dashes of salt, freshly ground pepper, and cayenne. Over the sink—right, you get it?—place calamari into basket and gently shake off any excess flour. At 375° F, fry for 2-3 minutes until brown and lovely. Don't overcook or the squid will get rubbery. Drain on a paper towel. Salt, pepper, and top with a few passes of freshly grated Parmesan. Serve with lemon wedges and a cocktail or garlicky marinara sauce. (If your timid beloved will only eat the rings, you'll have to separate the bodies onto your own plate. In which case, on principle, to make a surreptitious point, and just as a matter of practical mathematics, you'll serve yourself more.)

Back to your book. Fingers only.

Fried Tortilla Chips & Guacamole

The deep-fried chips are the centerpiece here and are going to drive you crazy with happiness. We were shuffling around lovely and lively downtown Asheville, North Carolina, one sunny October afternoon and stopped at an outside table at Havana Restaurant for a refreshing libation and rejuvenating snack. Although we had a big dinner planned for that night—a chef's tasting menu inside the kitchen of a restaurant over near the Biltmore Mansion—neither of us could stop eating these damned hot, salty, oily, crunchy chips.

When I got home, I promptly tried to replicate the chip, not to mention the effect, and found a reasonable facsimile easy to prepare. Decorum demands that you dip them in something and not just eat a bowlful of naked chips, so I've included a bare-bones guacamole both for that purpose and to give the recipe a little "healthful" cachet. Hot spinach and artichoke dip is another good match.

3-4 6"-7" flour tortillas

1 ripe Hass avocado

1 tomato

2 cloves garlic

½ small white onion (optional)

1 Tbs. mayonnaise (or more to taste)

¼ lemon

hot pepper flakes

sea salt & freshly ground black pepper

To make the superfluous guacamole, spoon the avocado into a small mixing bowl and add the diced tomato, garlic, onion, and the mayonnaise. Squeeze the lemon wedge into the palm of your hand (to catch the seeds) over the bowl. Salt and pepper liberally, add a dash or two of the pepper flakes, and mix and mash everything together, leaving some detectable chunks of avocado. (If you want to try, for fun, to root your avocado seed, impale with four sturdy toothpicks—or halved bamboo grilling skewers—and suspend in a glass of water on the windowsill. In a week or so, remove the slimy seed from the pestilent, mildewed glass and discard.)

To make the chips, use the basic, cheap flour tortillas—the smaller ones, sometimes called fajita size—common in most grocers in packs of 10-100. I suggest the refrigerated variety. With your kitchen shears, scissor 3-4 tortillas into triangles—let's say pyramids, for the Teotihuacán nuance—of roughly equal chip size. No need to be fussy about them. Deep-fry at 375° F for 1 minute or so until just beginning to brown, turning once with tongs or a fork. Drain on and pat with paper towels, then salt liberally.

That's it. Serve chips hot with the guacamole. They're addictive as hell.

Bonus Fry: Panko-Breaded Fried Oysters

Technically, I consider these a main dish for one, but since this chapter is a logical spot to insert the recipe, there's also no reason they couldn't be a contentious appetizer for two. It's my homage to *kaki fry*, which I got hooked on at Murfreesboro's first Japanese restaurant when it opened many years ago. I've quit going there for logistical reasons, but the fond memory of their deeply-browned, crunchy oysters remains. This breading is a heresy to my Louisville upbringing and that city's legendary Mazzoni's—the original location closed in 2008 after 125 years—but it's the only one you'll want to use from now on. So be it. *Sayonara*, Mazzoni's.

8-oz. container shucked, fresh oysters

⅔ cup plain panko breadcrumbs

½ cup flour

1 small farm egg

¼ cup milk

liberal shake garam masala

pinch cayenne powder

sea salt & freshly ground black pepper

for serving:

hoisin sauce

baby spinach or mixed greens + vinaigrette (optional, *vide infra*)

lemon wedges

This is another three bowl, "dry hand, wet hand" preparation. I trust the drill is habit by now. Drain oysters, check them for bits of shell, and place on a paper towel. If 1 or 2 of the oysters are conspicuously larger than the rest, scissor them in half. (If they're all monsters, I'd cut them all in half. More breading surface, don't ya know, plus a friendlier size for a reading snack and/ or the illusion of a larger portion for a single entrée.)

In the first bowl, season the flour with pepper, 3-4 shakes of cayenne, and a pinch of salt. In the middle bowl, beat the egg and milk together with a fork. In the third, add the garam masala to the panko crumbs. Bread the oysters 2-3 at a time, bing bang boom, covering each well and decisively with the ingredients of the three bowls, and place them in a single layer on a plate. Cover with plastic wrap and refrigerate. When you're ready to fry, hold the fryer basket over the sink—yes, yes, I know you know—add the oysters, and gently shake off excess crumbs. Deep-fry at 350° F for about 2 minutes. They won't take long to brown. Drain oysters briefly on a paper towel. Salt and pepper.

To eat as a happy hour/reading snack, divide onto two colorful plates and serve with a small bowl of hoisin sauce and perhaps a wedge of lemon. Better still, as a greedy meal for one, serve hot on top of a plate of baby spinach or mixed greens lightly tossed in a ginger vinaigrette (or similar), along with a lemon wedge and a dipping bowl of hoisin sauce (essential to the harmony of the dish). Eat with your fingers, plate balanced on the arm of the couch, while watching the game or, under duress, *House Hunters International.* Don't share.

CHAPTER 6

·

Risotto to Die or Kill For

Bone marrow and truffle risotto is one of the richest, most sublimely indulgent dishes I've ever tasted. (Needless to say, notwithstanding the foie gras-stuffed pig foot at that converted 17th-century church outside of Lectoure, and, yes, the unctuous, jaw-drop-inducing goat brain curry that I tracked down—twice—in the labyrinthine back alleys of Old Delhi, but let's not lose our heads here, people. Feet on the ground.) There's more good news: This preparation (a one-dish full meal), while perhaps cluttering the stove top, is well within the purview and skill set of the organized home cook.

Without hyperbole, I crown this my favorite dish that I make for myself, although, returning to an unfortunately recurring motif of this book, it's a lot of work—too much—just for one. This time I offer a happy solution. If your companion is unenthusiastic about bone marrow (startling, inexplicable, deeply troubling re. your future together, but in my experience not uncommon), below I offer a relatively simple compromise I've developed to ameliorate, to accommodate, to calm, to . . . perpetuate. Alright, it's a compromise that stings, but—gosh darn it—one that allows you to still "get yours" and the evening to proceed with luxurious promise. If your baby loves marrow, then the future looks even brighter. (Head spinning, *après*, you may consider proposal. Be careful.)

Bone Marrow & Truffle Risotto

6-8 2" pieces beef marrow

½ cup beef stock

1 cup Arborio rice

2-3 shallots, depending on size

1 Tbs. unsalted butter

1 Tbs. olive oil

½ cup dry white wine

4-5 cups low-sodium chicken broth

1 black truffle*

¾ cup freshly grated Parmesan

1 Tbs. fresh Italian parsley, roughly chopped

sea salt & freshly ground black pepper

black truffle oil (for gratuitous dribbling)

1 cup green baby peas

½ duck, roasted**

Important Miscellaneous Notes on Ingredients. *Risotto à la moelle et aux truffles* (so called if you're charging/paying 50 euros for it at the *auberge*) does, granted, require the stockpiling of some fairly exotic items in the pantry and freezer. Nothing so esoteric as to cause headaches, but a few well-spent guilders will be required.

The Marrow. Have your butcher cut you 10—for good measure—beef marrow bones, 2" long. Small to medium in diameter are preferable. Those 4"-wide monsters look impressive, and they're fine for soup and serviceable for roasting as an appetizer, but the marrow from smaller bones will come out whole and generally a lot cleaner. From the hole's larger end, push the entire cylinder of marrow out with your thumb, loosening around the edges with a small knife if necessary. Keep them whole. Continue until you have the requisite number of lovely, ivory and pink marrow bombs. If you have problems with any of the bones (that's why you bought extra) being "webby" or solid at the fat end, just dig out what you can with a paring knife or small spoon—raw marrow is delicate and friable material and will also start getting mushy as it warms to room temperature—and don't obsess. Keep the bits and move on to the next bone. (Caveat: I use a *lot* of marrow in my recipe, especially considering it may all end up folded into a single serving. I love the stuff and only eat it a couple of times a year, so embrace a what-the-hell philosophy. However, if you think you need to "wimp it down" a bit to avoid dizziness, hysteria, et cetera, suit yourself, but please use at least 4 whole pieces. You want the buzz and the bolt, right?) The marrow can be used immediately, stored in the fridge for a couple of days, or frozen for months. It needs to be thawed when you're ready to cook.

Roast the cleaned bones—no seasoning required—in the oven at 350° F for 50 minutes and until the kitchen smells good. When the bones have cooled, select a good-looking one, towel dry its excessive fat (liquefied vestiges of marrow, mostly) to spare the carpeting, and sadistically taunt the dog for a moment. He or she will be standing next to you trembling with love and longing. The affection (toward you) will be short-lived, however, once a command is perfunctorily followed, the bone's surrendered, and a flash of fur disappears around the corner. You won't see the mutt for a while, although you may appreciate a periodic "scraping" chorus from an adjoining room. (It's good to give, but make'm pay for it.)

   *The Black Truffle. The mythological stench and potency of the dirt-caked black winter truffle, fresh and seasonal, passed clandestinely between dark men in dark doorways—viz., the stuff of dreams—is out of reach for most of us, for both financial and practical reasons. The book from which I've adapted this recipe, however, contains my favorite single ingredient description I've found in any recipe: "1 black truffle, as large as you can afford, sliced thin." (The accompanying photo of a Provençal local, *Tuber melanosporum* the size of a golf ball nested safely on an impressive mustache and held tightly to one nostril, a look of religious ecstasy in his teary peasant eyes, communicates an earth of miracles.) For better or worse, packaged black truffles—usually 2-3 black balls the circumference of a dime up to a nickel and sealed in a tiny glass jar—are regularly available in chichi grocers and online retailers. Frankly, these generally don't have a lot of taste, but they're at least actually imported from France or Italy (otherwise, beware their dubious origin) and, anyway, are fun to play with, don't cost a fortune, and offer enough of a pleasant insinuation of the real thing to let you pretend you're playing in The Big Game. The black truffle oil—a nice stinky one, please—you're going to use for excessive dribbling will help augment the "truffleness" of the risotto.

   **Roasted Duck. ¼ of a roasted duck goes on top of each risotto serving when plating, did I mention? (I knew you didn't think we'd had enough duck earlier.) Frozen, pre-roasted half ducks are typically now available in supermarkets, and they're surprisingly tasty. You thaw, heat for 20 minutes according to instructions, divide with a knife, and serve. This dish is complicated enough that I mention, even endorse, the compromise. (Alternately, if I have offended your purist sensibilities with my suggestion, then go ahead and roast a duck two days before and [try your best to] save half for a simple heat-up. I recommend two days ahead so you're not in the kitchen laboring hot and heavy for consecutive days, but as ye will.) Against my own better judgment, I have topped this risotto with lobster tails rather than duck, fairly certain that the relative subtlety of the lobster would be lost among the bold, earthy flavors of the dish. I was right. Lobster risotto can be a remarkable and inspiring thing, conducive to *amour*, but the combination's strictly *verboten* in this recipe. Save your tails for your Valentine's Day risotto, if you know what I mean.

Okay: Let's cook some froufrou rice suitable even for the fickle gods! Follow me. The prep work is fairly simple: Finely chop the shallots, rough chop the parsley garnish, and thinly slice your black truffle. (Possibly two, if they're small to moderate in size and of the glass jar variety discussed above. Also, retain any liquid in the jar.) Grate the Parmesan.

I warned you that the stove top will be crowded. The recipe is a four burner affair. Steam your peas (if fresh) or boil them (if frozen) according to directions. Drain and keep warm on a back burner. In a saucepan, heat the chicken broth on a front burner. On a back burner in a smaller pan, bring the beef stock to a simmer over low-to-medium heat, add the bone marrow cylinders and loose pieces, and poach for 3 minutes. Cover and set aside. Heat your oven to 350° F and warm your roasted half duck for 20 minutes as you're making the risotto. (Set the timer. When it goes off, remove the duck from the oven and cover with foil.)

To make the risotto, place a heavy pan on your large front burner. Over medium heat, melt the butter with the olive oil. Add the shallots and rice and stir for 3-4 minutes. Pour in the wine, which will steam and quickly reduce/evaporate. Add ¾ cup of the chicken broth to the rice and stir frequently until all the stock has been absorbed, then continue to add ½ cup or so of broth, letting it be absorbed each time, until the rice has a creamy texture and is soft but still firm. This will take around 25 minutes. (Legend has it that the more constantly you stir, the creamier and better the result, but you needn't be fascistic about it. If you step away periodically—e.g., to grate the cheese you overlooked, fiddle with and divide the duck, uncork the wine you forgot to air, refresh the Martini [which you did *not* forget] in your non-stirring hand, or stare vaguely out the window at the darkening tree line—you'll still have a fine result. Just keep adding the broth, don't let the rice burn or stick, and stir as steadily and often as patience allows. You may find the stirring induces a calming, meditative state. You may not.)

Add the marrow slices and beef stock (I prefer my risotto almost—almost—soupy), truffle slices (and any truffle juice from the jar), Parmesan, and salt and pepper, and stir gently (to keep the marrow pieces largely intact). Cover, remove from heat, and leave for 3-4 minutes for the flavors to set.

<u>Promised Simple Variation to Accommodate Any Marrow-Wary (i.e., Repulsed) Companion</u>. Add truffle slices and Parmesan, salt and pepper, but *not* the marrow and stock. Stir, spoon half of the risotto into a bowl, cover with foil, and leave on the warm stove surface. Add the marrow and beef stock to the risotto remaining, stir, cover, and let sit for 3-4 minutes—the perfect amount of time for initiation of music and candles, placement of cloth napkins, et cetera. (Your portion will then be extra creamy, magnificently rich with marrow, and incomparably better than your partner's, as it should be under such strained circumstances.)

To plate, divide the risotto into wide pasta bowls, spoon the peas circularly around the edges, and top each serving with a quarter of a roasted duck and a sprinkle of parsley. Serve with hot, crusty bread, a bottle of black truffle oil to drizzle according to taste, and the sturdy French red wine you opened a half hour before, maybe a Côtes du Rhône with attitude (or for that matter, the Châteauneuf-du-Pape you've been saving for a special occasion—this is it). Cross yourself and dig in. Kiss your old life goodbye forever.

> . . . clawfuls of clamping
> shells as offering, forced stiff hinges,
>
> ate briny bodies for your amusement.
> You weren't amused.
>
> —*from* "Scalloping"

Scallop & Corn Risotto

Alright, alright. *Cálmate!* Once you've recovered from the meal above and have been released from the cardiac ward, you might also try this variation. The dish is a tad easier to prepare (you still have to stand there), not as dizzyingly rich, and less expensive. It's also not a holy experience, although it is excellent.

6 large sea scallops

1 cup Arborio rice

2-3 shallots, depending on size

2 ears white corn, double cut*

1 Tbs. + ½ Tbs. unsalted butter

1 Tbs. + ½ Tbs. olive oil

½ cup dry white wine

4-5 cups low-sodium chicken broth, simmering on stove

1 tsp. fresh thyme (optional, but recommended)

dash cayenne powder (optional, but recommended)

¾ cup freshly grated Parmesan

1 Tbs. fresh Italian parsley

spice rub of choice for scallops

sea salt & freshly ground black pepper

To begin, double cut 2 ears of white corn: *Stand each de-silked and rinsed ear on a cutting board and slice down through the kernels with a serrated knife, then cut around again, closer. Scrape down the cob with the knife blade and save any released "milk" with the cut corn. (If the summer corn season is over, you're much better off with a thawed baggy of the cut corn you froze in August, rather than the tasteless simulacrum you'll likely be subjected to at the grocer.) In a skillet, heat ½ Tbs. unsalted butter and ½ Tbs. olive oil, then add the corn, ground pepper, and, optionally, a tsp. or so of (preferably fresh) thyme and a dash of cayenne powder. Sauté (or if you're not sensitive about letting your southern roots show, "fry") the corn over medium heat until tender, 5 minutes. If the corn looks too dry, add a splash of the chicken broth and cook it out. Cover and set aside.

Press sea scallops in a paper towel to dry. Season both sides with paprika, salt, pepper, garlic powder, or as you prefer. (Yes, Mr. Lagasse's ubiquitous Essence is fine—that's why it conquered the world.) Set aside.

With our streamlined ingredients (sans marrow, beef stock, and truffle), prepare the risotto as indicated above. When the rice is creamy and voluptuous, stir in the corn until hot, remove from burner, and cover for 4-5 minutes. Sear scallops in a hot skillet (with a little olive oil) until the exterior is just browned and crisp, perhaps 2 minutes on each side, depending on their size. Or, broil them in the oven, on high, for 3-4 minutes. (N.b.: Sea scallops vary so much in size that you need some judgment here and also to watch them carefully. I'm assuming you've shelled out for 6 nicely portioned models. In any case, do *not* overcook them and turn them into rubber. You'll never forgive yourself, nor deserve forgiveness, if you do.) Theoretically, you could use bay scallops in this recipe, searing a skilletful for perhaps 1 minute and then gently turning them into the corn risotto. Alternately, you could also stir in those cooked chunks of lobster tail you've had frozen in reserve. However, I'd suggest sticking with the plan of the sea scallops, 3 medium-large per serving. If they're monsters, you can get away with 2.

On a personal side note, I find removing the foot of the sea scallop a silly, overly fastidious business, but it does have one benefit: Collect them in a small pile, sprinkle with truffle salt, and eat raw while you're standing there, ample reward for an unnecessary task perfunctorily performed. (If only one could procure those luscious Scottish diver scallops with the brilliant orange tail/roe attached. Or, for that matter, giant Georgia white shrimps, heads *on. Oh, righteous and misguided America* . . .)

Divide risotto onto plates or into wide serving bowls, top with gorgeously seared scallops and diced parsley—your gesture toward salad—and serve with hot crusty bread. If you can live without red wine for one night, pair with a Sauvignon Blanc, Viognier, or dry-style Sémillon, or, okay, maybe a Pinot Noir if you just can't help yourself. The idea is to enjoy.

CHAPTER 7

.

Bunny!

I'll be in my room upstairs,
you know where, slow sautéing
in virgin oil a fat rabbit liver,
local onions properly caramelized,
half bottle of Languedoc red
all that's left before the early train.

—*from* "Fête de l'Indépendance
(or, July 4th, Final Evening in France)"

Rabbit is wonderfully versatile. I adore it. Fried rabbit was a staple in my grandmother's kitchen when I was child—she kept a rabbit hutch for years for the purpose—and I'm delighted that the dish in its fancier iterations is making more frequent appearances on American menus. (Thursday night is Rabbit Fricassée Night at Table 3, a French restaurant in, of all places, Nashville. Hooray! Another fine [and sadly, now shuttered] establishment in the city, Mambu, when it opened offered a delicious—and beautifully colored—rabbit and beet stew. They were a decade ahead of their time in Music City and I think only I ever ordered the dish, but believe me I tried hard to take up the slack.) This ingredient is yet another under our consideration that might conceivably cause some turbulence in a dining room of hypersensitive political eaters (this time the "eat nothing cute" constituency), but with a hopeful heart and convivial spirit, let's blithely cook on.

The recipe below, though not the soup its title suggests, is a nod to *salmorejo*, a thick cold soup of puréed bread, garlic, vinegar, and tomatoes that originates from Córdoba. One reputed etymology for the name *España* itself is a derivation of the Punic *Isapanihad*, "land of rabbits." Fact or myth, Spaniards appreciate the bunny on a plate or in a bowl, just like we did in Kentucky.

Selecting/Purchasing a Rabbit. I have cooked almost entirely with frozen, domestic rabbits. If you are a hunter or know one and have access to the usually much smaller wild cottontail (or much larger wild hare), and you don't mind—or even enjoy—the gore, then have at it and good luck. You'll need to adjust cooking times. You will also, more importantly, need to practice the butchering. I butchered a rabbit (skinned, but head attached) only once, in the mountains of the Languedoc in southern France, with an inferior knife. It was a *lapin* "whole food" experience I'm not anxious to replicate. Luckily for the home chef, frozen rabbits have become much easier to find in grocery stores if you're paying attention. The brand I prefer—unpaid endorsement—is Pel-Freez. The rabbit is fully dressed, cleaned, and dissected. The product is well-packaged against freezer burn. The pieces are large and meaty, the offal is included, and they're relatively inexpensive. If you can't find the signature white box or any other brand in the local freezer section, ask. These days, any meatmonger worth his/her salt (and your commerce) should be able to order you a rabbit. You need not go to the pet store.

A Note on the Pieces. A rabbit has little fat, and of course you don't eat the skin. The saddle loin pieces (the rabbit equivalent of the chicken breast) tend to dry out, and I've recently stopped including them in sautéed dishes. At the end of the chapter, I'll suggest a simple recipe, with a southern insinuation, for a tasty appetizer or main course salad. It's up to you. The legs of one fat domestic rabbit (the hind legs are the money cut) and the tender, boneless, and underrated belly flap will supply a hearty meal for two. The liver, heart, and especially the round, darkly purple kidney (that's that strange organ one can't identify—*I think*—but whatever it is, it's *gooood*) are all delicious. They're also small as well as potentially off-putting to the anti-offal lobby, so I'll offer a selfish suggestion further down as to their preparation and surreptitious—*shh*—consumption.

> Four days surviving
> on hard bread, sticky jam,
> coffee and cheap wine fueled
> a *marché* thrill for *le lapin*.
>
> I couldn't help spreading
> tiny-toothed jaws with a thumb,
> softly touching each soft,
> opaque, sightless eye.
> Well, I'd lost a lost lately,
> and I wanted a lot.
>
> What was mutilation,
> what respect, what honoring

the appointed dead, I couldn't say.

—from "After Buying a Rabbit
at the Carcassonne Market"

Rabbit "Salmorejo"

1 rabbit, divided

1½ cups dry white wine

1+ Tbs. sherry vinegar

2 bay leaves

several sprigs oregano from the garden

3 Tbs. all-purpose flour

6+ Tbs. olive oil

6 large cloves garlic

6-8 oz. fresh pearl onions

¾ cup low-sodium chicken broth

1 dried hot chili, crushed

2+ tsp. sweet paprika

course sea salt & freshly ground black pepper

Italian parsley (for garnish)

gnocchi (for serving)

The paprika is the secret star of this recipe, believe it or not, so forego that dusty, decade-old lump (go ahead, throw it away—free thyself) in the spice cabinet and invest in some fresh Spanish or Hungarian paprika of quality (but not smoked, which would overpower this recipe).

Put the rabbit pieces in a bowl with the bay leaves and rinsed sprigs of oregano. Add the white wine and sherry vinegar, toss, cover, and marinate overnight in the fridge. Otherwise, the preparation is simple. Peel the fresh pearl onions by blanching them for 1 minute in boiling water, running under cold water until cooled, and then popping each onion loose by squeezing the fat/root end. This can also be done the night before or whenever is convenient prior to cooking. When you're ready to get serious, thinly slice the garlic. *Slice,* not chop. (Sliced garlic is the other secret star.)

Drain the rabbit and pat dry. Reserve the marinade and strain through a coffee filter. Coat rabbit lightly in seasoned flour. In a large, heavy frying pan or Dutch oven, heat 2-3 tbs. of olive oil, brown the rabbit on all sides, and remove to a plate. (You might as well go ahead and invest in a porcelain-enameled cast-iron Dutch oven if you haven't already. I suffered along for years without one and have no idea why. The Lodge six-quart is a good, useful size, I believe still comes with an eternal warranty, and costs a fraction of a comparable Creuset model. Yes, I'm enamored of nearly all things French, but the Lodge is good enough. The fact that I once received a fan note from the vice president of Lodge after my poetry reading at the Southern Foodways Alliance has nothing whatsoever to do with it, and I resent the inference. I had a lovely garden lunch there with a Goo Goo Cluster big shot, too, but you don't see me trumpeting the "classic peanut" over my Valrhona *Le Noir*, do you? Plus, by now your rabbit's cold.)

Heat more olive oil in the skillet, add the whole, peeled pearl onions until they brown a bit. Remove them to a bowl. Add the slices of garlic (and a splash more olive oil if necessary) to the skillet and fry briefly. Don't burn them. Add the strained marinade, the chicken broth, the crushed and seeded hot chili, and 2 tsp. (plus an extra dash for good fortune) of paprika from your shiny new tin. Return rabbit (and any blood/juices) and onions to the pan.

Cover and simmer gently for 45 minutes (or if you're using your new Lodge Dutch oven, you alternately could bake in the oven at 350° F for 50-60 minutes), until the rabbit is browned, tender, and beautiful. Taste, then as desired add more paprika, sherry vinegar, salt, and ground pepper. Plate with a little rough-chopped Italian parsley on top, over gnocchi (or, in a pinch, creamy mashed potatoes or rice), and serve with a good bottle of Tempranillo. The Three Tenors are meanwhile tearing it up, soaring (quietly) heavenward in the background.

This dish is irresistible to any romantic companion you serve it to. Unless, however, she or he doesn't eat rabbit, in which awkward situation you're in sudden and deep *mierda* (so make a lot of gnocchi). In any case, if you name your rabbit, absolutely keep that information to yourself. Please, please trust me on this.

> He cooks, cadaver incanting among cadavers,
> heats oils, slices and braises,
> sautés thick gravies
> with salting, always heavy-handed
> salting as the room glows in the amber of the fresh

frying blood of the world
—its abused flesh, its tender flesh—
while below his fragrant lumbering
beasts of the wood raise
bristled snouts, nostrils flare
and the ancient constellations glisten.

—*from* "Man's War against Depression"

Rabbit "Stew" with Pine Nuts, Mushrooms, & Pasta

1 rabbit, divided

1 cup red wine

3 Tbs. seasoned all-purpose flour

4 oz. pancetta or thick-sliced bacon

1 medium onion

4 cloves garlic

2 large carrots

6-8 oz. fresh pearl onions

4-5 Tbs. olive oil

8-10 oz. fresh shitake mushrooms

2 cups beef stock*

2 Tbs. fresh thyme

1 bay leaf

2 Tbs. pine nuts

3 Tbs. Italian parsley

coarse sea salt & freshly ground black pepper

5-6 oz. dried pappardelle or 6-8 dried lasagna sheets

While we're on a real hop with rabbit, let's try another dish, also adapted from a Spanish recipe—with Italian and even Asian influences—and similarly prepared, although quite different in appearance, eating experience, and flavor. (By the way, we'll leave the idiotic phrase "flavor profile" to the pundits. In this book we'll simply have "flavor," thank you.) Once you've mastered the techniques of the salmorejo, this one will be *muy facile* but allows you some variety for experimentation, self-amusement, and seduction. Again, you might consider retaining the rabbit loin pieces, as I'll proffer better uses for them nearer the end of the chapter.

Place rabbit in a bowl with the red wine and 1 Tbs. olive oil. Cover and refrigerate overnight.

Chop pancetta, onion, carrots, and garlic. (If you want to add a spear of chopped celery to the onion and carrots for a more traditional *mirepoix*, that's fine. Why not? I applaud your initiative in suggesting the addition.) Skin the pearl onions, *vide ut supra*. Chop the thyme and parsley. Clean and thickly slice the shitake mushrooms. (Use ubiquitous and inexpensive white button mushrooms if you like—smallish ones, quartered—but I prefer the more flavorful shitakes. Alternately, you might use button mushrooms and enliven them with a couple of ounces of dried shitakes reconstituted in advance in a few ounces of the stock. If you can find and afford fresh chanterelles/girolles, of course substitute with abandon.)

Once everything is cleaned, sliced, and diced, the methodology of the cooking is quite similar to the salmorejo, albeit with a longer cook time to tenderize the meat. In your Dutch oven (let's just assume?), heat 2 Tbs. of olive oil and add the pancetta or bacon, chopped onion, and garlic, and cook over medium heat until the pork's just cooked. Add the chopped carrot and pearl onions (and celery if you're tossing in a bit). Continue to sauté, stirring occasionally, for 6-8 minutes.

Heat 2-3 Tbs. of olive oil (adding more as/if necessary) in a large, heavy skillet. Remove the rabbit from the wine and dry pieces with paper towels. (Retain the wine marinade, of course.) Coat pieces with the seasoned flour and brown on both sides over medium heat. Remove the rabbit and add to the Dutch oven, along with the sliced mushrooms. Deglaze the skillet with the wine, scraping stuck bits loose with a spatula, and add all to the rabbit. Add the thyme, bay leaf, and stock. (*I'm inclined toward beef stock here, even if that might seem counterintuitive for a meat that's nearly in the poultry family in taste and texture. This is a hearty dish, however, and the beef stock seems an alchemical addition to the red wine. Use chicken stock if you prefer.) Salt and pepper. Cook over a low heat for 1½ hours, stirring now and then. (Or bake in the oven at 300° F for 2 hours or so.) Keep a periodic eye on the situation. When the meat is tender, remove from heat and allow to cool enough that you can strip it—left in respectably-sized chunks—from the bones. Return meat to the stew and stir in 3 Tbs. chopped parsley. Reheat.

Bring to boil a large pot of water (and a pinch of salt) and add the lasagna sheets, broken into pieces. Cook for 7-8 minutes, until *al dente*, stirring often enough that they don't stick. (The broken lasagna works fine, although of course long, fat, dried—or, happy days!, fresh—pappardelle noodles are preferable. I'm assuming you'll most likely opt for the lasagna default position, but if you're living a blessèd life and have ready access to fresh wide pasta, by all means proceed accordingly unto that blessing. Adjust portions and cooking times as appropriate.) Drain pasta in a colander, toss with a splash of olive oil, and add to the rabbit. Stir, divide among two wide bowls (or three or four, in which case include the saddle loin in the recipe, boil more pasta, and adapt accordingly to taste and however many *pignoli* you can afford), top with toasted pine nuts and remaining parsley, and dig into this fine, filling dish for a wintry evening. Toast your good luck and fortune in being together.

> Then, at the quiet table, a mystery
> still unto myself, with my hands
>
> I parted small teeth and ate its tongue,
> for speech and desire; swallowed
> both opalescent eyes, for failing vision;
>
> broke the skull between thumbs
> and scraped from within a nail's worth
> of warm, rich brain, as if for understanding.
>
> —*from* "More Honored in the Breach: Eating
>   the Rabbit's Head, Then Again Meditating
>   upon the Subject"

Fried Buttermilk Rabbit Tenders

saddle loin of 1 rabbit

¾ cup buttermilk

½ cup all-purpose flour

½ tsp. cayenne powder

1 cup seasoned breadcrumbs

sea salt & freshly ground pepper

optional salad:

frisée or assorted baby greens

2 Tbs. unsalted butter

1 shallot

2 Tbs. capers

8 leaves sage

1 orange

1 Tbs. olive oil

1½ tsp. lemon juice

Cut the meat free from the loin pieces, as close to the bone as you can. You'll probably find that the pieces will naturally come off the bone at a serviceable size, perhaps 1" x 2". They can be larger or smaller, but try to keep them approximately the same so that they fry evenly. Using three bowls, dredge tenders in flour (that's been mixed with the cayenne powder), dip in buttermilk ("dry hand, wet hand," Daniel-*san*), then roll them in the breadcrumbs. Over the sink (remember?), put them in your deep fryer basket and gently shake off excess breading. Deep-fry at 350° F for about 3 minutes, depending on the size, until attractively brown. Drain on a paper towel. Salt and pepper. As a happy hour appetizer (*vide* Chapter 5), the pieces from a single saddle will serve three to four, two if you want to overdo. Plate with your preference of sauce, sweet or savory (perhaps a mix of sour cream or mayonnaise and coarse mustard?).

If serving as a main course salad for two, melt the butter in a small saucepan, add chopped shallot, and cook until soft, about 1 minute. Add drained and coarsely chopped capers and sage leaves and cook on medium heat for another minute. Add juice and zest of the orange and cook until thickened and reduced by half, 3-4 minutes. Toss the greens with olive oil and lemon juice. Salt and pepper to taste. Divide on two plates, top with hot tenders, and spoon the sauce over the top. You've just put the Colonel and the Clown to shame.

We'll discuss buttermilk more—much more—later (*vide* Chapter 9). Meanwhile, go ahead and eat. (Of course, another obvious use for the loin— and you're probably way ahead of me—is to make a terrine for entertaining:

In the Cuisinart, pulse the meat with cream, walnuts, salt, and pepper, spread over a half dozen overlapped strips of raw bacon, stud with 3 rows of raw fois gras slivers, roll, secure in four layers of plastic, and simmer for 1 hour in chicken stock, turning once. Cool, slice, and serve with toast points. Easy!)

<u>Miscellaneous Last Thoughts on Mustard Sauce and Rabbit Bringing the World Together</u>. Sometimes, of course, all you want is a nicely skillet-browned rabbit on a nest of soft white rice, drizzled with a traditional mustard sauce (sour cream, yogurt, white wine, Dijon mustard, salt, pepper, some chopped fresh basil, just warmed together—Google the proportions). Sometimes, nothing could be better. It's really all you need, except your fingers and your yearning. Minimal utensils required, regardless of company. Let'm watch.

However, I'm also intrigued by the international possibilities I've not yet attempted. (The conundrum: I only eat rabbit a handful of times each year, and the recipes above are tried, true, succulent, hard to veer from, and make the mouth water.) But perhaps, in the spirit of the conquistador, a Mexican *conejo* in a jalapeño-tequila-lime-chili marinade? Or a Greek *lagos* with plums, onion, and cinnamon? An Indonesian *kelinci* in a curry-honey sauce with tart apples to solace a contentious world? A Polish *krolik* with cloves and baby turnips to quiet the tremulous heart? We'll need to get the Italians involved, the Germans, the Russians. I see walnuts and golden raisins, egg noodles, and horseradish. I see Mario's orange sneakers. I see a theme dinner for the ages. Hell, come on out to the house. We'll roll up our sleeves, tie back our "Kiss the Chef" aprons, get the pans smoking, the bunnies bouncing, and fly and fail together. Sounds like fun, don't you think?

CHAPTER 8

·

A Short, Personal History of Fried Chicken

> . . . not the worst, possum dumplings, mountain
> oysters, but the bad enough—the fried chicken and catfish,
> ham hocks and beans, butter-thick biscuits with sorghum.

—*from* "Apologia for Tuesday
Bachelor Dinners"

Full disclosure: My knowledge of fried chicken mastery is largely anecdotal, my expertise erratic—viz., as a home chef. However, as gourmand and glutton I am nearly unsurpassed in practical experience. Growing up in Louisville, I ate a lot of fried chicken. Grandma Brewer had strong and committed ideas on the subject, for example that a chicken should only *ever* be turned once in the skillet. (Cf.: She rather dismissively, as I recall, accused my mother of turning the pieces "to death." She further chastised my mother's mashed potatoes as overly soupy, ergo, ruined. Such fractious family observations were an assault on—indeed, a demarcation of—character. Grandma also periodically supplied for me my favorite childhood dish—slow-cooked pig feet and sauerkraut, so fatty the gelatinous feet had to be eaten with a wet hand towel nearby so that one's fingers wouldn't stick together. Photographic evidence of the corporeal effect of this healthful diet exists. However, my Crock-Pot variation of the latter dish, you'll be relieved to learn, is not included in this book. I indulge once each decade, when I have no other commitments, then go to bed for a few days.)

My mother got a bad rap, however, as her fried chicken, always prepared in an electric skillet, was heavenly. (I use the past tense here and following, as she recently informed me she has hung up her proverbial frying guns.) Even having watched the process for a lifetime, I can't figure out how she produced those crisp, dark brown cracklings, clinging to or independent of the pieces and, hot and greasy and liberally salted, absolutely transcendent on the tongue. I've never come close to replicating them in my own spotty history of attempted fried chicken. (The chicken was delicious cold, too—sometimes, it seemed, even better—and among my fondest memories is driving from weekend visits in Kentucky back to graduate school in Columbus, cold chicken and biscuits in aluminum foil in tow. I knew just the right midway rest area—now closed—with a pleasant view over the flat Ohio fields. I'd devote a sentimental moment to leave-taking and the unstoppable momentum of time, then attack a thigh.)

I warned you about the anecdotes. Fried chicken is a serious topic, debated not only in the American South but across nearly all social and geographic divides. I've produced a passable version in a trusted cast-iron skillet (by, um, Lodge), but nothing to equal what I was raised on. When I still occasionally make the attempt, I typically opt for the ease of the deep fryer, although of course this method leaves no drippings or cracklings with which to make milk gravy. There's a cost to everything in life, and that's a steep one. Too, the deep fryer method, while the result is crispy and juicy and tastes good, in general somehow feels a bit easy and soulless. Also, unless you have an unusually large fryer for home use, you'll probably have neither the space in the basket nor the time to bread and fry the back, which with its indecently high proportion of crispy skin, as well its succulently tender "lights" (kidneys) and coveted "pope's nose," is highly regarded by any true fried chicken aficionado. Recently, I've also experimented with adapting the Dutch oven as a deep fryer, with satisfactory results, *vide infra*. (N.b.: Obviously, folks, fried chicken is de facto *fried*, so we abrogate out of hand the pervasive and insidiously well-intended invitations to, rather, "bake." Concomitantly, corn flakes, crisped rice cereal, crushed saltines, dried onions, ground nuts and all similar "innovations" should be nowhere in the vicinity of your sacred fried chicken *mise en place*.

A Note on Brining. My mother dedicatedly brined chicken overnight, so that the flesh would be "nice and white" at the bone. Dark and discolored meat was considered grotesque and, most probably, again, a sign of the preparer's careless and faulty character—a social embarrassment. A metal bowl of chicken parts in vigorously salted water was a common sight in the refrigerator. I always thought this process overrated and never much bothered until I twice came upon recipes—of very different provenance (one Italian in origin from John T Edge's seminal *Fried Chicken: An American Story*, one from a Thomas Keller "at home" article from *Food & Wine*)—that suggested using lemon juice. Time allowing, I would recommend submerging your cut up chicken overnight in water containing the juice of 1 lemon, 1 tsp. of salt, and a pinch of sugar (and any other dry spices you feel strongly about). The result is a subtle, citrusy accent to the flesh (which is meanwhile, of course, "nice and white" all the way to the bone). Another playful possibility is the traditional Southern sweet tea brine.

All that said, please allow my humble submissions to the myriad variations on this timeless, essential dish (for variety, one fried in a deep fryer, the other in a Dutch oven). As you would guess from scanning the two recipes below, they produce a rather different product. The spice of life, and all that. They're both good. Neither is spicy hot. And a note before we continue: I suppose I must mention that I was made, *ahem*, a Kentucky Colonel back in the 1980s by then-Lieutenant Governor of the Commonwealth Steve Beshear (*vide* Chapter 30 for the further relevance of this entitlement), the same rank bestowed on tight-fisted ole Harlan Sanders (and Winston Churchill, for that matter). So:

Buttermilk-Battered Fried Chicken

1 3-4 lb. fryer chicken

2 cups all-purpose flour

1 tsp. sea salt

¼ tsp. baking soda

½ tsp. freshly ground pepper

¼ tsp. cayenne powder

2-3 twists freshly ground nutmeg

1 cup buttermilk

for brine:

juice 1 lemon

2 Tbs. kosher salt

pinch sugar

1 bay leaf

Cut up your chicken into 10 pieces: legs, thighs, wings, and halved breasts. (Save the neck, innards, and the divine back for a late night, invitation-only fry-up.) Brine entire chicken overnight in the refrigerator as detailed above.

In two large bowls, place the flour (seasoned with salt, pepper, cayenne, and nutmeg) and buttermilk. Remove chicken from brine, pat dry with paper towels, and using your hands coat lightly with the flour. (Some recommend using a gallon-sized zippered bag to coat the chicken pieces. I don't. Hands on.) Dip pieces into the buttermilk, then again into the flour mixture. Place pieces, not touching, on a cookie sheet or large plate. If at all possible, let the battered chicken rest in the refrigerator for at least an hour.

Deep-fry at 350° F, 2-3 pieces of similar size at a time, uncrowded in the basket, 10-15 minutes (again, depending on size—wings at the low end, fat thighs at the upper), until brown and crispy and bloodless. Raise basket, drain, and turn onto paper towels. Keep in 200° F oven until finished frying the entire bird.

Serve hot immediately, with lemonade or lightly sweetened iced tea with lemon and mint, coleslaw, hot biscuits and butter, hot sauce, ketchup (essential), salt and pepper, and, if you can divine a way, peppered milk gravy. Again, if there are leftovers—unlikely—they'll be just as good (and arguably better) cold the next day, out on the porch or at a favorite rest stop on the highway to your dreams. Serves one-four, depending upon cultural and philosophical prerogatives.

Sweet Tea-Brined Fried Chicken

1 3-4 lb. fryer chicken

2 cups all-purpose flour

1½ tsp. freshly ground black pepper

½ tsp. garlic salt

¼ tsp. baking powder

½ tsp. cayenne powder

4 farm egg yolks

½ cup water

½ tsp. Tabasco

2½ qts. vegetable oil

for brine:

4 Lipton tea bags

½ cup sugar

¼ cup kosher salt

juice 1 lemon

Fill a one-quart Mason jar with boiling water and 4 tea bags. Let brew until tea is strong and dark, then remove bags and let cool. To make the brine, in a large bowl add tea, ½ cup sugar, ¼ cup salt, and 1 lemon, quartered (squeeze the juice into the tea and then add the lemon quarters). Stir well until dissolved. Chill. Cut the chicken into 10 pieces (again halving each breast), plus back, neck, liver, heart, and gizzard, and add all to the tea. Coat well, cover with plastic wrap, and refrigerate overnight.

Remove chicken from tea brine and let drain on paper towels as you prepare the batter. In a wide, flat bowl beat together 4 egg yolks, ½ cup spring water, and ½ tsp. Tabasco, and whisk together well. (This latter won't make the chicken hot, just give a slight insinuation. If you want to kick up the heat, I wouldn't blame you, but I'm always concerned about overdoing it for others. After all, I'm already coercing my companion to eat fried chicken, ya know?) In a large second bowl, mix together with your hands the flour, pepper, garlic salt, baking soda, and cayenne. Coat each piece of chicken with the yolk mixture, dredge well in the flour, and put on a platter. (Again, the neck and back may be the odd pieces out, due to the size of the Dutch oven and the cumbersome matter of battering/dredging a back. Go ahead and fry it as a second batch if you like—there's nothing on earth like a crispy, deep-fried chicken back—or bake and brown unbattered the ostensible scrap pieces in the oven to share with the dog. Also, I'd suggest clipping the tips from the wings and discarding, just to maneuver, again, for a bit more space in the oil.) Refrigerate for 1-2 hours.

When you're ready to fry, pour 2.5 quarts (10 cups) of vegetable oil into a six-quart Dutch oven and, oven a high burner, heat to 350° F. It will heat faster than you think, maybe 10 minutes, and if you overheat the oil it takes a while to cool, so be attentive and use a good digital thermometer to test the temperature. (N.b.: Bear in mind, too, that when you add the cold chicken the oil's temperature will of course drop, so keep the burner cranked up. Once you're maintaining the 350° F consistently, you can turn it down to medium-high.) Add the thighs first, fry 2-3 minutes, then add all the other bits except the breaded liver and gizzard. You should have plenty of room. You'll also probably find that as the pieces are submerged and boiling away in a steamy miasma, turning the chicken, per se, becomes moot. Just give everything a good stir 2-3 times with the metal tongs, being careful not to ding the porcelain coating of the pot. Fry until golden and beautiful, about another 8-10 minutes. 2-3 minutes before you think the chicken is ready, add the liver and gizzard. (The Dutch oven works very nicely as a fryer, although my one hesitation here is the problem of what to do with the oil afterwards. Possibilities would be: 1] to let the oil cool, strain and refrigerate under the pretext of reusing, and then discard weeks later; 2] let cool, then go ahead and carry the Dutch oven outside and empty into the woods; 3] make suet for the birds, if you can be bothered; or, I suppose, 4] the jolly, heart-stopping option of frying chicken several days in a row, while you're on a roll of perfecting timing and technique, and making lots of friends around the neighborhood and in the office. Kidding aside, you'll notice the oil breaking down and needing straining even after the first batch. You won't get more than two fries out of it without some maintenance, so if you've decided, sensibly and after all, to commit from the outset to frying the back and neck, it's probably "olly olly oxen free" for the oil and problem solved.)

With the tongs, and again with care, remove the fried chicken to a paper towel lined platter. Lightly salt and pepper. Eat the hot liver and gizzard with your fingers while you're standing there, sharing with the dog only if necessary (viz., only if she's staring at you, not if she's gotten negligent and has to be called). Serve the rest immediately with coleslaw, hot biscuits and butter, hot sauce and ketchup on the side, and to drink either beer, lemonade, or more sweet tea. Theoretically serves two-four, and as reminded in the first recipe, any cold leftovers (for breakfast the next morning?) are as good or even better. But not as good as my mother's.

Bonus Faux-Southern Recipe: "Shake" Butter

1 pint heavy whipping cream

½ tsp. *sel gris de Guerande* (or salt of choice)

honey (optional, but recommended)

The mention of biscuits and butter, combined with the chapter's tenuous Southern theme, suggests as appropriate a place as any to mention this entertaining and astoundingly easy recipe. I suggest performing it for visitors, as it has the process and effect of a delightful—and delicious—magic trick and requires only a few minutes and a modicum of attention. The shaking can easily be accomplished during cocktails and conversation (or on the telephone, if you feel like narrating) and adds a dramatic flair to any bland occasion.

Let 1 pint of heavy whipping cream come to room temperature. Pour into a well rinsed 64-oz. (or thereabouts) plastic juice or soda bottle. Tighten the cap.

As you're discussing office back-stabbings or dismissing your parents' politics, give the bottle a firm shake once per second—a slow, steady (if harsh) rhythm. You'll feel self-conscious and silly doing this, until after about 4 or 5 minutes the magic happens, a profound alchemy takes place, and a lump of butter separates from the liquid. You'll know when it happens. Give the bottle another dozen shakes for luck, then drain off the milky residue. (Semantics aside, this pale "buttermilk" doesn't taste like anything you'd recognize, but if you want to retain it to drink cold later, out of curiosity, it's not bad.) Fill the bottle with enough cold water to cover and rinse the butter. Shake 4-5 times. Empty the bottle, collecting the soft, sexy mound in your hand. (You'll have to set down your glass for these last steps, but they're quick and worth it.) Gently squeeze excess liquid from the mass.

Mix in salt according to taste—still, gently. If you want to turn in a tablespoon of honey—perhaps sourwood, tupelo, or what's local—the resulting concoction is outstanding on hot biscuits, popovers, corn on the cob, or what you will. Spread into an attractive ramekin, cover with plastic wrap, and refrigerate, but try some while still silky and just shook. You might give your company a taste and watch their eyes roll up.

CHAPTER 9

·

Buttermilk as a Lifestyle Choice

When, to begin my poetry Invocation—at the barbaric hour of 9:00 a.m. —to a crowded hall attending the Southern Foodways Alliance Symposium, I pronounced that cornbread, sorghum, and buttermilk were the "greatest cure for a hangover in the history of humanity," this encomium was not greeted, unfortunately, as quite the valentine of endorsement I had intended by "Big" Earl Cruze, the patriarch of Cruze Dairy Farm on the bank of the French Broad River in East Tennessee. We'd all been mulling around (well, rather more like gorging around) outside the Commons that brisk October morning on the picturesque Ole Miss campus, many of us recuperating from a long and vague night dedicated to putting into practice the symposium theme of "The Liquid South." The breakfast of hot cornmeal hoecakes, slathered with butter and sorghum and washed down with ice-cold pints of churned buttermilk, was, I suspect, salvation for more souls than merely the morning's first speaker and his conspirators.

Earl *is* a big man, wide and tall (maybe 6'3" or so in his boots). The penetrating blue eyes in his craggy face reveal they know more than he's saying or that you're ready to hear. Later that day, he loomed over me, eyes narrow beneath his tawny Stetson, something that might have been the subtlest, faintest of a wry grin on the horizon of his lips, and let me know he'd been considering a revision to my diet. "*Waaal*, Gaylord, we're going to start you off slow. Half gin and half . . . *buttermilk*." His comment clearly referred to what he intuited as the rather disproportionate percentage of the former beverage in my daily maintenance program. Earl Cruze is a man confident in his knowledge that buttermilk can change the world, and I'm sure as hell not going to be the one who disagrees with him. (Cf.: For the rest of the weekend, admittedly, I entertained the fancy of marrying Earl's cute and utterly competent daughter Colleen, reflected upon the man I could become in the firm hands of their mutual tutelage: heir apparent, reflective and loose-legged in denim, working the udder and the churn. Wisely, I kept these ruminations to myself, wanting to experience a squinty reprisal neither from Big Earl nor, moreover, my wife.) But damn, that was a good bottle of buttermilk.

Drinking buttermilk is something of a lost/dismissed pleasure these days, but any cook's enjoyment and range would be diminished not to have it available as an ingredient in both savory dishes—*vide ante*, many batters, the occasional salad dressing—and desserts, *vide infra*. What you'll find at the store will be almost exclusively cultured buttermilk (i.e., milk fermented with bacteria that produce lactic acid). This will serve fine for cooking, but avoid the common low fat (or, gads, no fat) variety and seek out cultured buttermilk fashioned from whole milk. Of course, keep radar attuned—through a specialty food grocer or local small dairy—for the real thing, traditionally and essentially the byproduct of cream churned to butter. Maybe you'll get lucky and find a source. I recently sought out and discovered a cache of Cruze quarts and began playing with candies and desserts: buttermilk pralines (good), buttermilk caramels (good, although honestly I'd meant to make fudge and had to embrace a bit of linguistic reinvention to salvage the result), and buttermilk bread pudding (a disappointing waste of effort and excellent ingredients). I considered continuing the experiments with a buttermilk cheddar cheese bread and a new pie recipe but ended up drinking the rest instead. "Our wills and fates do so contrary run . . ."

Perhaps this chapter is overdue for some recipes to change your world. I hear Big Earl growling at me to get on with it.

> Somewhere I have lost my trepidation.
> There's no more time for foolishness.
> The last bite, and a dish to be licked clean.

> —*from* "The Hunter and the Figs"

Buttermilk Coconut Almond Pie with Sea Salt Bourbon-Caramel Sauce

1½ cups white sugar

4 oz. unsalted butter, room temperature

4 Tbs. all-purpose flour

3 farm eggs (out the fridge for 30 minutes)

1 cup whole buttermilk, preferably churned (*never* low fat in any recipes)

2 tsp. vanilla

½ rounded cup sweetened flake coconut

½ cup sliced almonds

1 unbaked pie crust*

2-3 turns freshly ground nutmeg

for bourbon-caramel sauce (optional—*ha!*):

4 oz. unsalted butter

¾ cup dark brown sugar

¼ cup bourbon

⅓ cup heavy cream

1 tsp. vanilla

⅛+ tsp. fine sea salt

As the name suggests, this is an ideal light dessert to follow a heavy meal. (Irony.) If you really want to gild the lily, add the bourbon-caramel sauce, which is otherwise optional. (Irony.) If you can't handle the action, serve cantaloupe. See how much love you feel returned from the table. As a theme dinner, you might consider just nibbling some crudités and then jumping right to the pie, those "Eat Dessert First" buttons proudly displayed on all lapels.

*A Note on Pie Crusts. I surrendered years ago trying to make my mother's light, flaky pie crust from scratch. The rolled pie shells in the freezer section are irresistibly easy, and once you practice eliminating their central flaw (a bottom crust that's either not properly browned or else sticks), they work satisfactorily. If this shortcut contravenes a deeply held tenet of baking purity on your part, then go right ahead and start raising a flour storm and cutting in that shortening. I commend you. (Cf.: It does seem to me, wistfully or not, that almost no one is making scratch crusts anymore and fewer still laboring over homemade biscuits—the latter not even my mother—understandably opting for the recently much-improved offerings in the grocer's freezer. This substitution will often be denied, of course, even in the face of demonstrable evidence of a plastic bag in the trash bin. As the man said, "Nobody's doing it, but there's an awful lot of people *doing* it." Okay, submitting to both packaged biscuits and crusts, now I feel guilty and compromised. Here's a quick and rich pie crust recipe that doesn't require chilling or rolling out. It's good. Whisk together 1½ cups of all-purpose flour, ¼ cup of brown sugar, and ¾ tsp. of sea salt. Slowly add 11 oz. of melted, unsalted butter and stir—with a fork, not with the whisk—until crumbly. Press into your pie pan and do what you will fancying the edges. That's it. As a primer on bisquits, try Nathalie Dupree's two ingredient recipe and variations. *Vide* Food and Literary Sources.)

To Make the Pie. So, your shell of preference is pressed/unrolled in your glass pie dish and artfully or sloppily crenelated around the edge. Preheat the oven to 325° F. In a large bowl, cream together the butter, sugar, and flour. Beat in the eggs, buttermilk, and vanilla. Stir in the coconut and, just because, 2-3 twists from the nutmeg grinder. Pour contents into the unbaked pie shell and sprinkle with the sliced almonds. Bake for 1 hour, until puffy and lightly golden. (I've always found "insert knife/toothpick to test doneness" quite a vague science. The top of the pie should be springy but firm. If in doubt, err on the side of removing it from the oven a few minutes early.)

To Make the Bourbon-Caramel Sauce. In a saucepan, melt the butter and mix in the brown sugar. Cook for 2-3 minutes at a medium boil, stirring continuously. Remove from heat and add bourbon and sea salt. (Cf.: I'm inclined to add as much as a rounded ¼ tsp. of salt, but then I'm a salt freak and consider it central to a happy lifestyle and complete nutritional/philosophical system. You might want to stick with ⅛ tsp., known where I came from as a big "peench"—i.e., pinch.) Return to medium boil for 4 minutes, continuing to stir. Remove from heat. Stir in vanilla and heavy cream. Makes one cup (1-8 servings, depending).

Serve pie warm, drizzled with a 1-2 Tbs. of the bourbon-caramel sauce and topped with a dollop of whipped cream, accompanied by an icy glass of whole milk or a quality cup of coffee (freshly ground Kona or Tanzania Peaberry if you can afford either, but anyway not Folger's.) Actually, earlier joking aside, if the sweetness and/or the calories are simply untenable, the pie's delicious without the sauce. Still, you only have one life, and after all how often do you make and eat dessert? (The pie's excellent either warm or cold. Personally, I'm adamant about mixing temperatures. If the pie's cold, I prefer a cup of coffee—a Sunday newspaper breakfast of champions. If warm, then icy milk, although this last mix is rather freakish and unsexy during dinner among adults. It'll be fine with the coffee.)

Vanilla Buttermilk Ice Cream

I've been using buttermilk in my ice cream bases for years. I'm hooked on the richness and the delectable but not quite identifiable flavor it adds. Here is the basic vanilla recipe and a few worthy variations. (My wife has a luscious recipe for pistachio ice cream that includes neither buttermilk nor, believe it or not, eggs, and ergo requires no cooking. This feels rather un-American to me, and I've therefore opted to exclude it. Add your eggs.)

3 local farm eggs*

1½ cups sugar**

2 cups whole buttermilk

2 cups heavy cream

3 tsp. vanilla

splash of vodka (optional)

butter waffle cookies (for serving)

A day ahead, place the quart-size cylinder of your ice cream maker in the freezer and prepare the ice cream base. In a medium saucepan, whisk together the buttermilk and eggs. (*Even leaving ethical issues—the deeply disturbing practices of big commercial egg producers—out of the matter, a local supplier of fresh eggs is one resource I would highly, highly exhort you to cultivate, and I'm aware I beat this drum ad nauseum throughout the book. It's well worth the effort and expense—although sometimes, direct from the farmer, a couple of dozen are an embarrassing steal—for the exponentially superior body, color, and depth of taste. Along the way, you'll likely come across some enjoyable surprises—I spent last summer playing with duck and guinea fowl eggs [ask me later]—and meet some interesting folks. And, anyway, why leave ethics out? Lay locally! *Vide* Chapter 14 for further obsessions regarding this all-important topic of eggs.) Whisk in the sugar. (**Buttermilk has a mild acidity and is sourer—for lack of a better word—than regular milk, and in my opinion requires extra sugar, thus the 1½ cups. Adjust according to taste.)

Over low-medium heat, stir continuously until thickened—stay especially attentive as the milk heats, and really do stir constantly once a low bubbling commences—perhaps 10 minutes. The mixture should be smooth and coat the spoon, but you can use your judgment about when enough's enough. (If you see a few specks of cooked albumen in the mixture, don't despair and don't try to pick them out. Take the pan off the heat, give it a brisk, authoritative whisking, and proceed. A few little flakes of egg aren't going to alter the taste and will in all likelihood magically disappear in the finished product. In the unlikely event that someone notices such a speck, claim it as artisanal design.) Cool, then stir in the cream and vanilla. If you choose, you can proceed to make the ice cream, but it will freeze better if the batter is chilled overnight.

Basically, then, all the work's done the day before. Making the ice cream merely involves returning the frozen cylinder to your electric ice cream maker—I finally, bitterly, and begrudgingly ceded my hand-cranked model two or three years ago. Turn on the machine, slowly pour in your base, and add the splash of vodka (to further help maintain a soft consistency in the finished product—vodka doesn't freeze at a normal home freezer temperature). Depending on the efficacy of your machine—my Cuisinart is methodical and fast, albeit noisy—let run for 20-30 minutes, then with a plastic spatula or wooden spoon (so as not to damage the cylinder), empty ice cream into a chilled glass container with airtight lid and harden in the freezer. (Eat a bit while it's still soft, however. A proper kitchen tasting is mandatory during cleanup and should involve at least a small bowlful.)

To serve, place 3 small or 2 medium *boules*, or a single large gob, into a bowl and add, upright, 1 crisp butter waffle cookie, preferably French. Top ice cream with a sprig of mint. (I'm assuming that the preferred alternate serving style is a given: Stand in front of the open freezer door, large spoon in one hand, open container cold in the other.)

Radical but Sublime Serving Suggestion. For either the vanilla or caramel (*vide infra*) ice creams, sprinkle a few flakes of Cyprus black lava sea salt over the bowl. The look is dramatic, and the sweet-salty taste and slight crunch are epiphanic. If you're not swooning yet, try a drizzle of good extra virgin olive oil over the top, then the black flakes. They didn't tell you life could be like this, did they?

Regarding Mix-Ins. This standard buttermilk vanilla recipe is delicious, and if you want to add an extra ingredient for texture and flavor, keep it simple to not overwhelm the flavor you've striven for. I'd suggest a single ingredient: 4 oz. of roughly chopped semisweet Callebaut (chopped squares of semisweet Baker's will suffice); ½ cup of toasted pistachios; chopped and mashed strawberries, cherries, or peaches in season (with a modest reduction of sugar in the batter); or, if you're feeling puckish, ⅔ cup of flaked and toasted coconut. These would all be agreeable choices. No marshmallows, potato chips, or Snickers bars, please, although the occasional broken Heath bar is debatably permissible.

Chocolate Buttermilk Ice Cream

ingredients for vanilla buttermilk ice cream, *vide supra*

⅓ cup European-style cocoa*

⅔ cup pecans or walnuts (optional)

After you've removed the hot mixture from the stove, sift in ⅓ cup of European-style cocoa powder—*Hershey's offers a credible version, called at time of writing Special Dark—and whisk. If desired, add toasted (and cooled) nuts, coursely chopped. Proceed as above.

Blackberry Buttermilk Ice Cream

ingredients for vanilla buttermilk ice cream, *vide supra*

1 cup frozen wild blackberries*

This is a personal innovation I'm proud of, worthy of its own designation. To your cooled base, add 1 cup of the wild blackberries you picked last August, washed and thawed from the freezer, then mashed. (*Admittedly, most of my favorite patches have been razed by rural "development." My father still picks some periodically, god bless him, and, believe me, a gift gallon bag of self-picked blackberries is very much an act of love, with the thorn scars and chigger bites to prove it. Currently, wild blackberries from any and all sources are running perilously low in my freezer, another bleak forecast of the future. Anyway, if you don't have access to small, wild berries, and are disinclined to contribute the sweat, time, and blood to their procurement, try to get something like the real thing, in season, from your farmers market. [Cf.: the enormous, testosterone-driven, picture-perfect, utterly tasteless models on display in the big-box grocers, grotesque and virtually inedible.] For further notes and reflections on blackberries, a subject of inexhaustible interest, *vide* Chapters 10 and 20.) Proceed as above. You'll be glad you did.

Caramel Buttermilk Ice Cream

ingredients for vanilla buttermilk ice cream, *vide supra,*

with 4 farm egg yolks substituted for 3 eggs

This version differs from the vanilla more in method than content. It's more labor intensive, but a flavorful change. Briefly: Melt the sugar in a skillet, stirring frequently until light brown, rock hard, and formed into frightening crystals. Pour scalded buttermilk (heated in a saucepan) over the sugar, and cook and stir patiently until the crystals melt. In a large bowl, beat 4 beautiful, bright, fresh yolks (substituted for the 3 eggs above), and slowly, slowly pour in the hot buttermilk/sugar liquid, whisking constantly. Return to saucepan and cook over low-medium heat, stirring regularly, until thickened. Cool and continue, *vide ut supra.*

CHAPTER 10

·

Grilling: A Reluctant Convert's Tale; or, Let Them Eat Plank

Coals
glowed with fine, low heat. I tasted my wine,
squinted through trees across late sun.

—*from* "Apologia for the Fish
I Overcooked on Good Friday"

<u>Charcoal vs. Gas</u>. Since I was a young man living in his first ratty apartment, I happily grilled over charcoal, slowly upgrading from a wobbly tabletop grill to a proper stand-up model with a hinged lid and rudimentary vents. Somewhere along the line, my introduction by a friend to the charcoal lighter basket/chimney, and the brilliant simplicity of its design, allowed me to put aside those fumy pre-soaked coals and get serious. Something about the ritual and romance of properly filling and stacking the basket, striking a long match, and stepping back, never failed to please. Once the coals were a lovely glow, emptying the basket—sparks exploding in the face and on the collar—throwing on a handful of soaked hickory chips, and loosing your inner Primitive Man or Woman. Coals are an inexact science, of course—e.g., prone to flare-ups and premature burnout—and thus the challenge and danger, ecstasy and defeat.

Things change. Several years ago, my in-laws gave me the generous and unwanted gift of a top-end Vermont Castings gas grill—a costly steel monster. I recall vividly, in high definition, a delivery man removing the grill from the truck, the behemoth rising in air on the prongs of his forklift and hovering martially, inexorably, through the yard and toward the back deck. Only a strain from the woods of "The Ride of the Valkyries" was missing. Upon inspection, the grill was undeniably a beautifully designed piece, sturdy and broad and implacable, loaded with bells and whistles. I hated it. I wrote an ungracious (and lousy) poem about the aggressiveness of gift giving, then for a year left the eyesore dismissed and unused as I continued to light the coals of my now suddenly shabby and flimsy former grill and make whatever inchoate point I intended to make.

Things change. For better or worse, that rusted charcoal grill has long since been ignominiously consigned to the trash heap, and I am fairly well hooked on the convenience, consistency, and increased control of the gas grill. I.e., I have been weakened and reduced by the habit of how nice it is to just light that big boy, wait twenty minutes, and have at it. (Aside to my in-laws: Thanks for the great gift, guys!) I'm still attracted to the (spurious? whimsical?) notion that food grilled over coals tastes better—due to the supposed carcinogens, I theorize—and I still can't find a useful, practical place for wood chips (either loose or in a smoking box) beneath the gas grill's racks, but I'm otherwise a happy bourgeois sell out who's unlikely to go back to all that fiddling around. (Cf.: I realize, too, that the true grilling freak needs to have both. *Needs* to. Well and good, but for the modest approaches of this chapter we aver gas.) Yes, there's the omnipresent anxiety of the tank, and perhaps you, too, don't feel comfortable with an extra fifteen pounds of propane sitting in storage in garage or mudroom. So, since few grills have a gauge for fuel level, attend to the tank that's your lifeline, give it an inexact "lift" now and then to test the weight, and don't take unnecessary chances when you're having guests or doing something special or complicated. (Yes, once or twice each grilling season you'll be sabotaged by a sputtering, empty tank, and yes this is frustrating well out of proportion. With a modicum of luck and foresight, that calamity will befall midweek Chicken Night, not during the Wild King Salmon Payday Grill Party.)

Personal Reflections on the Terms and Limitations of Grilling. I rarely participate in "tailgate" grilling (burgers, brats, hot dogs) and seldom, anymore, undertake the stress of trying to tailor red meat—in which category I include not only beef but also fresh tuna—for a group with individual, unreliably stated, and unsatisfiable needs. (The exception to this rule is, of course, 4 nice fat lamb loin chops for two, rubbed with olive oil, chopped garlic, and peak season rosemary from the garden. Sear those little beauties at a high temperature and bring them off rare.) That limits the field to chicken, to ribs, to shrimps and prawns—with dry rub, marinade, or brushed sauce, and often actually improved by the char of an inadvertent flame-up (claim it was intentional) while you're refreshing visitors' drinks—and to the suggestions I make below, especially in the implementation of the cedar plank. If cooking for two, you can more attentively accommodate by request a marbled porterhouse or ribeye or thick pork chop (as well as the silent ridicule attendant upon failure with the proverbial tongs). Otherwise, consider taking my advice, eliminating virtually all grill anxiety, and matriculating to the plank school. (N.b.: And do not, under *any* circumstances, not over gas and especially not over coals, ever, ever attempt to grill strips of bacon. This is one of the few sustainable truths I learned during graduate school, and I offer it freely.)

Now, let's first briefly address and close an earlier matter.

> Indulge the mood, Ghost, celebrate
> the light that never fades until it does.
> Salty grilled vendace—*better than sardines,*
> *my friend*—eaten with the fingers . . .

> —*from* "Ghost Attends the Midnight Sun
> Festival as a Special Guest"

Grilled Shellfish

1-2 dozen unshucked oysters (or 1 lb.+ of mussels in shell)

coarse sea salt to taste

appropriate condiments

Due to the speed at which these shellfish will cook on the grill and the management they require, you might consider this a fun, interactive snack for two rather than an appetizer, although of course you could increase the portions, add a green salad, and call it a light meal. Eating these al fresco, right off the grill, is mandatory.

Grilled Oysters in the Shell. These are, you'll recall, the dozen or two oysters impulsively purchased for the previous day's festivities—Thanksgiving or just a spontaneous moment unfortunately failed (*vide* Chapter 4)—and now languishing, cursed and recriminating and locked tight in their jagged and unforgiving shells, in a Styrofoam tray of melted ice in the refrigerator. Today you exact a qualified revenge.

Place the oysters, the curved "belly" of the shells downward, directly onto the rack of a medium-hot grill and close the lid. Cook for 5-6 minutes, until the shells open. They will not spring open in the generous manner some contend, but they will, mostly, part to a perceptible crack. Remove with tongs to a large serving platter, trying to lose as little liquid from each as possible. Eat immediately, at the table on the deck, prying the shells open with the knife that failed you yesterday. Serve with melted and salted butter, lemon wedges, Tabasco, saltine crackers, and cold Pilsners in frosted glasses. As I said, the oysters won't open as easily as you'd like, but they will open, and shared with a partner who's into the absurd spirit of the enterprise (i.e., revenge), it's a playful snack (even if, finally, just not quite worth the effort). Most significantly, the oysters are, so to speak, off your back, and you've shown an undefeated character and resilient perspicacity.

> Endure their briny effluvia.
> Raise each ebony bivalve
> to running water,
> burnish away all grit,
> all residue of sea possible.
> Discard the crushed and broken.
> Detach each coarse
> beard with whatever force
> necessary. Ice the survivors.
> Tap parted shells,
> allowing the rest a moment
> to pull themselves together.
>
> Most won't. Discard the dead.
>
> —"Cleaning Mussels"

Grilled Mussels. While we're at it, let's grill some mussels, too, which are easier to handle and tastier to boot. Thoroughly clean the mussels—a shared pound for a snack, at least one pound each as a main course—brushing them under cold water with a toothbrush and debearding them. Discard any mussels cracked and/or clearly dead and give any questionable specimens a tap and a few minutes to think about it. Arrange the living on a medium-hot grill, sprinkle with sea salt and cracked pepper, and lower the top. (I used to try to employ a foil-wrapped rack to preserve the liquid. Forget it.)

Grilling mussels is virtually foolproof. All you need to decide is how cooked you prefer them—soft and a bit "wet" and chewy, or cooked longer until the edges just begin to char/crisp. They cook fast, and within 3 minutes the shells should begin to open. You can then eat them any time. On the grill, I prefer mussels cooked a bit more—to maximize the smokiness—than when steamed in wine or hard cider on the stove, so take a peek and perhaps grill another 3 minutes with the lid up. When you're happy and satisfied with the result, remove the mussels with tongs to a serving platter. Sprinkle some chopped Italian parsley over the top if you're feeling fussy. Eat them immediately, at the table on the deck, with lemon wedges (melted butter and hot crusty bread optional, but recommended). If the weather's nice—and why wouldn't it be, if you're outside grilling mussels?—pair with a chilled bottle of semi-dry Gewurztraminer or Riesling, although a Sauvignon Blanc is the standard choice. Said bottles would also complement the oysters.

·

> Forgive me, my compatriots,
> if I reject the rusty hot dogs
> and leather burgers of your grill . . .
>
> —*from* "Fête de l'Indépendance
> (or, July 4th, Final Evening in France)"

Grilling with Cedar Planks. The pre-cut cedar planks—usually shrink-wrapped in packages of three—readily available at the grocer work fine (in fact, they're so thin that they blacken and buckle quite dramatically on the grill), but they're expensive, and of course the lengths are prefabricated. You're going to want to plank a lot to master your technique, so go to the local home improvement retail monster—a lumberyard would be even better in terms of personal involvement and culpability, if you can find one patient with such a small order—and pick out the cheapest, roughest untreated cedar 1x6s that you can find. Two 8' pieces will produce enough planks for a season's worth of play and experiment, trial and error and triumph. Ask the sales assistant to cut the lumber in half, which he'll do for free. The 4' pieces are easy to transport in the car, and you can saw your own planks at home to accommodate specific and varying needs, meanwhile feeling like a grilling warrior. A 10" plank is ideal for a fat Cornish hen, while you'll require 14"-16" for a rack of ribs or side of salmon.

Before grilling, you need to soak your plank in water for at least an hour. It floats—stubbornly and aggressively—so weigh it down in the sink with the large Mason jar of dry beans (or whatever you use for pie weights) from the pantry. If the plank is longer than 15" or so, it won't fit flat in a conventional kitchen sink, so you'll have to soak it vertically, exposing as much surface as possible to water and alternating the submerged end every 15-20 minutes.

A Note on Grilling Accompanying Vegetables. It's desirable and pleasing to pull an entire meal (or close to it) off the grill whenever possible, since you're already going to the trouble. Grilling vegetables along with planking, however, presents a challenge in the sense that the secret of the planking is that your entrée, after initially smoking on a high heat, then cooks slowly on a low heat, and crucial to the proper result is that, once begun, *you do not lift the lid.* The ease of this constitutes much of the charm of the method, and is quite amenable to concentrated drinking, but it's not a technique perfectly conducive to turning, properly charring, and granting the general attention most grilled vegetables require.

Moderately sized baking or sweet potatoes are one good option. Rinse, dry, rub with olive oil, and wrap each snugly in aluminum foil. Place on the grill rack as you are heating it, turning once in the interim. Once you place the plank on the grill, depending on the size of the taters, either simply move them to the side or, perhaps more wisely, lift them with tongs to the raised rack off of direct heat and let continue to cook. I'll make a few other suggestions according to the meats and variations discussed below, but first I'll offer one specific favorite that can be adapted according to the plank or enjoyed anytime you're grilling during the summer. For our purposes, I'm assuming here grilling for two, but obviously this is infinitely (well, infinite at least to the limits of your grill size) expandable.

Grilled Corn on the Cob

2 ears white, small-kerneled sweet corn (local and in season)*

2 oz. softened herb butter**

*I prefer sweet white corn when/if I can get it, and I'm sure you do too, so let's use that. The in season requirement is, of course, non-negotiable, and I'll make my fiercest pitch to also go to the slight extra effort of staying local. (If you're going to the farmers market every Saturday morning during the summer, as are any right-thinking, fun-seeking citizens who love quality produce and admire and support their farmers, then it isn't any extra effort.)

**Herb Butter. This is so delicious, so calming, and so pleasant and convenient to have around—and since it's a bit of effort to make—you might as well go ahead a whip up at least ½ lb., which will last in the refrigerator for weeks, if it makes it that long. In a mixing bowl, chop up 2 sticks of unsalted butter and let soften. From your garden, and in another bowl, cut a handful of oregano, a handful of thyme, and a handful of basil. Soak, rinse, drain, and pat dry with paper towels. De-stem and finely chop the herbs, then mix them into the butter with a fork or your clean hands, along with coarse sea salt and freshly ground black pepper (and perhaps just a few crushed red pepper flakes—"devil or angel, do whichever you are . . .") according to taste. Roll the butter into a log, wrap snugly and well in plastic wrap and store in refrigerator or freezer according to frequency of use.

Shuck and rinse your corn, cut any bald ends/stubs from the ears, dry them with paper towels, then with a knife and with love spread 1 oz. (or so) of softened herb butter up and down the rows of kernels of each ear. Wrap tightly and individually in aluminum foil. (While I'm attracted to the romance of grilling corn in the shuck, cleaning the cobs sufficiently so as not to get a stringy mouthful of silks never seemed worth the considerable effort. Plus, all that charred shuck is cumbersome on the plate. Let's leave it to the food truck vendors and to enjoy as we stroll around Arts in the Park.)

Place wrapped ears on a medium to medium-hot grill and cook, covered, for 20 minutes, turning periodically and evenly. Adjust cooking time according to taste. I like grilled corn on the cob to know it's been there and have a few black kernels. With tongs, remove from grill and place directly onto the individual plates at the picnic table. Let the lucky recipient participate by unwrapping his or her own hot foil for the steaming reward that awaits. No pain, no gain. Eat immediately, gnawing left to right, not even pretending to care about anything else on the plate.

> This is the holy day, fête, glass of wine raised
> to animal heaven in blood communion.
> Greasy mortality and the well-gnawed bone.
> Pallid over nests of lettuce, carrot and radish,
> vegetarians size you with nervous glances.
>
> —*from* "Ghost Holds His Vow of Fasting
> for Nearly Twelve Hours"

Cedar-Planked Baby Back Ribs

1 2-lb. side baby back ribs

for dry rub:

⅔ cup dark brown sugar

4 large cloves garlic

1 tsp. sweet and spicy paprika

1 tsp. onion powder

1 tsp. ground ginger

½ tsp. cayenne powder

1 tsp. freshly ground black pepper

1 tsp. coarse sea salt

Mixing together a dry rub demonstrates ideally how recipes—especially in regard to ingredients and to a lesser degree technique—are essentially approximations and suggestions relative to taste. A recipe requires, however, authority, specificity, and, of course, dogmatism to be useful. So, do exactly this: Peel and chop your garlic and mix in a small bowl with all of the dry ingredients. It's a mix of sweet and savory and heat that I like, but let your conscience, if it speaks, be your guide. Dry mustard? Garam masala? Curry powder? The smoky paprika you bought as a lark and can't figure what to do with? More cayenne? Hell, chili powder if you like. (I wouldn't, but you can.)

Massage dry rub into the rack of ribs on both sides. Wrap snugly in aluminum foil and place in refrigerator, on a platter, overnight.

Soak a plank of sufficient length. Preheat the grill to high. (If you're also grilling wrapped corn on the cob or potatoes—*vide supra*—place them on the rack as soon as you ignite the grill. Put the top down. Midway through the grill heating—mine takes about 20-25 minutes to get to 500° F—turn vegetables once with tongs and close lid. Before you begin planking, move them to the raised shelf of your grill off direct heat and continue cooking at the low temperature—*vide infra*—for the duration.)

Unwrap ribs and place on soaked plank. If you've any extra room, you might also place on the plank, rubbed in olive oil, a peeled and halved onion, flat side down, and/or a quartered red or yellow pepper. Place the plank on the hot grill, lower the top, and let the plank smoke for 15 minutes. Reduce heat to low and continue to cook for 45 minutes. (N.b.: Do *not* lift the lid again after putting the plank on the grill. Have faith. Have a Martini.)

With sturdy tongs, lift the entire plank from the grill and put it directly on the table, either on a platter or board if eating inside or on a tablecloth, or directly onto the wrought iron deck table. With the slightest hint of dramatic flourish, slice the ribs while still on the platter. They will look, smell, and taste spectacular. You are a magician.

Serves two gluttonously, three adequately, four skimpily.

> Festivities unraveled into night,
> as festivities should. Beaded sangria,
> roast chicken al fresco
> from two greasy fists, crisp skin
> and moist flesh. Sunset
> behind the mountain where the old town
> fell to pieces. Earth claimed the ruin.

—from "Ernesto's 109th Birthday Party"

Lemon-Scented Cedar-Planked Cornish Hen

1 fat Cornish hen (or 2 small ones)

¼ cup local honey

several sprigs fresh thyme

several large cloves garlic

juice 1 lemon

2-3 sections preserved lemon

coarse sea salt & freshly ground black pepper

Rinse and pat dry your hen, then season as you prefer. I suggest mixing the honey, 1 Tbs. cleaned and chopped thyme, 2-3 chopped garlic cloves, the lemon juice, and salt and pepper to taste. Place the hen in a snugly fitting bowl, pour the marinade over it, rub the bird thoroughly all over until well-coated, and leave in the fridge for 2 hours, turning once.

When ready to grill, stuff hen with a few sprigs of thyme, a few garlic cloves, and sections of preserved lemon from the jar in the fridge (*vide* Chapter 17). Place on soaked plank and place plank on hot grill (*vide ut supra*). With lid lowered throughout, smoke plank for 10 minutes, turn heat to low, and cook for another 45 minutes. Pull gently on the leg to check doneness, remove plank with tongs, and deliver the bird whole to the table. Slice in half on the plank and serve.

I'm a fan of Cornish hens, and a single plump specimen serves two as an entrée just fine. If they're small, prepare 1 bird for each and check for doneness 5-10 minutes earlier. They're a lot of fun to eat, but resist, no matter how jovial the mood, comparing the adorable little wing or drumstick to that of any former avian pet now deceased. Otherwise, you should have a good time. Perhaps jasmine rice as accompaniment?

> Later, we ate your fresh and tender flesh,
> grilled, coarsely salted, the cold wine
> succulent river of our gathering.
>
> —*from* "Apologia to the Trout at Meadow Farm"

Cedar-Planked Wild Salmon

1+ lb. side fillet fresh king, coho, or sockeye salmon

⅓ cup molasses

4 large cloves garlic

coarse sea salt & freshly ground black pepper

1 lemon (optional)

1 lime (optional)

This is the sine qua non of all grilled plank recipes, the one that started it all, the reason we're gathered here together in this chapter. Wait until king salmon season (roughly, late May to early July) or, a bit later, coho—you'll also come across the more ubiquitous sockeye somewhere in there—then splurge and keep splurging until it's all over and you have to wait until next year. This is the definition, my friend, of luxurious summer grilling and good, appreciative living. (Remember, too, that prices tend to drop as the season proceeds and peaks. Get to know your fishmonger, flirt and flatter away, and don't be shy about asking questions regarding anticipated price and availability. If you're not getting straight, informative answers, or if the fish isn't stunningly beautiful in color, buttery in texture, and head-shaking, smile-inducing in taste, then get another fishmonger. Just bring your debit card, swallow slowly, and remember, as the man opined, "That's why they call it money.")

Scale the skin side of the fillet with a keen vegetable peeler, then give the flesh side a nice, sensual massage (no reason to have anyone else around during this) to remove any pin bones. Use tweezers. Rinse and pat dry. Rub flesh side with molasses and finely chopped garlic, salt to taste, and pepper generously with the grinder. (You may have noticed throughout this book my fondness for garlic. Well, why not? Also, my mother for many years charmingly believed that a clove of garlic meant an entire *bulb*, followed recipes accordingly, and thus raised us boys sweet-breathed at the table. I believe this story to be actual history rather than family folklore. If it ain't true, it oughta be.) If you prefer, concoct a dry rub of your own, but the molasses/garlic rub is a personal favorite and tested date pleaser.

As the grill heats to high, grill 1 lemon and 1 lime, halved and placed flat side down on the grill. (*Vide ut supra*: Remove these halves, with tongs, to the indirect heat of the raised rack when you begin planking.) Place fillet (or whole side if you're flush) of salmon onto soaked plank and put on grill. Lower the lid. Assuming a fillet thickness of about 1", cook on high heat for approximately 15-20 minutes. Do not overcook this special piece of fish. Check the doneness of the flesh with a fork and try to bring it off the grill at medium-rare (any rarer than that and you won't have adequately benefited from the planking). Place the grilled lemon and lime halves around the fillet and with sturdy tongs bring the plank to the table. Slice and serve with a salad of mixed greens and whatever else sounds good. (If you simply *must* pair with a Chardonnay, if you just can't help yourself, please make sure—as a personal favor to me—that it is un-oaked.)

If at all possible, eat outside on a balmy evening under the strings of deck lighting, listening together to the chittering screech owls in the woods lamenting the lost day and cooing forth the night. Leave your wristwatch inside.

•

Barbeque Sauce

Since I'm certain you're not going to give up on a good sloppy grilling of chicken, ribs, steaks, and so forth just because I'm bullying you into finessing your plank technique, below are two dynamite sauce recipes using, respectively, blackberries and blueberries. Barbeque sauces are amusing to cook up and can be tinkered with and adjusted ad infinitum according to good or bad taste and what's on hand in the kitchen. I've tried to keep the ingredients lists here relatively concise and at the same time offer two sauces with radically different layers of flavor.

The sweeter blackberry sauce is unbeatable on both beef and pork ribs, while, of the two, the smokier blueberry is the better choice for chicken. Either, I imagine, would complement a venison loin, a nice ostrich steak, and possibly even salmon. (If you think this latter heresy, please consider that I'd never even heard of barbequed salmon until I was up at the Last Frontier Theatre Conference in Alaska, a state that takes its salmon *very* seriously. Q.v.: At unpretentious Oscar's restaurant in Valdez, approach the window in the screened-in patio and order whichever of three [or all three] distinct local types of just-caught salmon are on the grill that evening, all lathered in a tomato-y barbeque sauce and all finger-licking sensations.) Consider, too, spooning a bit of either warmed sauce over a nicely blackened, medium-rare duck breast sliced on a bias and served over polenta. Experiment with other game, as well. (If you're up in Quebec in August, the blueberry season, you can buy fresh berries from the roadside stands to augment your craving until dinner, when the rural Québécois restaurant will likely treat you to *bluets* on your salad, drizzled as a sauce over your rare elk fillet, and integral, naturally, to dessert. Wonderful, although surely we can also concoct a potent blueberry cocktail of some sort to initiate the proceedings? *Bluet* beer can't do it all.)

Bear in mind that if you wait for fresh berries, you'll be well into prime grilling season, especially regarding (in my area, anyway) the blackberries, so you may want to raid last year's stash from the freezer. If using frozen berries, rinse quickly—don't thaw, or they'll begin to lose their juice—under cold water, shake dry, and use immediately. Lastly, I'd suggest you make both sauces simultaneously. Since you're already in there mincing, measuring, and messing around, why not? Then you'll be ready to attack the grill like the force of nature—locked and loaded with tongs and sauce brush—you truly are. (If either sauce gets thicker than you like while cooking it down, simply add a splash more wine or beer. If you already—mea culpa—drank all the wine and beer during the reduction process, then vinegar, chicken stock, or even, obviously, water will suffice. Please remember, too, that these sauces are *not* to be used in conjunction with the planks, which mostly require dry rubs.) Taste as you proceed and adjust as inspired.

Each recipe yields 2 cups. Pour into a one-pint Mason jar, cool completely before screwing on the lid, and store in the fridge for a month or longer.

Blackberry & Red Wine Barbeque Sauce

2 rounded cups wild blackberries

½ cup dark brown sugar

½ cup organic ketchup

2 Tbs. red wine

1 Tbs. red wine vinegar

1 Tbs. canola oil

½ medium white or yellow onion

2 large cloves garlic

1 Tbs. fresh ginger

1 tsp. Tabasco

2 tsp. soy sauce

½ rounded tsp. coarsely ground black pepper

Zest the ginger, mince the onion and garlic, and add all ingredients to a medium sauce pot. Bring to a boil, lower heat, cover, and simmer for 30 minutes. Remove pan from heat to a coaster and mash the sauce and berries a bit with a potato masher. Don't overdo. Lumps are fine, even preferable, and will remain regardless. (*I know we largely addressed this in the previous chapter, but allow me to repeat that if, unfortunately, you're reduced to using those huge, dubious tasting, suspiciously grown, ghastly steroid berries from the grocer, you may want to scissor/slice the largest behemoths in half before cooking. They may require, too, an extra press or two with the masher for their discipline.)

Return to heat, bring to low boil, and cook down for about 15 minutes, stirring occasionally, until thick and rich. Remove from heat and cool.

If your nephew or a former student or any other maniacal kid with a gun has "gifted" you a venison loin, don the carnivore's apron. Or, if you're simple folk like us, have your baby back ribs positioned nearby, trimmed and ready.

> . . . pluck each ashy-dark berry that remains.
> It's late season but I harvest
> an awkward fistful. Then I kick the door in
> and enter with spoils to announce.

> —*from* "Blueberries and Corpses"

Blueberry & Stout Barbeque Sauce

2 rounded cups blueberries from your bushes

1 cup homemade oatmeal stout

⅓ cup molasses

⅓ cup organic ketchup

1 Tbs. Worcestershire sauce

1 Tbs. canola oil

1 giant or 2 medium shallots

2 large cloves garlic

2 large chipotles in adobo + 2 tsp. adobo sauce (from can)

¼ tsp. smoked paprika

5-6 turns freshly ground black pepper

pinch sea salt

Mince the shallot, garlic cloves, and seeded chipotles. Add all ingredients to a medium sauce pot and bring to a boil. Reduce heat to medium and reduce, at a low boil/high simmer, uncovered, for 45 minutes. Stir occasionally. While you're waiting, pour the remaining 4 oz. of cold beer, careful of sediment, into your special "tasting glass" to ensure it hasn't spoiled and has, indeed, lagered properly. At some point, remove the sauce from the burner—*vide ut supra*—give it 3-4 quick presses with the masher, and return to heat. When thick and deeply colored, remove from stove and cool.

And, again, why wait? Maybe a mixed grill tonight? Wouldn't this be enticing on a pound of those wild fresh prawns you saw at the counter yesterday?

CHAPTER 11

·

Chili: A Man's Man vs. a Foodie's Foodie

Or a woman's woman, for that matter. Chili is for the People.

Two general matters to begin: First, I always make chili in a simple stove-top wok. I like the large, curved surface both for the initial sautéing/searing and also for the subsequent slow cooking that melds the many ingredients. Plus, a wok easily facilitates a lot of turning and stirring. If the technique seems eccentric, let's just call it fusion and double the price. My wok is of the no-frills, inexpensive, indestructible metal variety, nicely and irredeemably blackened by 30 years of use since one of my brothers gave it to me when I was in college. The box (long ago disintegrated) included the base that goes over the burner, the wok, a metal spatula, a removable half rack for steaming, and a virtually weightless aluminum top. I'd suggest you make the small investment in a similar setup (no electric woks, please), as it will prove indispensable not only for stir fries and Chinese steamed buns, but also, as you know now that the secret's out, for murderous chili. (Metal woks are prone to rust, however, so treat respectfully and don't ever soak overnight. After the meal, scrub it, dry it, and put it away.)

Secondly, you have to work very hard and really apply yourself to make bad chili. It can be accomplished, through utter ineptness or a dedicated application of arrogance, but not easily. Below, I offer my own amped-up take on the matter with black beans and two cuts of lamb. (N.b.: Absolutely *no* kidney beans and *no* spaghetti. If you want to add diced tomatoes, okay, but since it's winter—right?—you're better served using canned.) This is excellent chili, spicy, aromatic, fortifying, and requiring sufficient effort and cost to make it worthwhile. Plus, the philosophical foundation is solid enough, confident enough in its quirky yet hearty personality, to allow lots of variation.

Actually, the recipe's versatility suggests a third point, or anyway an important corollary to the second. Don't make chili with a rigid or even fully predetermined list of ingredients. It's one of the classic—again, operating within the proven basic matrix of the recipe—"toss it in there" dishes, and spontaneity and calculated risk from a crowded counter (and skewed imagination) of possibilities are part of the fun. E.g.: This time around—in a last refreshing-the-memory test batch, and for the first time ever—I added cumin seeds because they were in the spice rack and seemed like a good idea. Sometimes I've used white onions and maybe thrown in a shallot. This time, the small yellow onions at the grocer looked shiny and appealing. In an increasingly jolly mood, I added chipotles in place of the usual mix of cayenne powder and red pepper flakes—I don't like punishing heat in chili or want eating it to be a competition in suffering, so something had to give, but by all means please thy sadomasochistic self—because: a) they were open in the fridge, b) to celebrate the new high our Chipotle stock had hit that afternoon, and c) I felt like it, and the cook is both god and fool of his own kitchen paradise/purgatory. The seeds and the peppers were successful tweaks and acceptably within the original premise. (Cf.: I briefly considered adding red wine, then came to my senses and drank it instead. No wine compromising *my* chili, thanks very much. The last thought was cocoa, which I'd been mulling over earlier, a conquistador temptation I resisted or anyway deferred. *Vide infra*: I experimented later with the leftovers rather than risk the whole batch.) Just don't get *too* goofy and screw it up.

Vide ut supra for meatloaf, also. Enough chitchat. Tie on your apron and let's cook. This makes 4 substantial bowls, meaning it serves two with minimal and fought-over remains. Don't be nonplussed by the ingredients list. Be plussed.

Lamb & Black Bean Chili

1 lb. ground lamb

1 lb. boneless leg of lamb

7 (yes, 7) large cloves garlic*

2 small or 1 large yellow onion

1 Tbs. all-purpose flour

2 Tbs. olive oil

1½+ Tbs. ground cumin

1½+ Tbs. chili powder

2+ Tbs. Worcestershire sauce

1 Tbs. molasses

3 chipotles in adobo sauce (from can)

½ tsp. cumin seeds

½+ Tbs. freshly ground black pepper

½ tsp. sea salt

15-oz. can black beans

2+ cups organic tomato juice (*not* V-8)

accompaniments for serving, *vide infra*

With a good carving knife, cut the leg of lamb into small, ⅓"-½" pieces, somewhere between cubed and diced. (You want them to be distinguishable from the ground meat in the cooked down finished product, but not chunks. Think, perhaps, "large bits.") Dust the pieces with flour and set aside.

Heat 1 Tbs. olive oil in the wok. Over medium heat, add the coarsely chopped onion and cook, stirring to keep from burning, for 2 minutes. Add the chopped garlic and cook and stir for 2 more minutes. Add the ground lamb, salt and pepper lightly, break up the meat with a spatula, and cut in with the onions and garlic. Cook about 5 minutes. Turn once or twice, but don't pester; leave it alone enough to brown a bit. With the spatula, remove all to a bowl, heat remaining olive oil, add the leg of lamb pieces, lightly salt and pepper, and stir-fry for another 5 minutes—claiming a clandestine rare piece before all are gone—until pink inside. Turn down the heat to medium-low, return the ground mixture to the wok, then add cumin, chili powder, Worcestershire sauce, molasses, chopped chipotles, cumin seeds, tomato juice, and a hearty grind of pepper. Mix it all together well, return to a boil, then turn burner to low and cover the wok.

Let it simmer a while, 2-3 hours, stirring and tasting occasionally. Add a bit more tomato juice if the chili overly thickens and adjust spices according to taste. My deeply felt advice is *not* to skim off any slight bit of grease but rather to covet it. Your lamb should be less fatty than a cheap cut of ground beef, and anyway that's why you added the flour. Tennessee Williams: "In the time of your life, *live*." (Granted, he was referring to a different matter than lamb grease.) 20-30 minutes before serving, empty the black beans into a colander and rinse and drain well. Stir them into the chili.

When you can't wait any longer, call in the lover you ran off earlier for lifting the lid, stealing smells, and generally mucking with your Process. Don't worry—all is forgiven. Serve in wide, flat bowls with accompaniments of sour cream (mandatory), shredded cheddar cheese, diced white onion, Tabasco, and either saltines, white corn tortilla chips, or cornbread muffins. (I give a slight nod to the humble saltines.) To drink, beer in frosted glasses. (I brewed a nut brown ale with Tettnanger hops and brown sugar that matches superbly.) An icy hard cider will also complement and gratify. Flannel shirts, wide-wale corduroys (okay, kids—sweatpants), wool socks, a fire lit in the grate if you have one, in your heart if you don't. Peer through the window into the early dark. It's cold out there and the wild world's on its own tonight. Music, not compulsory, should also be warm and robust and remind you how lucky you are to be here.

Postscript: The Great Cocoa Experiment was inconclusive. I separately reheated 3 cups of chili, adding ⅙ tsp. of Hershey's Special Dark cocoa to one, ¼ tsp. of shaved Baker's unsweetened baking chocolate to another, and leaving the third as the tasting baseline. Both of the chilies with cocoa, not surprisingly, turned brown ["rich" or "muddy" according to one's point-of-view]. The consensus of our panel of two seemed to be that the chili with shaved chocolate tasted slightly more "chocolaty," maybe, while the cocoa powder seemed to mellow—mute?—the slight heat of the chipotles. Maybe. Both variations were intriguing, although neither, by unanimous vote of the panel, necessarily improved the original, but it was an entertaining snack. Next time? That encrusted jar of *mole negro* in the fridge? Maybe. Maybe not.

CHAPTER 12

·

Home-Dried Foods

Okay, the wrapping has been shredded, and you are on the floor staring a bit vacantly at the Ronco Food Dehydrator your sibling or colleague has offered as the "perfect present for you." If you weren't sure your brother/peer loved you and was a person of character and good humor, you might naturally think you've just been re-gifted. Regardless, the moment confirms again your conceit that gifts are acts of aggression, enacted on the battlefields of birthday and Christmas/Hanukkah/Kwanzaa.

Stay on your game. Nod. Smile. That box is going to be a terrible space-eater in the "gift closet," but don't show your pain. Remember that you're a professional. After all, this *is* a food gadget, and there's considerable time to be wasted on another hobby, so all's not lost. From his wide-eyed photo, and as seen on TV, Mr. Popeil *does* appear an earnest, handsome man, or at any rate a man giddy at the prospect of all things dried—fruit, vegetable, and flesh alike. (Truthfully, I'm being disingenuous in these paragraphs. My father gave me my dehydrator, which I was perplexed but pleased to receive. No reason was ever tendered for his generosity, but I assume it constituted an offshoot, of sorts, of the legendary beef jerky that he makes in his own machine and distributes in Ziploc baggies over the holidays—a nod to legacy.)

Ignore the included recipe book's zealous embrace of dehydration (you can reduce just about anything to leather), followed by its Orwellian zeal for "rehydration" of all the lovely fresh produce you just laboriously destroyed. Keep an open mind. Think post-Apocalypse, bomb shelter, survivalist, and just plain ole having fun frigging-around-with-food-for-no-good-reason. (According to Mr. Popeil, the Egyptians and Vikings had a blast with this technique.) Forget, however, most of the recipes presented. Viz.: dried mango (too hard to peel and slice), dried "raisins" (too cutesy and pointless), dried fruit roll-ups (too damned stupid), apple pie (huh?!), and dried flowers and herbs (not worth dignifying with a response—hang'm upside down on a nail in the kitchen, folks).

For your salvation, here are three satisfying, insultingly easy recipes to make all that circulating low heat worthwhile. Each will take in the ballpark of 36 hours, more or less, as indicated below and according to your machine.

Don't forget to bring a bulging baggy of product to the sister or boss responsible. Make her masticate a piece while you watch: It feels good to pay it forward.

Honey-Glazed Banana Chips

10 unblemished, just-ripe bananas

¼ cup local honey

¼ cup spring water

These are delicious—tastier than anything you'll get at the store. Mix honey and water. Take 10 beautiful bananas (which will approximately fill a five tray dehydrator) and slice ¼" thick. Mix the slices in the honey-water, coating thoroughly, shake off the excess, and load trays. Rotate trays according to diagram. Dry to a definitive crunch. (Caveat: One downside to this recipe is that the honey caramelizes on the trays and leaves them sticky. You'll have to briefly soak afterwards for cleaning. Did that stop the Egyptians?) Store cooled chips in a gallon-sized storage bag in the refrigerator.

Sweet Tater Chips (for the Dog)

3-4 sweet potatoes

When in season at your farmers market, hand select a bagful of sweet potatoes, remaining undistracted by the proprietor's mantra—*them there's some good eatin' sweet taters darlin'*—and keeping in mind that, obviously, the size of the potato determines the size of the chip. Sliced thinly (⅛" or so?—don't hurt yourself with the big knife), 3-4 potatoes fill up the trays quickly. Put no seasoning on the slices, just load up the trays. Rotate the trays for 24-36 hours, according to the diagram, until the chips are firm. The result is bland for a human, but apparently deeply gratifying, in my vicarious experience, for a dog. Stored in a gallon-sized bag, these will last for months in the fridge, but they won't need to. (Slip a few in the pocket of your denim jacket before those brisk and self-reflective autumn walks with the mutt. A large chip for behavioral reward, a medium just for fun, and a last small one just because you love your little pooch-pooch and are amazed she tolerates you.)

Goat/Venison Jerky

meat, *vide infra*

marinade, *vide infra*

Jerky is the Big Daddy, the raison d'être, of the dehydrating universe. Its preparation is not something the devotee jokes about, speaking rather in hushed and secretive tones.

Selecting and Purchasing the Meat. In a pinch, lamb. To separate yourself from the pack, you'll of course want to use something other than beef. If you have a friend who's a hunter ("hunter-friend" need not be oxymoronic, at least not until the meat's safely in your fridge), venison is an excellent option. Otherwise, goat—the world's most widely eaten red meat, although its charms have largely been lost on Americans—is an appealingly eccentric option and available at a reasonable price from your local carnicería. (If the butcher tempts you with an entire leg, resist the conceit to bring it home and trying through culinary alchemy to coax it into a succulent baked leg—i.e., somehow turn it into lamb. *No, gracias.* I implore you to trust me on this [*vide* Afterword]. The magic of red wine and braising can only do so much, and your conjuring will end in a stringy, distasteful evening of harsh recrimination and domestic tragedy. The tender goat *nyama choma* I had while teaching in Kenya, however, was superb.)

Or, you might undertake some quick research for locally sourced farm goat. (Transferring butcher-papered white packages of goat loin from trunk to trunk, cooler to cooler, in the deserted parking lot of a closed blues club, while the farmer and I glanced nervously side to side, remains a special memory.) Keep in mind, though, that unusual meats get expensive at your foodie grocery or specialist online site. Otherwise, theoretically elk, buffalo, and/or wild boar would all make good options. (No poultry, however, not in the USA, unless you want to die.) In any case, go for whatever lean, cheap cut is available: round or flank steak, rump roast, et cetera. The rib, chump, or even neck chops might work, too, but bear in mind you'll be trying to carve some nice strips of lean red meat out of these, and a lot of bone, fat, and tendon could be your undoing.

Preparation of the Meat and Marinade. Cut your peculiar meat of choice into ¼" strips. (Some jerky nerds advocate wrapping the meat and freezing for 30-60 minutes to ease cutting. This seems superfluous. Use a decent knife and proceed.) Or course, strips will be different lengths, widths, and shapes, but try to keep the width consistent. Trim off all the fat and discard, however much this pains you philosophically. (It will tend to turn rancid and, anyway, doesn't dry properly.)

I prefer a wet marinade, and you can let your taste, instinct, and daring be your guide here: brown sugar, molasses, soy sauce, Worcestershire, Tabasco, finely chopped chipotles in adobo, hoisin sauce, a splash of ketchup or tomato paste, garlic and/or garlic salt, lots of freshly ground pepper, hot pepper flakes, herbs and spices as you like. Lean a little Tex-Mex, lean a little faux Asian. Use what's on hand in the fridge and pantry. I'm inclined toward sweet-hot-peppery. Stir meat and marinade well together, cover, and refrigerate for 24 hours.

Making and Distributing the Jerky. Shake marinade from meat. Towel strips dry a bit, too, if you like, but I wouldn't. Load up your trays. Dehydrate 24-36 hours, depending on the size of your strips. Keep an eye on them. Rotate your trays every 8-9 hours. Sample, cool, re-sample. (Cooling a piece determines its true consistency.) Stored in baggies, the jerky will last for weeks or longer in the fridge. If excellent, keep most for yourself. If unremarkable, give away most as gifts, using those very smallest half-pint Ziploc bags to exaggerate the jerky's rarity and "perceived value" (and, therefore, your generosity, thoughtfulness, and craftsmanship).

Theoretically, you can make jerky in a conventional oven, set at 140° F (apparently the approximate standard temperature of a dehydrator), the meat distributed directly onto the racks (with or without the oven door partially open, depending on your source—it generally works either way). It will turn out alright, but is that really the kind of person you want to be? I thought not. No guts, no glory. No dehydrator, no jerky!

Follow the time and tray rotation directions for your particular size and model of machine. My dehydrator runs a little hot, I think, and hardly anything takes more than 36 hours. Often 24 hours do the trick. If your situation is similar, it's a good idea, as I said, to rotate trays every 8 hours, rather than the 12 hours generally recommended, unless the idea bores you. Dehydrating isn't rocket science, so don't fret about any of this. Just rotate the trays evenly and keep an eye and tooth on what's happening. Again, items will harden a bit as they cool. If trays seem to be drying unevenly, remove them as appropriate according to your good sense or forgetfulness. We don't want limp and we don't want brittle. Isn't that the truth?

CHAPTER 13

·

Duck Redux: Finally, Some Foie Gras; or, An Author's Ethical Dilemma

The ungainly title above is appropriate, perhaps, to my hesitation in writing this—yes—thirteenth chapter (and has nothing whatsoever to do with various specious arguments against foie gras production). The attitudes in this book I'd like to believe are uniquely its author's, or fairly so, but certainly the recipes herein, those favorites that I've revised and modestly refined and shared and greatly enjoyed for many years, are an amalgam of ideas, ingredients, theories and methods borrowed, bastardized, and stumbled upon. Sometimes the origination of a particular recipe is easy for me to recall. Other times, I'm a little foggy on the details. The book's spotty reference pages are offered in the spirit of full disclosure (or as full as memory allows) and to earmark some useful resources by my culinary betters, where you might enjoy browsing and, perhaps, shoplifting a technique.

"Amateurs borrow, professionals steal" is the cheeky mantra you'll hear attributed in various versions to Pablo Picasso, Malcolm McLaren, and others (even Anthony Quinn). So, let's gently borrow. This chapter focuses on a rich meal of seared scallops and lobes of foie gras served atop a silky parsnip purée. I've made the dish many times, tweaking, testing, and always trying to streamline the process for the ease of the home cook (as it were, me), so over time I've come to feel a bit proprietary. Still, it's obviously a specific and eccentric alchemy of elements, one that can, I believe, be traced back to Las Vegas guru Scott McCarter. I've conflicted feelings about the notion/argument of recipes as intellectual (or for that matter, artistic) property. Would the most rarefied and scientific molecular deconstruction, produced in a food laboratory in Barcelona, be the exception? Even a genius like Sr. Adrià—although I'm not sure that "like" is an operative word regarding him—gleamingly acknowledges, as I interpret, that not only are recipes not created in a vacuum, but that the entire process of gastronomy is an integrally social act (and inarguably one, however pleasurable, with serious moral overtones and political implications).

Such were the heady and rambling thoughts I was sharing with my lovely companion as we drove to Nashville for a celebratory (why not?) Friday night of dinner and the symphony. (At the Mad Platter, ricotta gnocchi with crab and smoked Gouda mornay sauce and truffle oil? Are you kidding me? Ohlsson playing Chopin? The old boy's still got it!) She suggested I begin the chapter by writing about my hesitation, get in front of it rather than cloak or avoid it, and then get on with the cooking. I thought her advice brilliant. Enjoy, experiment, respect the ingredient, serve, share. Appreciate your privileged life, its good company, and what time remains. If the originator of the following is indeed solely Mr. McCarter (and whatever conflation of influence brought him to this delicious marriage of tastes), I hope he would be pleased that I've appreciated and studied it and want to pass it along. If he disagrees, please go to my website—www.gaylordbrewer.com—to contribute to the legal fund. But no hurry. Flirt first with this recipe and impress somebody you'd like to impress. Use the truffle butter if you can—I don't know why no one thought of it before I did. The fig preserves are my idea, too. Claim them as your own.

Seared Scallops & Foie Gras with Puréed Parsnips & Port-Fig Reduction

4 large sea scallops

2 1" slices foie gras

2 large parsnips

2 + 1 Tbs. unsalted butter

1 Tbs. black truffle butter (optional)

1 Tbs. grapeseed oil

2 Tbs. heavy cream

3 oz. port wine

3 Tbs. homemade fig preserves, *vide infra*

white pepper (optional)*

sea salt & freshly ground black pepper

microgreens, parsley, or chives (for garnish)

This dish is not as succulent as the multi-duck feast of Chapter 1, not as varied in texture and taste, but it is attractive, elegant, extravagant, and impressive both on the plate and the palate. Obviously, the prestige ingredients of scallops and foie gras are front and center, and these should be of the highest quality you can hunt down. A single portion of scallop and the trimmings would be an ethereal first course, but the preparation here is sufficiently time consuming that I highly recommend a "full" serving of 2 scallops, with a green salad on the side, and calling it a meal. And indeed a fine meal it will be, colorful and luxurious, but not deadly. (The portions are rich but moderately sized.)

That said, the preparation isn't overly taxing. You can make the parsnips the morning or day before and reheat, and I've streamlined the port-fig reduction—aside from the addendum of cooking your own preserves—for simplicity while maintaining maximum depth of flavor. Be forewarned, though, that—similarly to marrow risotto (*vide* Chapter 6)—this is a full stovetop, four burner commitment, so cleanup constitutes something of a chore . . . tomorrow. (Try this: The following morning, pretend to be deeply asleep—from your culinary and amorous exertions on your beloved's behalf, et cetera—and perhaps you'll hear the heavenly sound of him/her in the kitchen clacking, clicking, and scrubbing with appreciative reciprocity.

(Hey, it was worth a try.)

<u>Puréed Parsnips</u>. Rinse the parsnips—preferably locally grown. Cut off the hard stem ends and discard, and chop into 2-3 inch chunks. Put in a medium-sized pot, cover with water, add a pinch of salt, and bring to a boil. Lower to medium and cook at a low boil until fork tender, around 20 minutes (they take longer than potatoes). Drain, retaining a bit of the cooking water. Let cool a bit, then peel. (I would like to be able to honestly tell you that you can finish these satisfactorily with a manual potato masher, and that the lumps won't matter, but forsooth you really need to use the Cuisinart. A good blender with a sturdy engine and sharp blades might contrive a passable result.)

Add warm parsnips to Cuisinart, along with 2 oz. of chopped butter, and purée. Add a tablespoon or so of the cooking water—if you forgot and discarded it, *duh*, use chicken broth—and purée further. Add the cream and purée until curvaceous and silky. Scrape sides, add salt and white pepper to taste. (*The white pepper is a thoughtful, invisible touch, and a disposable white pepper grinder is something worth investing in, as you can use it variously, including for your gravlax—*vide* Chapter 14—and it will last indefinitely. It's enjoyably eccentric, but after you've emptied one if you're like me you're unlikely to bother with another. In the case of this dish, if you're taking my good advice and using the truffle butter, its black flecks of love will render the white pepper's invisibility meaningless, so arguably you might as well grab your standard, sturdy, black peppercorn grinder.)

Add black truffle butter, purée, test for taste with a pinky finger, smile, and give it a final spin. (N.b.: If you believe me re. nothing else, please take as an article of faith that you should *always* have a cache of D'Artagnan black truffle butter, cut by your own hands into 1-oz. triangles and double-wrapped in plastic, in an undisclosed but easy to reach spot in your freezer. Wait until you taste what it does for your Thanksgiving turkey—to be detailed, reader, in this book's publicly demanded sequel—or, for that matter, any handy shoe leather or cardboard. Of course, it's up to you . . .) Spoon into a smaller pot and keep on a warm burner or seal in the refrigerator, depending on when you're using it.

> I balanced on a rail, stretched my length,
> pulled two soft, syrupy
> teardrops from a high branch. Black Missions,
> velvet and warm.
>
> I cradled my spoils in sticky fingers
> and hurried from God's eyes, and man's.

—*from* "1ˢᵗ Baptist Fig"

Sidebar Recipe: Fig Preserves

12-15 ripe Brown Turkey figs

1-2 stems fresh rosemary

¼ cup (or to taste) white sugar

generous splash (to taste) sherry vinegar

Make during fig season, approximately July-September, preferably from fruit you picked yourself. (I'm a bit too far north for figs but had a peculiar local source. In a windless alcove next to the heating unit, the First Baptist Church of Murfreesboro sheltered an old, enormous, heavily producing Brown Turkey fig tree. I would never have given you the address, and after all you wouldn't have wanted a woman to rush out of the sanctuary and come at you with a broom, as once happened to me. I didn't mind risking a little damnation for fresh figs, although it's challenging to run with a shirttail full of sticky fruit cradled like a child to your chest. Into the car then, escaped, gleefully postlapsarian, criminal bounty warm and just-picked, enjoying the happy life of the fallen. When I saw they had downed the tree and poured concrete in its place, I almost cried. *This* was their faith's vision?)

To make the preserves, simply clean and chop a bowlful of figs, cook them down with a modest amount of white sugar and a stem of fresh rosemary, then add a splash of sherry vinegar (or similar). Can according to the hot pack directions of your water bath canner. Ball makes a wide-mouth glass jar that holds about 6 fluid oz. and is perfect. (If you prefer to avoid the ordeal of sealed canning, a jar of fresh preserves will last a month or longer refrigerated.) If necessary, use store-bought fruit. Or, if that's the way you want to be, go ahead and use store-bought fig jam/preserves, but where's the fun and danger and fall and redemption in that?

Port-Fig Reduction. Pour port into a small saucepan and cook on medium-high heat until reduced by half, approximately 15 minutes. If you overly reduce the port, just add a bit more, have a sip yourself, and play with it until syrupy and sexy. Stir in the fig preserves and reheat. Whisk in 1 oz. of room-temperature butter. That simple, excluding the hours you spent canning—and driving back and forth to the church—months before. Cover and keep on a warm burner until ready to plate.

Finishing the meal involves two small skillets and some fairly quick timing, but otherwise it's a snap. (If for some reason you prefer to escape with a single skillet, then cook the scallops first and keep them in a warm oven, but I recommend the two-handed method.) Season the scallops on both sides with Chinese five-spice (a fresh jar, please, not the dusty and tasteless antebellum stash discovered in the back of the spice cabinet) and a pinch of salt. If you've been able to procure 2 nice, thick slices of foie gras (note I recommend 1" thick), then slice each horizontally. If they're thinner and wider, then cut in half vertically. Gently score and season with sea salt and ground pepper (white if you're also using it in the parsnips).

With your parsnip purée and jammy port-fig reduction warm on two burners, on the other two burners heat ½ Tbs. of grapeseed oil in each of two small sauté pans. Bring to high heat and add the scallops to one, the foie gras slices to another. They cook similarly and fast. Don't lose your nerve. Don't flinch. It all comes down to the next minutes, soldier. Cook both scallops and foie gras until a nice brown crust forms, then flip and sear the other side, 1-2 minutes on each side for the scallops, 30-45 seconds for the foie gras. The foie gras may cook even faster. Do *not*, for the love of Mary, overcook either.

To plate, spoon the parsnip purée onto the center of plum and cobalt blue Fiestaware plates. (I neglected to mention earlier—whoops—but you'll need an array of Fiestaware place settings to match courses with pleasing colors. Here, the dark plates beautifully contrast with and also complement the nearly white parsnips and deep purple reduction.) Top the purée on each plate with 2 scallops and top the scallops with the foie gras slices. Spoon the warm port-fig reduction around the edge of the plates. Garnish with the microgreens. Magnificent. My god. Raise a toast to yourself. Remove your metaphorical paper toque and take a bow.

Serve with a green salad, both for texture and—as Grandma Brewer used to explain—to "cataract" the richness. Your companion may mock all the fuss and expense of the ingredients, or anyway will likely raise an eyebrow or shake the head, then devour every bite. You could do worse for a St. Valentine's Day dinner. Finally, the wine pairing is a bear. Maybe a Viognier, or go ahead and pop that chilled Sauternes (although if that's a bottle you typically have on hand, you're leading a sweet life, friend—pun always intended). Something bubbly wouldn't hurt anyone's feelings, either, I wouldn't think. If you simply must have a red, then have it. It's your meal.

CHAPTER 14

•

More 5:00 P.M. Snacks,
More Happiness—Non-Fried

Further options here for happy hour happiness. As I insinuated—well, mandated—in Chapter 5, the 5:00 p.m. snack, accompanied by the first sip, the latest John le Carré or Robert Crais novel or posthumous collection of Bukowski poems in hand, is hard to argue against as the best part of the day. For better or worse, richer or poorer, the work is done. Soon—let's say it's autumn—there will be a walk with the dog at sunset, and beyond that the temptations and beckonings of the night ahead. First, though, there's this hour to relax: the breeze of a cracked window on your neck, a silent toast, a physical book (*not* a monstrous Kindle) open across your legs, and a tasty nosh. A nearly perfect gestalt. We'll start with three finger exercises, then move on to the main event, the beautiful and irresistible gravlax.

> Low-fat milk and a dozen
> free-range eggs. I squeezed
> the bread, six grain,
> announced it still as giving
> as a woman's thigh
> and soft enough to eat.
> Our bed restored and tucked.

—*from* "Apologia for a Shopping List"

Deviled Eggs

3 large farm eggs*

5 anchovies fillets rolled with capers

1 tsp.+ olive oil**

½ tsp. Dijon mustard

1 Tbs. + 1 tsp. mayonnaise

1 Tbs. finely chopped dill pickle

¼ tsp. lemon juice (optional)

freshly ground black pepper

smoked paprika

Don't laugh. This is a flavor-packed variation much sexier than your great-aunt Dorie's pasty effort of memory, left too long in the sun. These are good. The integral ingredient is the anchovies. (I've no idea how anchovies developed such a fear-inducing reputation in America. I celebrate them in all their incarnations: from the beautiful and fragile Mediterranean white anchovy fillets—*boquerones*—packed in small trays in sunflower oil, vinegar, and spices, to the fun-as-hell-to-eat whole fried anchovies, the popular Spanish tapas *anchoas fritas*. We were even eating these latter in Finland last year. You can keep your soggy French fries. [Adapting a recipe we enjoyed while staying at a farm in Chianti, my wife folds sage leaves around tinned anchovies, dips the leaves in a batter of white wine and flour, and fries them in a cast-iron skillet. It's become a new staple snack, one of our favorites.]) Here, we use an inexpensive 2-oz. flat tin of anchovies rolled around capers, ubiquitous even in the big chain grocers. The tin I'm considering as I type this has a charmingly crude cartoon drawing of a woman in red dancing flamenco while a skinny blue fish peers up at her adoringly. It's imported from Morocco.

Bring the eggs to a full boil in a pot of water. (*Here we continue our earlier disquisition—i.e., discursive rant—on eggs, *vide* Chapter 9. Random notes on eggs, judgment, and perspective: Chicken eggs are the obvious and easy choice here, but if your farmer at the market or down the road offers some alternatives, happily accept the chance to mess around. Last summer, I amused myself with duck eggs. Their rich yolks and high-protein whites, which whip like a meringue dream, are a treat for baking, and they're also delicious soft-boiled on a spinach salad. An unanticipated largesse of guinea fowl eggs, meanwhile—hard-shelled and about two-thirds the size of a medium chicken egg—did yield up some cute deviled eggs.

(I made deviled eggs—once—from quail eggs. This is a perverse act, and if so tempted you will find yourself, great and clumsy hands trembling as you try to peel the little bastards, with time to reflect on where you've come to in your life and how. Quail eggs are often available at a good Asian grocer, in adorable Lilliputian cartons that beg to be cradled and bought. Not only, however, are they not worth the effort of tiny deviled eggs, preemptively they're also not worth the task of hard-boiling. [Cf: the economical and prepared can of quail eggs, god bless it, contents easily drained and patted dry.] As a snack, quail eggs bring inexplicable amusement to folks. They make me silly. Serve the can of eggs on a platter accompanied by an appropriately miniature—i.e., to scale—bowl of celery salt, for rolling the eggs, and a shot glass full of toothpicks, for spearing them. Good with beer. [I have a long, supermodel-skinny dish where I line up the eggs side by side, with a 3" ceramic fisherman I stand up amidst them, but you can, possibly, get by alright without these accoutrements.] Yet, disclaimers aside, a dozen fresh quail eggs are worth amusing and abusing yourself with at least once. They're cute as a button—and not much larger—fried sunny-side up and served on toast points, or think small and use your imagination. Just don't let them break your heart and don't try to devil them. If you persist in the folly of the latter, all you'll get for your shot nerves are odd, oblique looks from folks who care about you. In other words, definitely try it.)

Gads, we've forgotten our boiling eggs! Just in time, turn down to medium. Let them jiggle for 8-10 minutes. Drain, cool the eggs under cold running water, and peel. (N.b.: If using local farm eggs, remember that fresh eggs won't peel cleanly without an extra step. If you don't believe me, try it and make a mess. The extra step, however, is easy and a good trick, and it does *not* involve baking soda or pricking holes. Once the eggs are cooked, remove them to a bowl of icy water for 30-40 seconds. [If you're only boiling 2-3, you might just hold each under cold running water with tongs.] Return the eggs to the hot water and count to ten. They should now peel easily. The "science" of this, I believe, has something to do with the interior of the cooling eggs shrinking, then the shells re-expanding when returned to the hot water, creating a small space of air between. If your eggs are a few weeks old or from the grocer—where they're always old—then of course you needn't bother.) Slice each egg in half and, using a small spoon, remove the yolks to a bowl. (If the yolks pop out cleanly, great. If not, be gentle with the albumen and don't tear it. Rinse the whites off and drain them if they get messy with the friable yolks.)

To the bowl of hard-boiled yolks, add the finely minced anchovy-caper rolls, the chopped dill pickle (1 oversized cornichon is about the right amount), the olive oil (**from the tin of anchovies), the Dijon mustard, the mayonnaise, a liberal grind of pepper (perhaps ¼ tsp.), and, if desired, the lemon juice. (There are already a lot of powerful flavors slugging it out here, but I like the fresh note of the citrus.) Mash everything together well with a fork. If it needs to be a bit smoother, add a splash more olive oil from the tin. Do *not* add salt. The eggs will be plenty salty from the cured anchovies, and that's the way you want them. If you're nervous about it, begin with 3 or 4 anchovies and taste as you go, but don't be shy. The whites, remember, are there as antidote. (In any case, you'll have a few of the rolled anchovies left in the tin. Go ahead and eat these so you won't have to fret about what to do with them.)

Spoon yolk mixture back into the whites and sprinkle with smoked paprika. To my mind this is classic bar food, meant to make you thirsty. You can eat these velvety spice bombs with anything, but an icy IPA or similar, in a frosted glass, is obscenely appropriate. Serves two, barely. Why didn't you make more?

Blue Cheese Crackers with Pepper & Cayenne

1½ cups all-purpose flour

3 tsp. coarsely ground black pepper

½ tsp. cayenne powder

½ tsp. coarse sea salt

8 oz. blue cheese

⅓ cup unsalted butter

1 cup coarsely chopped walnuts

2 farm egg yolks, slightly beaten

I believe my mother passed this recipe on to me a few years ago, from what newspaper or magazine I've no idea. In any case, I have the ingredients jotted in my handwriting on a crumpled and only slightly stained piece of notebook paper. My innovations were to keep walnuts, butter, and cheese coarsely chopped and to include the cayenne, which adds a lot, and extra pepper. In a medium-sized bowl, combine the flour, black pepper, cayenne and sea salt. Add the softened blue cheese (buy something decent and nicely marbled) and butter and cut in until crumbly. Add the egg yolks and mix.

Roll the dough into a ball and knead for perhaps 1 minute. Divide and shape and roll into 2 9" logs. Wrap well in plastic wrap and chill for at least 2 hours. Slice the desired number of ¼" crackers and bake 8 minutes at 425° F. Eat hot from the oven. I like these peppery and salty and to be able to definitely taste the heat of the cayenne. You can adjust the ingredients accordingly, of course, and/or sprinkle with more salt and cayenne when they come out of the oven if you're feeling feisty. The rolls last forever (but won't) in the freezer and there's no need to thaw before slicing. When you're in the mood for hot, spicy, homemade crackers, which require no other accompaniment, simply remove a roll from the freezer, lob off the number you think you and your partner will want (and then add a couple more) with a sharp knife—the blade periodically run under hot water if necessary—rewrap the roll well, and bake the crackers at the high temperature indicated. You can thank my mother for the delicious, cheesy-buttery result, if you like, and curse me for the gratuitous heat.

Cheddar Cheese Straws

The blue cheese crackers were so tasty and disappeared so fast, let's try another variation, quite stylish, on the same theme.

1 cup grated sharp cheddar cheese

¾ cup all-purpose flour

¼ tsp. paprika

¼ tsp. cayenne powder

⅛ tsp. coarsely ground black pepper

½ tsp. coarse sea salt

1 Tbs. spring water

1 farm egg

4 oz. unsalted butter

In a medium bowl, add the cheddar cheese, flour, paprika, cayenne power, pepper, and salt, and mix well. Chop the cold butter into the flour, then cut the butter in with a pastry cutter until it is small and luminous pearls. Add the beaten egg and spring water. Knead with your hands until you have a ball of dough. (You can then refrigerate the dough for later use, if you like, but set it out a while first. It'll be easier to roll and handle, and the straws twist better as the dough softens.)

On a floured counter, and with a sprinkle of flour on top of the dough, roll out flat, ⅛" or thinner. With a knife, demarcate a rectangle, collect the rough edges to roll out again, and slice your rectangle—which will naturally be about the right length, 8"-9"—into ⅓" strips. (Don't grow frustrated if they stick and tear at first.) Twist each strip and arrange on a cookie sheet. (You can put them fairly close together.) Once you've repeated this process with the remaining dough, the recipe will produce about 20 straws. Bake at

400° F, with the oven shelf fairly high, for 10 minutes or until the straws are bubbling and starting to brown and crisp. Let cool slightly, but eat them hot, compulsively. For a little flash, arrange straws upright in a tall glass, which will soon be empty.

(Cf.: Vis-à-vis the two cheese recipes offered here, you can make quite a tasty cheese cracker using no flour, butter, or eggs at all, only cheese. Grate a few ounces of aged Parmesan, mix in some salt and cayenne powder and a few generous grinds of black pepper, and spoon in small heaps directly onto a glass or enamel cooking dish. Bake at 375° F for 5 minutes, then finish under the high broiler for 2 minutes. Let cool slightly. These are oily and delicious warm.)

Bourbon-Cured Gravlax

2 1-lb. fillets fresh wild salmon

1 cup kosher salt

¼ cup sugar

1 Tbs. white peppercorns*

1 oz. bourbon

several sprigs fresh dill

2 bricks**

accompaniments for serving

This is an involved preparation that takes three days and a modicum of casual attention, but the elegant, succulent result, sensual in color and rich in taste, belies that the recipe is basically indestructible. The ideal time to make gravlax is during the aforementioned wild salmon season (*vide* Chapter 10), perhaps later in the run as prices drop slightly, but if you need a fix at another time of year, any fresh salmon that is attractively (and not artificially) colored, firm in texture, and smells of the sea's cold depths will yield a satisfactory result. Consider it a practice batch to limber you up for the wild sockeye's buoyant return. I'd recommend you make at a minimum the 2 lbs. indicated here. You'll be surprised, the first time, how quickly you and a loved one will eat it up over consecutive days. If serving to friends, leave them wanting more. You don't want to spoil them, after all. Maybe, too, you should consider doubling the amount of the rub and curing an entire side (maybe 4 lbs.?). I've never seen gravlax last long enough to go bad, but it does freeze superbly, retaining its body, if you were (theoretically) to do so.

Try to get thick, center cuts of fish of nearly the same size and square shape. If you must settle for triangular end pieces of varying thickness, don't despair, just make sure that the rub and dill are covering all the flesh of both pieces, match them up—*vide infra*—as best you can, and wrap tightly. To begin, scale the fish with a sharp vegetable peeler, pull pin bones out of the flesh with a pair of tweezers, and rinse and pat dry. (As I mentioned earlier in preparing the cedar-planked salmon, feel along with your fingers to find the pin bones. You and this fish are going to be spending some intimate time together, so you might as well initiate the relationship now.)

Combine the kosher salt (which is slightly less salty than table salt and generally coarser in grain), the white peppercorns broken with a mortar and pestle, and the sugar. (*Re. the peppercorns: I'm assuming you bought a white peppercorn grinder for the parsnip purée—*vide* Chapter 13—and are itching for ways to use it. If not, use black peppercorns or even a black and red blend, although I list the three options in my diminishing order of preference. White is best here if you have it.)

Place the salmon skin side down on a large piece of plastic wrap. Massage the bourbon (or scotch if you prefer, lassie) into the fish. Spoon over with the salt-sugar mixture, spreading carefully over the flesh. Massage this in. Cover one fillet with your washed and towel-dried dill sprigs (use a big bunch), place the second fillet on top of the first, flesh sides touching, and wrap tightly within the plastic. Wrap a second time with plastic, and perhaps a third. The fish will be generating a lot of liquid from the dissolved salt-sugar mix—minor seepage is acceptable, perhaps unavoidable—and you want the pieces tightly and securely packaged.

Place wrapped salmon in a glass baking dish, weight with two clean bricks wrapped in aluminum foil, and place in the refrigerator. (**Bricks really do work best, but you can substitute a thick telephone directory and another heavy book—say, your *Riverside Shakespeare* from graduate school or last year's edition of *The Bedford Introduction to Literature* you're not teaching from anymore but can't sell back—on top of that. The books can get perilously tall and unbalanced, however, both in the fridge and when lifting the dish. Really, better this time the bricks than the Bard.) Turn the fish over and replace the weights every 12 hours for three days.

Unwrap the fish and scrape off the dill and excess pepper and other seasoning. Rinse the salmon briefly under cold water and towel dry. Firmly rewrapped in new plastic wrap, the gravlax will last a week in the fridge or months (in plastic wrap and aluminum foil) in the freezer. Your best option is to attack with delicate zeal and eat it all at 5:00 p.m. over the next few days.

Beginning at the fattest end, slice paper-thin and at a slight angle with a sharp knife, only as much as you are eating at the time. For the easiest serving, arrange slices—surrounded by lemon wedges—on an olive wood cutting board or platter of complementary color (Fiestaware persimmon or turquoise?) with water crackers or rye bread squares and small bowls of chopped capers, diced red onion, and sour cream or crème fraîche. Ignore suggestions for some fancy mustard-dill sauce and forget the vodka. The brightly colored and prepossessing slices, however, with their subtle nuances of dill and spice and just a touch of salty bourbon sweetness, pair ideally with a properly made Martini—*vide* Chapter 22, yet again—its icy surface a cold and uncharted sea you peer across as you raise your glass for lips to navigate.

Crucial postscript: The accompaniments above are how I have served the gravlax for years, and they're a delightful combination of on-hand ingredients that can be put together quickly. However, I've recently become head-over-heels enamored with egg salad as the sole topping, the beautiful, bright, thin slices of gravlax topped with a small dollop of the eggs, both balanced on a small square of coarse pumpernickel. The combination of colors, tastes, and textures is dynamite, appealing to the eye and an explosive pleasure to eat. So if you can think ahead enough to make the egg salad (hey, you just devoted three days to curing the fish), then by all means do so.

Gravlax & Egg Salad on Pumpernickel Canapés

2 large farm eggs

1½ Tbs. hot bread-and-butter pickles

1 Tbs. chives

1 rounded Tbs. scallions

½ cup mayonnaise (less 1 rounded Tbs.)

sea salt & freshly ground black pepper

squeeze of fresh lemon juice (optional)

gravlax—*vide supra*—thinly sliced at an angle

pumpernickel bread*

Hard-boil the eggs and try not to overly harden the yolks. (Jokes aside, I choose not to discourse here on the lore and debate of hard-boiling an egg—how many minutes based on its size, beginning in cold water or hot, et cetera. Devise and commit to a system that works.) Coarsely chop the eggs, pickle slices, and cleaned scallions and chives. Mix all in a bowl along with the mayonnaise, a few turns of salt and pepper, and a squeeze of lemon. This will make sufficient egg salad happy hour snacks for two for consecutive days (and you really don't want it sitting longer than that).

*The pumpernickel bread is important. I got lucky, finding a vacuum-packed German pumpernickel with whole rye kernels. The thin, pre-cut slices are nearly black, wonderfully chewy, and each, squared, is the ideal size for small canapés. If you can't locate a similar product, try to do better than the long, small, ubiquitous, and generally slightly stale loaves found around the deli case at the grocer. (Cf.: These loaves suffice, even excel, however, for a fine, stinky Limburger cheese left on the car dashboard or in a sunny windowsill until the smell announces the time has come, then cut thick, along with a crunchy slice of red onion, piled on the tiny bread slices, all washed down with cold beer. But for the hard work and subtler flavors of our cured salmon, you and the fish both deserve better.) Try to find the densest, darkest bread you can and slice very thin. (A friend bakes heavy loaves of pumpernickel in a bread maker that would adapt well here. You might consider.)

Bonus Snack: Grilled Piquillo Pepper Dip

I append this fiery and delicious dip/spread with a degree of personal bitterness, as the recipe is all that remains of a proposed full chapter: "Waffles: Morning, Noon, and Night." The dip was to accompany the spicy couscous lunch waffle. For dinner we feast on fun and festive clam-hash waffles with poached eggs and coleslaw, then follow up with a decadent dessert of buttered chocolate-banana buttermilk waffles with maple syrup. I was being facetious, of course, with the requirement of eating them all in a single day, but who doesn't like waffles and fiddling around with the waffle maker—the hopeful and authoritative lowering and lifting of the lid of that arcane little iron maiden, mechanical bird call announcing the golden result? In terms of cooking for the proposed chapter, however, I did, in fact, proceed with preparing the recipes in quick, successive order and, if I may, in a professional manner. By evening's end, however, my tasting companion ungraciously announced she had waffles coming out of her ears—I paraphrase—and enough for a lifetime. (This judgment did not bloom the roses of romance that April night.) The *coup de grâce* to the feast, prior to the delivery of hers to the chapter, was to be crunchy cornmeal waffles planned for the next morning's breakfast, the yeasty and aromatic batter already rising. They went uncooked, the waffle maker wiped clean and returned to its ignominious purgatory on a back shelf—between the wooden crab hammers and toothless mandoline—beneath the counter.

However, even the most ungenerous and curmudgeonly of waffle detractors—I'll name no names; you know who you are—would (and in fact did) admit that this dip is a winner.

1 8-oz. jar Spanish grilled or roasted piquillo peppers

2 large cloves garlic

3-4 small dried chili peppers, seeded

1 rounded tsp. tomato paste

3 Tbs. olive oil

15 pitted black olives

generous pinch sugar

generous pinch sea salt

several grinds of black pepper

In a mini-chopper (large enough to hold and efficiently process 1+ cups), add all ingredients except the black olives. Pulse/chop until smooth, scraping down the sides of the processor once or twice as needed. You needn't process it to death, just until well blended. Add the black olives and pulse/process in 2-3 brief intervals until evenly chopped but still visible. The consistency should be about right, but add a splash more olive oil if necessary. Taste. Delicious, eh? Like me, you probably thought dedicating an entire jar of piquillos, succulent on their own, to the chopper was a bit excessive. Live and learn, about ourselves and others.

Makes approximately one cup. May be prepared ahead and refrigerated, but serve at room temperature with pita chips, hot fried tortilla chips (*vide* Chapter 5), or, *ahem*, spicy couscous waffle squares, which pair ideally.

Postscript: In addition to my deep commitment to the preservation of the happy hour sacrament, I'm also a dedicated fan of small plates in general—unshared—which allow both variety and the indulgence of rich ingredients. They may sometimes seem a disproportionate amount of work for a modest yield, but think rather in terms of bounteous taste and always, of course, of amusing and surprising yourself. The alternative to a three day preparation of gravlax would be, perhaps, an inspired spontaneous use of leftovers. Last night, out on the deck with a few fat snowflakes drifting, I grilled squares of chilled polenta left over from the evening before (from by-request coarse white cornmeal stone ground nearby, pardon my redundancy) and rubbed with olive oil, along with enormous white shrimp I'd marinated in spicy pesto (made and frozen into cubes last August before the last of the basil shriveled), everything on high heat, uncovered, until black-striped. On small plates, 2 shrimp on 2 "toasts," a spoon of warm marinara sauce, and clumps of radish sprouts and watercress. (For us, the greenery courtesy of nearby 4K Farm and its astounding greenhouses. Chris and Russ supply delicious and photoworthy produce year-round.) Less work than it sounds, really, easily executed and enthusiastically received. Finicky? Sure. Pedantic? Perhaps. But better froufrou than Fritos, and a far fairer appreciation of our earth and privilege.

CHAPTER 15

·

Blood Sausage & the Rudiments of Love

But here, you dig in with the natives
at crowded tables, pierce skin
with tines designed to free the soft
black guts. Taste it, the richness

of death: blood-aroma in nostrils,
hot pudding in the mouth. Ghost food,
indeed.

—*from* "Ghost Visits the Quay in
Tampere, Eats Blood Sausage"

As I write this, it is Valentine's Day morning. The pressure's on, the fat's in the fire, and I, of course, am dreamily reminiscing about blood sausage. *Boudin noir, biroldo, blutwurst morcilla, morcella*—all the world pays tributes to the lyricism of thy names, the smooth bulge of your physique and dark center of your truth, yielded to the fire. A Neruda ode is due, but I can offer instead only this modest personal recollection of our long relationship. Reader, I suppose it began with the slices of broiled white and black puddings included in any self-respecting and heart-mauling English or Scottish breakfast, a proper "fry up" to send you lurching out in a sweat into the cloudy day. I loved the stuff immediately and have ever since, crossing paths with various incarnations—in Spain, Portugal, Mexico, New Orleans—occasionally but not nearly often enough.

In preparation for an artist residency in Finland last summer, I'd read that the Fins also take their blood sausage seriously, but I wasn't prepared for the creamy, voluptuous local version, *mustamakkara*, discovered on a sunny day when I was randomly exploring the pleasant city of Tampere. I'd hitched a ride in from the hinterlands of the lake country, primarily to see in person the grotesque and stunning Simberg frescoes—even better than advertised—in the cathedral, and wound up strolling the quay, admiring the impressive produce and equally impressive prices of the farmers stalls. My shoulder bag, recently deceased and that I had worn for nearly 30 years when travelling (a

World War II Austrian artillery bag bought at a pawn shop in Louisville, *not* a purse), already stuffed with a sack of fresh peas in shell (never waste space in your bag with a camera or whatnot), I moved over to the crowded kiosks to consider the lunch options. My Finnish being what it is—*nada y pues nada*—I waited in line, gave the universal "I'll have what he's having" blasé nod, and at a small shared table devoured the two most delicious, depraved, creamy and steaming blood sausages I'd ever eaten. Everyone with the same paper boat of sausages and healthy red dollops of lingonberry jam like accusations of congealed blood, plastic knives and forks, and cartons of milk, the sun gleaming off the pedestrian suspension bridge across the Tammeroski, the brick factories smoking in the distance, Simberg's ghouls and wounded angels quiet behind us, we were all in it together. (Actually, I had a light beer to refresh me from my perambulations. The milk looked good, though.) And hurtful gossip notwithstanding, I did *not* lick clean the paper boat.

Nor did I have any intention of including a chapter on blood sausage in this book, since my personal cooking experience was limited to grilling a few links. In an epiphanic moment, however, I realized any résumé of my very favorite foods had to include these sultry wonders. Odd, since I'm not a sausage man, per se. So, while nearly every recipe in this book is an old favorite, tried and true and thoroughly (mostly) kitchen tested, this chapter is a fraud. I needed a blood sausage recipe to claim as my own, so here's what I've been concocting and adapting in the kitchen for the past several days, an homage of sorts to cassoulet with a tip of the hat to the Portuguese bean stew *chispalhada*, and other cues appropriated (i.e., stolen) from other sources. Actually, blood sausages are outstanding—*vide ut supra*—merely grilled or broiled and served with fried eggs and the requisite lingonberry jam, but that's not much of a recipe to write a chapter about. (The Finns' enthusiasm for the wild, forest-picked lingonberry is surpassed only by their passion for the small, extremely tart, bright yellow wild cloudberry, an acquired taste.) You can find lingonberry jam at some high-end grocers in the US, expensive and probably imported from Sweden. You have to have it, though, as I now hold—though only recently converted—the taste to be integral to the pleasure of the sausage, and, again, there's the curiously pleasing "blood effect" of the bright red jam. You've already emptied the coffers ordering the sausage from some online retailer. Don't get parsimonious now.

(Excuse me: The recipe that follows is a good one, one I welcome to the repertoire, but it will to have wait. It's Valentine's Day, as I mentioned, now late afternoon, and I have a dinner for two to tend: lobster and corn risotto [with a secret splash of cream for richness] and yeasty whole grain organic rolls—currently proofing on the counter—from a local artisanal baker [the same folks who mill my cornmeal, by the by]. For appetizer, D'Artagnan's French Kisses, Armagnac soaked prunes stuffed with foie gras mousse—easily and even better homemade, when time allows—and a cold brut rosé. For dessert, I haven't decided: either a board of Manchego, quince paste, and hot, sweet-savory pecans; or simply petits fours. Either will go fine with coffee [Tanzanian peaberry] and a lovely Riesling ice wine from the Columbia Valley. Except for the risotto all largely prepared foods, yes, but I don't want to be in the kitchen all night. Not tonight.)

Blood Sausages with Flageolet Beans & Roasted Tomatoes

4 4-oz. or 1 1-lb. link blood sausage (or ½ lb. + ½ lb. andouille, *vide infra*)

1 12-oz. bag dried flageolet beans

1½ lbs. fresh Roma tomatoes (about 8-10)

1 large + 1 small carrot

1 medium white or yellow onion

1 large shallot

2 ribs celery

5 large cloves garlic

1 Tbs. olive oil

¾ cup low-sodium chicken broth

2 bay leaves

2 Tbs. hard pork cracklings* (optional)

several sprigs thyme, rosemary, & Italian parsley

1+ tsp. sea salt

1+ tsp. freshly ground black pepper

Alright, back to the serious business of blood sausage. Cover your dried beans in a bowl with spring water and let soak for 6-8 hours. One caveat on the front end of preparing and assembling this meal is that it's not overly complicated, but it does take considerable (non-engaged) time. The tomatoes cook for 4 hours, and after soaking the beans they will still take forever to cook, probably 3 hours. So get an early start on this—soaking the beans the night before or as soon as you get up, getting the tomatoes in the oven by early afternoon, et cetera—if you intend to serve that night. Otherwise, the cooked beans will last fine, cooled and in their cooking water, overnight, and the roasted tomatoes can be covered with olive oil in a jar and placed in the fridge. (Make these days ahead, if you care to and it occurs to do so.) So if time gets away from you as the clock is spinning out the inexorable hours, one option is just to stop, take a breath, give up, pour some wine, have a salad, and treat yourself to an easy finish the next night. (This fallback option doesn't work terribly well if you have guests, however, and since this is one of the few recipes in the book that will serve four if you double the sausage, get started early, like I said. If your beans aren't soaking by 8:00 a.m., you've probably already lost the battle. ["Quick soaks" don't set right with me.] Anyway, do you have friends who will appreciate blood sausage or really deserve it?)

Rinse and pat dry the Roma tomatoes. Halve them lengthwise and clean out ribs and seeds with a grapefruit spoon. Place cut side up on a foil-lined cookie sheet, sprinkle with the kosher salt, and cook for 4 hours at 250° F. They should be dry but also sweet and soft, not tough or crunchy. Cool. Cut each half in half again with kitchen shears, and store appropriately until ready to use.

Drain the beans and put them in your Dutch oven along with the large carrot (sliced into 3-4 thick pieces), the peeled onion (sliced in half), 2 bay leaves (fresh or—since this is a wintry dish—perhaps dried from last summer's plant), and the fresh rosemary, thyme, and parsley all cleaned and tied with string into an attractive bundle. (No need to wrap the herbs in cheesecloth. What pieces cook off into the beans will be fine. Ditto for renegade bits of onion.) Cover beans with 2" of spring water (and no salt in the water, please). You might stop a moment and appreciate the vivid canvas of uncooked ingredients in front of you. The lightly green flageolets like pebbles in the bottom of the Dutch oven. (My Lodge's exterior is Caribbean blue, which heightens the suggestion of a lake- or riverbed.) The bright carrots, the vivid verdancy of your bushy *bouquet garni.* The dark, sure contours of the floating bay leaves. Just lovely, eh? Bring to a boil on the stove, stir with a wooden spoon, lower to a simmer, cover, and cook for eternity—2-3 hours. (Check periodically. You may prove me wrong about the cooking time, but I don't think so. Bear in mind, though, that the beans should retain some body. A touch beyond *al dente*, perhaps, but you don't want them soft. You'll be cooking them a bit more after you assemble the parts.) Cool, cover, and store in fridge. Or, if you're continuing on to make the dish now, discard the carrot, bay leaves, larger pieces of onion, and bundle of herbs. Retain ½ cup of the cooking liquid. Drain beans in a colander but don't rinse.

Clean and dry the Dutch oven and return it to the burner. Bring 1 Tbs. olive oil to medium heat, add chopped garlic, celery (cleaned and cut into ¼" slices), and chopped small carrot and sauté 2 minutes, stirring occasionally. Add the roughly chopped shallot and cook another 2-3 minutes, until the celery just softens. Add the beans, ½ cup of the cooking liquid, and ¾ cup low-sodium chicken broth. Add the roasted tomatoes. (If you've had these keeping in olive oil, don't worry about minimal extra oil in the beans. Just give the tomatoes a shake out of the jar and add to the rest.) Stir everything together and salt and pepper to taste. Leave the lid off and cook down the liquids a bit, maybe 20 minutes. Add the pork cracklings and stir. (*By pork cracklings, I mean the hard type used for cooking, as in making cornbread, not the pork rind snack. Clifty Farm makes a fatty, salty, hard crackling—probably found near the country ham display—that's impressively bad for you on all fronts, although I don't know how far they travel outside of Tennessee or the South. You can leave these out, but I like the elusive depth of flavor and odd surprise crunch they deliver. In fact, if you wanted to delete the cracklings and the sausages, this would be a fine, robust vegetarian dish. But, especially following the panegyric that begins this chapter, why on earth even entertain such a mad notion? You'll already have the cracklings on hand, anyway, since they're indispensable for cracklin' cornbread and corn muffins.)

Taste the beans. If they're ready, they're ready. They should be fine, covered, burner on low, for an hour or so. If you want to serve immediately, then during the sautéing of the vegetables and cooking down of the liquids, cook your sausages in the oven at 400° F for 20 minutes, turning them once. If the skin hasn't cracked by that point, finish them with a couple of minutes under the broiler. Serve the beans in wide, flat dinner bowls with the hot sausages whole on top and, just in case, hot sauce and lingonberry jelly close at hand.

There should be sufficient beans here for four normal humans—with the number of sausages adjusted accordingly and perhaps a salad and/or bread—or for two with leftovers that reheat wonderfully. (Thickly slice any remaining sausages and stir into beans before refrigerating.) I deluded myself that the two of us would get two meals out of the ingredients listed above, then of course we sat down and ate ⅔ of the beans and all of the sausage—half of a 1-lb. ring of black sausage for me, 2 4-oz. links of andouille for my lovely, albeit squeamish and unenlightened, companion. (Yes, I recognize the "unadventurous date" as a sad, recurring motif from earlier chapters and, likely, future ones, but peace, tranquility, and romance above all! Anyway, this is at least an easy recipe to compromise without destroying your own pleasure and/or the evening's motives. By the way, I don't know why eating blood sausage seems so superbly decadent and wrong. Perhaps a bourgeois middle-class American sensibility? Self-consciousness certainly wasn't present on the quay, nor, I'm certain, on the Brewer farm for generations, but the illicitness does add to the enjoyment.) No apologies, though, and after all isn't pleasure central to our humble thesis? Set blood sausage in front of this author—the dark and aromatic custard of its center, the taut robe of broken skin—and that's the end of that. To drink, a red wine with a little sass—perhaps a Syrah—or a cold hard cider. Or milk?

CHAPTER 16

•

Summer Seafood of Love

The alternate and preferred title of this chapter, really no more inaccurate, is "Let's Grill Again, Like We Did Last Summer," homage to Chubby Checker's *other* hit, the summer after "The Twist." I'm a big fan of self-cannibalizing. Looking back over the earlier chapters of this book, it strikes me that many of the recipes are on the heavy, wintry side, perhaps because I began the writing a few days after Thanksgiving. (If I'd known, I'd have kept closer records. E.g., of two scrumptious—if I may say so—dressings ["stuffing" to you non-Southerners] I made: cornbread with corn, apple, walnuts and sausage, and an oyster dressing with pine nuts, both loaded with the last sage of the year and other fresh herbs. I also experimented with salting the turkey and leaving it uncovered in the fridge for 24 hours before roasting, and I'll be damned if it didn't seem it *was* the moistest turkey breast I'd ever cooked. I had been skeptical at best of the boasted effect.) Much of the rough draft, as well as nearly the entire lineup of recipes, was concocted, furiously, during the winter months that followed. I do have a propensity for rich, heavy flavors and dishes, but let's blame the cold weather.

In these later chapters, let's also consciously start looking more toward summer, its long nights, sandals, silk shirts, and cotton dresses, with dishes that emanate at least a semblance of meals (slightly) lighter and perhaps more "healthful"—a term I'm still learning to accommodate. (I'll try to sabotage this healthfulness at every opportunity, of course, in my role as devil in your ear, but with two big, multi-section chapters on desserts approaching, I thought it sporting to don the façade.) This chapter presents a copious variety, a virtual seashell's cornucopia—i.e., a dodgy hodgepodge—of seafood dishes anxious to please and guaranteed to delight: two returns to the grill, one to the deep fryer—*healthful* deep-frying, friends!—and one boil. Calibrated another way, two appetizers, one complete one-pot meal, and one course-indefinable recipe for marinated shrimp on the barbie that defies pigeonholing. You'll just want to eat them with your fingers (and mouth, of course), as many crustaceans as you have, and not worry about tables, times, or etiquette. And perhaps a bonus shrimp recipe as well. Good lord!

Later, I will blacken these odd creatures
on the grill, serve with roasted lemons,
sea salt, another drizzle of good oil . . .

                              . . . another day
mortgaged to darkness in a summer barely
begun. When this one's over, one fewer
will remain. I'll drink the wine, eat

the hot, charred bodies with my hands
and await the owls who come at evening.
I will butcher their purrs and soft trills
as the dark ones marvel at my distorted aria,
the rituals and long shadows of our table.

—*from* "Squid"

Calamari Stuffed with Feta Cheese & Black Olives, Two Ways

8 medium-sized calamari bodies/mantles

4 oz. feta cheese

25 black olives*

¼ cup Italian parsley

1 Tbs. lemon juice

¼ cup walnuts

1 Tbs. sun-dried tomatoes in olive oil, + ½ tsp. olive oil**

⅛ tsp. white sugar

⅛ tsp. sea salt

¼ tsp. freshly ground black pepper

8 thin bamboo skewers or toothpicks***

Frozen calamari is now readily available at grocers and, luckily for all, is already cleaned: the head/beak divided from the tentacles; cartilage/cuttlebone, ink sack, and membrane removed from the body (aka, the tube or mantle). From this point forward we may gladly concern ourselves only with the good bits—the wonderfully adaptable tentacles and body tubes. (If you have some arcane source for fresh squid and a desire to get your hands in the murk and muck to clean them, then go forth, pilgrim.)

Thaw your calamari in water, rinse, divide tentacles from bodies and drain on paper towels. Each tube has a small, nearly transparent "fin"—I don't know what they're called or what they are, but I don't like the look or notion of the dag-gummed things. Cut these off with cooking shears. You can probably just pull them off, but do so gently. You don't want to tear the tube. (A 1-lb. package of calamari will contain around 15-20 small-to-medium bodies and a roughly equal volume of tentacles. This recipe will stuff 8 medium-sized bodies. (Keep everything barely thawed in the fridge until you see exactly what you have and need, then cut the remaining tubes into ⅓" rings, mix with the tentacles, and refreeze to either fry later [*vide* Chap. 5] or to sauté with garlic and tomatoes and toss with [squid ink] spaghetti/fettuccine.)

In a bowl, crumble the feta cheese with a fork, then add the roughly chopped olives. (*I'm trying to be rare with brand endorsements, but I'm addicted to Lindsay "Naturals," both their black and green canned olives. They're inexpensive, pitted, and minimally processed in only water and sea salt. They're also delicious. You'll need these or something equally good and natural for your Martinis—*vide*, always, Chapter 22. [You skipped ahead long before now, right?]) Add the chopped walnuts and parsley, the lemon juice, salt, pepper, sugar, olive oil, and chopped sun-dried tomatoes. (**If you think you'd like a touch more sweetness and less tartness in the mix, you might substitute dried cherries, cranberries, or currants for the sun-dried tomatoes, omitting the sugar.) Mix/mash everything together well.

You can try to manipulate a small spoon to fill the bodies, but you'll soon discover this is more trouble than advantage. Go ahead and use your hands. Hold open the body cavity and, as best you can, patiently stuff with bits of the mix, squeezing the feta down toward the pointed end. You won't want to undertake this when you're nervous, anxious, angry, or in a hurry. Don't worry about spilling or smears of cheese on the outside. Commit to a little bit of a mess and enjoy it as play. The mantles are fairly durable, but try not to tear them (a very small hole or squirt out the tip is manageable). Fill up your tube, leaving a bit of space, then "knit" the lip together twice with the 3" pointed end of a broken bamboo skewer so that the body is puckered firmly closed. (***Of course, you can also use a toothpick, but if you choose to do so you'll need a sturdy, round toothpick, preferably with an attractive turned end—again, these latter are required anyway for Martinis—not those flat, masquerading wood splinters 750 to a box. I prefer the bamboo skewers, though, if you can find thin ones. Don't bother trying to cut or scissor them, just break off the pointed end like the savage that you are. [Moreover, the skewer tip renders a dramatic effect to the stuffed body, holds up well on the grill or in the fryer, and can be used to lift and eat the calamari, which should be tender enough that they won't require knives and forks when served as a snack.]) Gently rinse off the stuffed tube, pat dry, and place on a plate. Continue with the others. (They freeze very well, by the way, and, *vide ante*, a 1-lb. package of calamari should contain enough bodies to make a double batch, and if your nerves can stand it you'll be glad you did. They are delicious and impressive, and once the slightly arduous stuffing is done there's nothing to the cooking. I'd love to have a bagful in the freezer at all times.)

To Grill. Heat your grill, spray the calamari on both sides with olive oil, and grill at a high temperature, top down, for 3 minutes, until marked by those beautiful black grill marks that they paint on in advertisements. Yours are real. Turn and grill for another 3 minutes, leaving the top up so you can admire your handiwork. Remove to a plate, squeeze a wedge of lemon over all, sprinkle with a pinch of coarse sea salt, and serve immediately as a happy hour snack (3 or 4 each) or as exotic accompaniment (perhaps 2 each) to a green salad as a first course.

To Deep-Fry. Use the same batter as for fried calamari (*vide* Chapter 5). In two wide bowls ("dry hand, wet hand," please), dip the bodies in milk and then in an equal mixture of all-purpose and semolina flours. This is a light breading, but cover them thoroughly. Deep-fry at 350° F for 2 minutes, no more. Place on a paper towel for a moment, salt and pepper lightly, and serve with individual small bowls of marinara sauce for a happy hour snack or first course. (I believe I actually prefer the grilled version to the deep-fried, an odd concession for this author. I'm determined to keep sampling both, however, until I'm absolutely certain. If you *really* want to gild the lily, serve both preparations as a snack or, with a little token greenery, a salad: 2 grilled and 2 fried stuffed calamari artfully, symmetrically arranged on small plates the color of the sea. Who won't be impressed by the fortitude of your will, the whimsy of your vision, and the palette of your design? And then just wait until they taste them.)

> But, my tender *loup de mer*,
> my industrious *dorade*,

my simmering *soupe de poisson*—
the wife has other tastes.

—*from* "Apology to the Fish Girl in Forcalquier"

Gaylord's Low Country Boil

I started doing this simple boil a couple of years ago, when I got the Dutch oven I'd long coveted (and continue to tediously laud). Adhering my name to the dish is just being cheeky, as the contents of a boil are fairly standard. I suggest you do keep it simple. If you want to add some small red potatoes, that's fine, although I prefer the boil without them. Anyway, this is classic, incontrovertible summer fare. Putting the Dutch oven in the middle of the deck table, lifting the lid to *oohs* and *aahs* (easily earned this time around), and digging in for a leisurely feed is enormous fun. My god, as I type this I'm remembering those plump, sweet white shrimp on St. Simon's Island, just off the boat and purchased for a song, and my mouth's watering at the thought. It's summertime and we're feeling easy and social, so I'm going to alter our book's usual approach and whip up a boil for four hungry folks, seafarers and landlubbers alike. If it's just the two of you everything's easily halved, and it's still a lot of fun.

2 lbs. raw, unpeeled, wild shrimp (if possible, with heads on for sucking)

1 lb. smoked sausage ring

4 ears local corn

1 large white onion

3 celery stalks

4 Tbs. Old Bay seasoning

2 bay leaves, preferably fresh

In your Dutch oven, bring enough water to boil to cover all ingredients except the shrimp. Add the sausage cut into 4 equal pieces, corn (each ear de-silked, rinsed, and broken in half), onion (skinned and quartered), celery stalks (rinsed and chopped into ½" slices), bay leaves, and Old Bay seasoning. Cover and cook for 15-20 minutes. Add the shrimp and cook another 3-4 minutes, depending on their size, until pink. Don't overcook the shrimp. Drain everything in a colander in the sink, remove the bay leaves, and return the boil to your Dutch oven.

That's all there is to it, and don't let anyone tell you differently. Place in the center of the table, outside on a sultry afternoon, and eat immediately. (You'll need utensils to cut the sausage with, but otherwise this is mostly hands on.) Bread or crackers, optional. Cocktail sauce and cold beer, mandatory. Cloth napkins, much appreciated.

Asian-Marinated Grilled Shrimp

These shrimp are irresistible and impossible to classify as a course. Appetizer? Snack? Main dish? Any definition's irrelevant. We're hooked on this hot, spicy, easy to prepare dish, adapted from *The Splendid Table*. The shrimp are ideal for summer (and pretty damned congenial for winter, too, if you don't mind grilling in the dark and cold).

1 lb. large wild shrimp

2 cloves garlic

1" knob fresh ginger

½ tsp. freshly ground pepper

1 tsp. sesame oil

2 Tbs. rice wine

3 Tbs. soy sauce

3 Tbs. hoisin sauce

1 tsp. sugar

Peel and finely chop the ginger and garlic. Devein and pull the legs from the shrimp, but leave the shells on (which enables these sweet crustaceans both to take the marinade and to grill superiorly). Rinse and pat dry. Mix all of the ingredients in a bowl, add the shrimp, coat thoroughly, and refrigerate for at least 30 minutes and up to 1 hour.

Spray a hot grill with vegetable oil. On high heat, grill the shrimp for 2 minutes. Brush with any remaining marinade, turn them with tongs, and cook 2 more minutes. Don't overcook. Serve immediately. Don't bother trying to pretend to have simultaneous side dishes. Set out a bowl for shells and dig in, fingers only. 1 lb. of shrimp will leave two people wanting more, regardless of what course you decide it is. (Consider grilling 2 lbs. and eating half as an appetizer and half as an entrée. Dilemma solved!)

<u>Bonus Shrimp Happy Hour Snack</u>: <u>Spicy Baked Shrimp with Smoked Paprika</u>

10 large wild shrimp, peeled and deveined

1 Tbs.+ olive oil

2 tsp. smoked paprika

½ rounded tsp. garlic powder

3 shakes cayenne powder

½ tsp. sea salt

Perhaps these don't attain the sublimity of the grilled shrimp above, but they're quick to make and, as they require neither marinating nor heating the grill, can be made spontaneously according to inspiration.

The spice amounts above will produce shrimp with a piquant spiciness but not an unpleasant amount of heat, at least according to my taste buds. Adapt accordingly, easing off or piling on as inclined, and of course make twice as many shrimp as I'm suggesting for this austere snack for two.

Heat oven to 425° F. Devein and shell—leaving tails on—rinse, and pat dry the shrimp. Oil or spray medium-sized glass or enamel cookware and place in oven to heat. In a bowl, mix all remaining ingredients together well. Add the shrimp and coat thoroughly with smoked paprika mixture. In hot cookware, bake shrimp for 4 minutes, turn them, bake for 4 more, then finish under a high broiler for 2 minutes. Serve on small plates and devour hot, holding by the tail.

CHAPTER 17

·

Fruits & Vegetables, Why Not?
Part I: Simple Canning

Cucumber Relish

Cucumber relish, meanwhile, may strike you as about as sexy as deviled eggs (*vide* Chapter 14), but trust that this relish is outstanding. I've made it the past three summers as soon as cucumbers are plentiful at the farmers market. It's become a seasonal staple. My folks and anyone else to whom I've given some return the (small) jar and ask for more. Ideally this is a perfect condiment for grilled burgers, hot dogs, or sausages, but I find that a good portion simply and mysteriously disappears from the refrigerator. The level in the glass jar lowers and spoons multiply in the sink. The recipe below could theoretically be halved, but I wouldn't advise it.

6 medium cucumbers

1 large white onion

1½ tsp. + ½ tsp. sea salt

½ cup sugar

1 cup white vinegar

2 tsp. cornstarch

red pepper flakes

Skin the cucumbers, slice them in half lengthwise on a cutting board, and scoop out the seeds with a grapefruit spoon. (Even if you're using the thin and reportedly seedless English cucumbers, I'll still recommend de-seeding. Also, if the dark, warty, so-called pickling cucumber is available from your farmer, great. Otherwise, about any sort will suffice.) Finely chop the cucumbers until you have 4 cups. Skin and finely chop 1 cup of white onion. Toss cucumber, onion, and 1½ tsp. salt in a colander, place in a large bowl, and let drain at room temperature for 3 hours. Heap drained cucumber-onion mix into the center of a clean kitchen towel (*not* paper towels or cheesecloth), twist into a ball, and squeeze hard to eliminate additional liquid.

In a pot, combine sugar, vinegar, and remaining salt and boil as the sugar dissolves, then cook down on medium heat for 4-5 minutes until the mixture is reduced to 1 cup. Add cucumber and onion and cook, stirring, for 2 minutes, no more. Don't overcook. You want a little crunch in the finished relish. Add the cornstarch dissolved in 2 tsp. spring water and cook, stirring, for 1 additional minute. Remove from heat, spoon relish into a bowl, and add several hearty shakes of red pepper flakes. (Their heat complements the sweetness.) Cool in the fridge for 2 hours, then distribute to several small, decorative glass jars. The relish will last several weeks in the refrigerator, but this really won't be an issue. If you're going to serve it with grilled burgers or sausages, plan on doing so soon.

Preserved Lemons

These salty, intense cured lemons are a must to have in the back of the refrigerator. They're essential to cooking in the tagine—such as a pungent fish stew with tarragon, tomatoes, and almonds, or savory-tart chicken thighs with green olives—for stuffing a whole bird, or any of the other uses you'll improvise for them, either chopped finely or used as whole quarters. (Cf.: By tagine, I mean of course the shaggy real deal of curiously smelling clay, lopsided and oddly other-worldly in its conical appearance, needing to be cared for properly. No enamel tops, Teflon bottoms, or celebrity chef brand names, thank you.) As an additional bonus, the lemons are rather fun to make and look vivid and lovely in the jar, clearly deserving of an ode, so let's insert the obligatory Neruda quote here (*vide* Food & Literary Sources): "you spill / a universe of gold, / a / goblet yellow / with miracles, / one of the aromatic nipples / of the earth's breast, / the ray of light that became fruit, / a planet's miniscule fire."

1 bag nice, firm, spotless lemons

5 Tbs. coarse sea salt

one-quart Mason jar

Rinse lemons, cut the nubs off the stem ends, and quarter with a sharp knife. If there's a thick string of pith in the center, you might gently and moderately slice the worst away and also pick out the most obvious and accessible seeds. (Symbolism aside, you never know what you're going to get when you cut open a lemon, but if you're lucky, yours will be glistening and clean inside with few seeds.) Layer the quartered lemons into a one-quart Mason jar, pressing them in tightly and sprinkling liberally with the salt as you go. Depending on their size, about 5 quartered lemons will fill the jar. Juice 3-4 additional lemons in your juicer (sometimes known in familiar circles as your fist, although I use my Oster citrus juicer regularly and recommend it). Fill the jar of lemon quarters with juice.

Screw on a new lid, shake the jar a few times to help dissolve the salt and make sure all the lemons are well-coated, and refrigerate. After two days, turn the jar upside down, and continue this rotation every two days for two weeks. The lemons are now ready to use and will last for a year.

Lift that alien-looking tagine from above the kitchen cabinet, rinse it off, start it soaking in the sink, grab the chicken and dried fruits and homemade harissa, and get your Moroccan mojo rocking. Wait, damn it: That's not vegetarian. Let's try again:

CHAPTER 18

•

Fruits & Vegetables, Why Not?
Part II: Salad, Sides, & Entrées

A woman weighs
butter lettuce, radishes, three fistfuls
of *petits pois* in shell. At the boulangerie,
where the girl, I believe, recognizes me,
I pretend to study her wooden racks
before choosing Monday's simple baguette.

—*from* "Lost Poem Regarding the Museé
d'Orsay, Rescued by Renoir"

Keeping to the fraudulent theme of relative healthfulness propagated in the previous chapter, let's consider some token fruit and veggie dishes. Actually, you'll notice throughout this book that I'm a big advocate of a green salad—simply prepared with local greens and scallions and lightly dressed—as a standard accompaniment (i.e., defensive strategy) to the author's proclivity toward heavier and more elaborate main dishes. (The one exception to the "simple" theme, but staying local, is a spinach salad with thinly sliced red onion, a poached farm egg on top, crumbled bacon [or mini crab cakes on the side], perhaps according to mood some chopped sun-dried tomatoes or roasted piquillo peppers, and a light dressing of choice—I make a pear vinaigrette that complements nicely [although, if you're using a jar of Spanish piquillos, you might just opt for a drizzle of that sublime oil they're in]. With a hot, yeasty roll or crusty loaf on the side, a spinach salad is a fine summer meal that nevertheless offers the semblance of being good for you.)

As a change of pace, here's a salad sans greens that is easy to assemble and a pleasing blend of sweet and savory. I associate it with summer and the Mediterranean.

Orange & Olive Salad

2 good oranges

12 black olives

1 small white onion

2 Tbs. good olive oil

sea salt & freshly ground black pepper

microgreens for garnish (optional)

Peel the oranges and carefully remove as much as you reasonably can of the white pith, but do not pull apart the sections. Thinly slice the whole oranges and arrange on an attractive Fiestaware plate of a complementary color (perhaps lemongrass, turquoise, or—why not?—tangerine). Sprinkle with a pinch of sea salt, then add the onion (peeled, thinly sliced, and separated into rings) and pitted and halved black olives (*vide* Chapter 16 for a note on olives, recall). Drizzle with the good olive oil and finish with several coarse grinds of black pepper. If you like, garnish with tart or spicy sprouts. This is a handsome, flavorful, and refreshing salad that pairs well with pasta, tomato-based sauces, or whatever's coming off the grill. As usual, serves two.

Whole Steamed Artichokes

2 large, whole artichokes (preferably in season)

1 qt. low-sodium chicken broth

2 lemons

¼ cup white wine

4 large cloves garlic

2 fresh bay leaves

several sprigs Italian parsley

1 Tbs. Italian breadcrumbs

sea salt & freshly ground black pepper

2 Tbs. olive oil (plus more for dipping)*

How could the artichoke not be included, its lovely armor opening to the flesh, the tender heart that epitomizes summer? Yet for years, and for reasons now unclear to me, I was intimidated by the idea of steaming artichokes, which seemed a complicated and arcane affair, and was more than content for my wife to undertake the task whenever she or I found and brought home a couple of fat, dark green specimens demanding to be deconstructed and demolished.

Hard to say whether she was relieved or saddened or largely indifferent when I recently discovered how simple they are to prepare. She seemed willing enough to eat the artichoke. 1 large choke makes a first course or snack. 2 each and call it a veggie meal.

To prepare the artichokes, rinse thoroughly under water and pull off any outer leaves that seem extremely tough. Don't overdo the stripping, though, as most recipes seem to encourage. Another common practice I decry is cutting off the stems, which I think are perfectly edible and tasty—albeit just a bit stringy—after steaming. (Most folks don't recognize that the stems are desirable, so if you've better sense and keen instincts, you're likely to get all of them at the table for your good taste.) On a cutting board, with a sharp knife, cut off just the tough tip of the stem and about 1" of the top of the artichoke. If you want to try to clear out a few of the interior thistles—i.e., the choke or beard—with scissors or a grapefruit spoon, you may, but I don't encourage wasting much time on this. They'll separate easily after steaming.

In a large pot with a top, you can add anything reasonable for the steaming, conceivably as simple as water, salt, pepper, and a splash of olive oil, but my recommendation is this: In the pot, combine the chicken broth (or vegetable broth or, I suppose, water), the lemons rinsed and halved, white wine, peeled garlic cloves, bay leaves, rinsed parsley, seasoned breadcrumbs, olive oil, and salt and ground pepper. Bring to a low boil. This combination is fast and easy and includes nothing you don't already have at hand, so you may steam artichokes any time, spontaneously, when you find some nice ones (in season somewhere, and carbon footprint, just for the moment, be damned). Notice, too, how attractive and healthful the mélange looks as you nestle the artichokes tops down in the simmering goodness. (Along with excessively peeling outside leaves and the discarding of stems, assign to the myth pile the need to rub the cleaned chokes in lemon, soak them in a prepared acid water, or generally murmur a special invocation to keep them green. Just clean your chokes, get your broth and wine simmering, and get on with it.) Cover and simmer for 30 minutes. (They may take a few minutes longer if enormous, but don't steam them into mush. You want the leaves to come off easily and yield as you pull them through your teeth like a rabid animal, but you want, just as in love, the heart to have a little texture and "give" when you partake of its gift.)

To serve, place each artichoke on a plate or in a serving bowl, with an additional plate or bowl for the leaves once you've scraped the flesh off with your teeth. I used to eat artichokes exclusively with a dipping bowl of melted garlic butter, but now in my matured and philosophical years I prefer a good virgin olive oil—simpler, better, and healthier. Each leaf: rip, dip, scrape. (You may also opt to simply drizzle oil over the entire choke and simplify the process to "rip, scrape.") They're a fun, dripping mess to eat, so cloth napkins, rather than paper, are highly recommended. When you reach the center, you should be able to pull/peel out the inedible thistle florets with a single deft maneuver. If they're resistant—meaning the choke may be just a tad undercooked, but no worries—carve the mothers out with the always useful grapefruit spoon. Nothing is going to stop you now from your craved and earned reward, toward which the leaves have teased and directed you: the succulent, exposed, naked surface of the heart, cut into pieces and dipped in oil and eaten with the fingers or on the tines of a petite fork. No metaphor required.

Roasted Cauliflower with Anchovy Sauce

1 large head cauliflower

3 Tbs. + 3 Tbs. + 4 Tbs. olive oil

2 thick slices leftover homemade bread

2 cloves garlic

4 anchovy fillets (in olive oil, from a tin)

1 tsp. lemon juice

1½ Tbs. fresh Italian parsley

½ tsp. sea salt

freshly ground black pepper

I'm uncertain how hamburgers and sausages and fish and chicken so easily violated our previous vegetable chapter, but no need to be overly vigilant about vegetable matters, and anyway I was already determined to include this unusual and addictive roasted cauliflower. Anchovy sauce hardly violates any open-minded diner's ideal of vegetarian, don't you agree? Cauliflower is a fine, underappreciated plant, and I dedicate this recipe to the haunted and brilliant Bernard Loiseau, who before his suicide (apparently due in great measure to the rumor, perhaps largely self-perpetuated, that La Côte d'Or would lose one of its three stars in the next *Guide Michelin*) was reportedly obsessed with his late, eccentric *choufleur caramelizé* (caramelized cauliflower). Years before Loiseau's death in 2003, during my stay for a few weeks at a writers' retreat/wine cave in Burgundy—I'm not kidding—one of my hosts treated me to a driving tour on a sunny afternoon, the white Charolais cattle grazing the hillsides, for a "taste" of the area's heralded sights. Of course, we stopped at La Côte d'Or in Saulieu, got out of the car, and stood quietly and reverentially for a moment, as we couldn't afford to eat there. Then we went to find some snails (which were hot, buttery, tender, large, and excellent). Let's roast some cauliflower in M. Loiseau's memory and flatter ourselves he might have enjoyed this simple but rich dish.

Clean any leaves from the head of cauliflower, place stem down on a cutting board, and with a large knife slice the head all the way across into approximately ¾" slices. On a large platter, massage the slices (and all bits and pieces) of cauliflower with 3 Tbs. olive oil, sea salt, and ground pepper. Arrange slices in a single layer on a large metal baking sheet and cook for 1½ hours at 350° F. (The cauliflower might be done in 1 hour, but I doubt it. Be patient. You want the slices to not only tenderize, but to shrink, brown, and, yes, caramelize and sweeten.)

Meanwhile, cut side and bottom crusts from bread and discard. Tear the bread into fine pieces in a glass cooking dish, mix well until wet with 3 Tbs. olive oil and a dash of salt, and bake at 350° F in the smaller oven for 15 minutes. Toast and brown them, but be careful the crumbs don't burn. (Obviously, you can do this and all of the sauce preparations earlier, if you prefer, and leave the crumbs covered on the stovetop.) With a mortar and pestle, crush the garlic cloves and add the lemon juice to them. Chop the anchovies and add. Let stand 10 minutes for the lemon juice to tame the garlic, then grind everything into a paste. Slowly pour in the remaining 2 Tbs. olive oil, as if you were making aoli, and further mistreat with the pestle as you go.

To serve, place a warm cauliflower slice (and a few browned bits) on each plate, spoon over with the anchovy sauce, and top with the breadcrumbs and a large pinch of roughly chopped Italian parsley. Yes, this is a lot of work for cauliflower—I understand that diners never quite, not fully, appreciated Loiseau's effort—so serve with a simple main course of, for example, roasted chicken. Dig in and see if it wasn't danged nearly worth *your* effort, which is more than one can say for so much of our lives, *non*?

Now, I need more of the small, sweet onions . . .

—*from* "What Is It You Would Seek?"

Onion Tart

If your companion, however comely, generous, and kind, suddenly discovers he or she is lactose intolerant, in addition to the perhaps just slightly finicky eating habits iterated upon occasion earlier in this book, you'll find your life further and dramatically diminished. With no "cheese love," you can kiss goodbye, so to speak, those silky ice creams, your beloved, luxurious quiche Lorraines, and any picnic worth a damn. To salve the pain of unrequited loss, you might attempt a bright lemon sorbet (*vide* Chapter 19) as substitute for the ice cream and, *vide infra*, a rich onion tart—with only 3 Tbs. of dairy, discounting the *touch* of butter—as palliative for the quiche. As for the picnic? Your rented Peuguot twisting up through the Alpes-de-Haute-Provence, a wheel of Muenster warm and oozing on the dashboard, the morning's baguette, a local bottle of red, the yawning afternoon hours of June and the anticipation of all to come? Well, love hurts, as does the sharp edge of memory. Maybe the tart will lift your spirits.

for the crust:*

5 oz. + 2 oz. unsalted butter

5 Tbs. vegetable shortening

2 Tbs. cold spring water

2 cups + all-purpose flour*

⅛ tsp. sea salt

for the filling:

2 yellow & 2 white medium onions**

3 large farm eggs

3 Tbs. heavy cream

2 tsp. sugar

chives from the garden

¼ tsp. freshly ground nutmeg

additional sea salt & freshly ground black pepper

*The crust here is easy enough to make, but it does require some delicacy and patience in the rolling and handling. You might instead use a puff pastry from the grocer. I've made the tart both ways, and, to be brutally honest, the puff pastry is at least as good as the homemade crust, maybe better depending on your preference of texture and the particular result. But the Calvinist roots of a Presbyterian upbringing run deep, and as I'm feeling residual guilt for store-bought frozen pie crusts and biscuits recommended elsewhere in this book, let's go ahead and make the crust from scratch. Or just watch me, then you can sensibly head off to buy a box of frozen puff pastry sheets. No judgment.

In the Cuisinart, place the flour, shortening, 5 oz. cold, unsalted butter cut into chunks, and ⅛ tsp. fine sea salt. Pulse until well mixed into crumbles, 1 minute or so. Continue to pulse as you add the water. Remove the dough with your hands, shape into a ball, wrap tightly in plastic wrap, and refrigerate for 20-30 minutes. While you're waiting, skin and thinly slice your onions. (**I chose a white and yellow mix because they were hanging in the basket and I was curious to compare their response. Use what you have and like, although if you're using Vidalias—which I wouldn't recommend here—you might consider deleting the sugar.) Separate the slices into rings in a pile on the cutting board and cover with a towel until you're ready for them. To complete the crust, on a floured counter or marble slab roll out the dough into a circle of about 10", sufficient to cover the bottom and sides of a 9" tart pan (i.e., with a removable bottom). The dough will be friable and break and tear easily. Just be patient, show it some love, and use a long spatula to help you lower/shape it into the pan. You can mold in any broken pieces and smooth tears with your fingers, so take your time and massage the crust evenly in the bottom and up the narrow sides. Slice away any extra along the edge with a paring knife. Cover pan snugly with aluminum foil and refrigerate for at least 2-3 hours.

In a large sauté pan, melt the remaining 2 oz. of butter. Add the onions, the sugar, and a pinch of salt. Mix well with a spatula, cover, and cook over low-medium heat for approximately 30 minutes, until the onions soften and turn a pale gold. Stir 2-3 times. Don't turn them into mush. Remove onions from heat and allow to cool.

The rest is a snap. To bake the crust, fill the foil-covered tart pan with dried baking beans and place in a 450° F oven for 10 minutes. Reduce the heat to 375° F and cook for 5 more minutes, then remove from oven. Remove the foil and funnel the beans back into their jar.

To complete the filling, whisk together the beautiful farm eggs (which you remembered to take out of the fridge 30 minutes earlier), the cream, a few twists of coarsely ground pepper, 10 turns of your nutmeg grinder, and perhaps another pinch of salt. Stir in the onions, spoon evenly into the shell, and sprinkle a handful of rinsed and diced chives on top. Finish with another twist of pepper and nutmeg, for luck and fortune.

Bake in the 375° F oven for 25-30 minutes, until the center has the consistency of a sturdy custard. Serve warm slices of the tart, nearly vegetarian and virtually—to the author's mind, although his curmudgeonly confidante disagrees—dairy free, with a green salad and a dry, cold, fruity white wine. (I'll fall back on my workhorse, go-to white, Alexander Valley Vineyards' inexpensive and unpretentious—and organic—Gewürztraminer, which has a nice, citrusy nose and good acidity.) Have I managed to distract, or are you still lamenting the bacon and Swiss cheese quiche, the Muenster, the alps, the dissipated dreams of once-immortal youth? "When you love you wish to do things for, you wish to sacrifice for, you wish to serve," the priest explains in *A Farewell to Arms*, shortly before Frederic Henry is AWOL and on the run. You'll be alright. Try the tart.

.

A Light Vegetarian Meal For Two (No Kidding)

The three dishes below look lovely together on the plate, the dark green kale specked with sesame seeds stunningly complementing the blackened and deeply orange carrots and the white-stalked bok choy. Served on Fiestaware of sunflower or lemongrass, these plates will be so bold and beautiful you'll almost forget you have only rabbit food in front of you.

Oven-Roasted Kale

2 small bunches locally grown kale, any variety

3 cloves garlic

1½ Tbs. olive oil

1½ tsp. sesame seeds

sea salt & freshly ground black pepper

Toast sesame seeds for 4-5 minutes, until they just begin to brown. Wash and carefully dry the kale. Tear or cut the whole leaves from the stems. Discard the latter. On a large cookie sheet, mix leaves with the chopped garlic, olive oil, a few grinds of pepper, and 2-3 pinches of salt. Don't overdo the salt. Toss everything well with yours hands, then bake at 350° F for 12-15 minutes (turn once during the cooking time). Sprinkle with the sesame seeds.

Baby Bok Choy with Pistachios

4-5 bunches (6-8 oz.) baby bok choy

5-6 medium scallions

3 cloves garlic

1 Tbs. olive oil

⅔ tsp. sesame oil

2 rounded Tbs. salted pistachios (or cashews)

sea salt & freshly ground black pepper

dash red pepper flakes (optional)

First, take a moment to admire the beauty of the baby bok choy, the dark round leaves and tubular white stalks reminiscent of mushrooms. Is there a lovelier green? Soak the bunches in a large bowl of water to clean, then rinse, cut the leaves free from their base (leaving the stalks on the leaves, of course), and drain on paper towels. Chop the nuts and toast them for 4 minutes or until just beginning to brown. In a large skillet, heat the olive oil to medium high. Sauté the green onions for 1 minute, then add the garlic and cook for 1 additional minute. Add the bok choy leaves, the sesame oil, a pinch of salt, a dash of red pepper flakes, and a liberal grind of pepper. Cover and cook 3 minutes. Mix in the pistachios or serve them over the top of the plated cabbage.

Sautéed Candied Carrots

10 small locally grown carrots, tops on

1½ oz. unsalted butter

3-4 sprigs fresh thyme

2 tsp. local honey

sea salt & freshly ground black pepper

Rinse the carrots, peel them just enough to remove any hair and give them a roughly uniform shape, and trim the tops, leaving 1" of green. Melt the butter in a large skillet, add the chopped thyme, and cook on medium for 1 minute. Raise the heat to medium-high, add the carrots, cover, and sauté for 5 minutes, jostling/turning occasionally. Add the honey and coat the carrots well. Lower burner to medium and cook for another 2-3 minutes. Don't overcook. The carrots should be slightly blackened, but still firm and opinionated.

To serve, divide the kale, bok choy, and carrots onto the Fiestaware indicated above. Not only are the colors dazzling, but the light crunch of the kale (which dissolves in the mouth), spicy, vaguely Asian bite of the bok choy—as well as the continued motif of the sesame—and the sweet, slight resistance of the carrots combine for an oddly pleasurable mouthfeel. Of course, you could still salvage this meal with just about any fish, chicken, or red meat. These are eminently versatile sides. Tonight, though, you've played the trump card to impress and deceive your lovely vegetarian partner, so stay strong. Focus. Remember that the pre-dinner Martinis and the cool, dry white wine with dinner are also vegetarian, not to mention vegan, so possibilities and expectations endlessly persist. Also, to my mind, neither kale nor carrot necessarily requires flatware, if you care to further reconsider lifestyle choices.

•

Roasted Green Beans, Two Ways

Another dish difficult to categorize. These will work well as a side, with a modicum of imagination could easily be manipulated into a salad, and they're also an enjoyable and (relatively) healthy snack. Since over and over we've eaten all of the test batches as soon as they came out of the oven and were cool enough not to burn the fingers (the beans often didn't even make it onto plates), I incline toward and suggest the latter—an anytime snack. (Cf.: There's nothing especially or necessarily even vaguely "traditional"—*vide infra*—about the first option offered here, but the title provides a convenience in separating it from its variation.) These are a world away from the cooked-into-submission, bolstered-with-hunks-of-pork-fatback version of Southern green beans, god bless'm, that I grew up eating and enjoying. No apologies! Besides, you'll see that I pay my homage by chapter's end. The rather arbitrary numbers of beans indicated are merely meant to suggest a happy hour snack (if any make it into the living room) or side for two. By all means, make as many as you like.

Traditional Roasted Green Beans

14-16 fat green beans, locally grown

olive oil

dried thyme or herbes de Provence

red pepper flakes

sea salt & freshly ground black pepper

Rinse your green beans, scissor off the ends, and dry trimmed beans on a paper towel. On a cookie sheet or in a pie pan—this is important, as glass won't crisp the beans properly—thoroughly cover the beans with a healthy drizzle of olive oil, 3-4 shakes of the dried herbs, 2 shakes of the red pepper flakes, a few turns of pepper, and salt to taste. Use your hands and massage the green fellows well. Make them happy. Cook at 500° F, the shelf raised one notch above the center of the oven, for 6-8 minutes depending on the size of the beans. (It's not a bad idea to preheat the cookie sheet, in which case you'll need to toss the beans in a bowl or on a plate.) Don't overcook. Pull them out of the oven, let cool a moment while you find napkins, then call in someone you love (or intend to) to stand at the stove and dig in, one delicately raised bean at a time. Feeding each other or creating some spontaneous food game—rules best kept privately between the two of you—is neither recommended nor discouraged.

Bacon-Wrapped Roasted Green Beans

9 fat green beans, locally grown

3 strips thin bacon

Any deserving chapter on vegetables needs to end on a note of bacon. This is a deeply held conviction of mine that I hope you share. The thinnest, cheapest bacon you can get is ideal here, as it tends to stretch, wrap, and hold more effectively than its thicker kin, and one can't really toothpick a green bean effectively. Okay, listen carefully: Cut your strips of thin, cheap, fatty bacon into thirds and curl/stretch 1 piece diagonally around each bean. This is a sensual activity and I feel strongly that you will enjoy it. (Another option would be to wrap each piece of bacon around 2 beans, rather than 1, to raise the green bean ratio vis-à-vis the bacon and ergo moderate your guilt, although why you'd want to do this I have no idea.)

Two ingredients. That's all you need. If you have extra strips of bacon, feel free to wrap them around liver, oysters ("angels on horseback," with a squeeze of lemon juice just before eating—heavenly indeed!), scallops, shrimps, olives, prunes, bananas, plantains, or whatever's handy. In the meantime, carefully place your bacon-wrapped beans in a metal pie pan and broil on high for 8-12 minutes, depending on the ferocity of your broiler. (For ease and out of habit, I broil exclusively in our smaller top oven, which doesn't have quite the bite of the full-size lower one.) Turning really isn't necessary and risks the calamity of dislodging the secured bacon. When the bacon's crispy and browned on top, remove from broiler, drain for a moment on a paper towel or don't, and eat, to paraphrase the popular expression, "like you were dying."

And as to that ninth bean? Well, that's just how the bacon math worked out, right? It's nothing to do with power dynamics or who loves whom more. Remember that.

Okay, are we all feeling healthful and good about ourselves, our right choices and prudent restraints? Excellent. I applaud you. Can we hurry on now to dessert, for pity's sake, while there's time?

CHAPTER 19

·

Vita Brevis: Desserts for All Seasons
Part I—Spring & Summer

I slice cherries thick enough to attack
like apricots or plums. The knife we bought
together enters the waxy skin of each,
separates glistening pink flesh,
reveals a dark center. Even to my taste
for excess, they are sweet.

—*from* "After a Disagreeable Conversation
One Continent Away"

Early Spring: Olive Oil Almond Cookies

2½ cups all-purpose flour

1 tsp. baking powder

½ tsp. sea salt

½ tsp. freshly ground nutmeg

1½ cups sliced almonds

¾ cup white sugar

½ cup dark brown sugar

½ cup olive oil

1 Tbs. unsalted butter

2 Tbs. finely grated orange peel

2 tsp. vanilla extract

2 farm eggs

First, I won't try to describe in too fine detail the seductive texture or subtle flavor of these thick, delicious cookies. Rich but not overly sweet, with an accent of salt, they actually remind me a bit of shortbread, ironic considering the lack of significant butter. These are fine cookies with a slightly unusual consistency and taste. Anyone you serve them to will eat several and want to know the truth of the ingredients. The secret, of course, is the olive oil, so be very coy about that. Admit nothing.

Second, this is also a winning recipe because it requires two simple but essential kitchen gadgets: a nutmeg grinder and a fine grater (i.e., zester). Freshly ground nutmeg is unmistakably piquant and aromatic. I'm addicted to my Williams-Sonoma grinder—already employed in this book—love loading the whole nut as if locking a weapon, delight in cranking it inappropriately and indiscriminately where nutmeg has no business, and don't know how I ever lived without it. A Brewer Christmas or two ago, my brothers were mocking me for traveling with my grinder (there are people who *don't?*), until, that is, they tasted the eggnog I'd made. Well, yes. Lick the glasses clean, unenlightened *fraters*: behold and learn. As to the zester, it too is a must. You may fool yourself that that old box grater you inherited as a family legacy suffices as well for zesting as for grating cheese or potatoes, but once you use a proper zester you'll be convinced. Microplane makes an excellent model. I use it constantly for oranges, lemons, ginger, and the occasional tip of finger.

Okay. In a medium bowl, blend the flour, baking powder, freshly ground nutmeg, and salt. In a larger bowl, whisk together the white and brown sugars, the olive oil, the orange zest, the eggs (which you remembered to set out 30 minutes earlier), and the vanilla. Whisk hard for 1 minute until a pale gold. Gradually, by thirds, add the dry ingredients to the wet and blend well with a fork. (N.b.: Do *not* whisk the dry and wet ingredients together, as the whisk will immediately be a gloppy mess that you will regret. Use a fork.) Fold in the almonds and mix with your hand. Blend thoroughly but gently. If you break some of the almond slivers, that's fine, but don't be brusque.

Divide the dough and roll with your hands into 2 6" logs. Double wrap each tightly in plastic wrap and freeze for 2 hours or until ready for use. To prepare, cut desired number of cookies (the recipe makes approximately 36 cookies, a few more if you prefer them thinner) from the logs in ¼" slices. On a cookie sheet, bake at 350° F for 8-9 minutes. Don't overcook them. Remove from oven, sprinkle with sugar, and let set for 1-2 minutes before dislodging with a spatula. Eat warm.

> What of theoretical salt burning eyes,
> symbolic shirt stained to chest, and later,
> at last, what of that first taste,

ripeness judged sweet but not, perhaps,
to her thematic tongue, quite sweet enough.

—from "Blackberries"

Late Spring: Orange or Lemon Soufflé

The prose poem, Canadian literature, an "easy" soufflé recipe—most of us at adulthood put aside such oxymoronic myths. I am here to debunk the casual ease with which food magazines and cookbooks notoriously tout their airy sweet and savory concoctions, their delicately risen ramekins. I am here to tell you the truth: There's no soufflé that isn't a royal pain in the arse to put together. Still and all, about once a year you just simply have to tackle one if you're living a fully lived life, yes? (Anyway, the upcoming berry cobbler—*vide* Chapter 20—is so insultingly easy that we need some toil to restore a karmic balance.) That settled, I offer the version below. A winning alchemy takes place in the oven as the cake more or less separates into a pudding-like bottom with a light and pillowy top. To my mind, this would probably need twice as many eggs to certify as a true, anxiety-inducing soufflé ready to implode at the jar of an opening oven door or an errant heavy footstep. A truer name might be something like "pudding cake," but hey, who wants to argue semantics? Soufflé is close enough for country dancin'. Anyway, you won't seduce anyone with a pudding cake. But a citrusy soufflé? *Ah oui!*

2 juicy oranges + 1 lemon or 2 large & juicy lemons

¼ cup all-purpose flour

⅓ cup sugar

¼ rounded tsp. fine sea salt

1 cup whole milk

4 oz. unsalted butter

3 large farm eggs

2 Tbs. Grand Marnier (optional, and for the orange version only)

This is time-consuming enough that you might consider doing a bit of prep in advance (viz., whisking the dry ingredients, zesting and juicing the fruit). Also, undertake this on a night when the rest of the meal is by and large taken care of—a one dish meal in the oven or slow cooker, for example.

Zest 1 Tbs. orange peel with your new zester. (If you're preparing a lemon version, substitute 2 lemons for the orange directions, juice them entirely, and leave out the Grand Marnier. You can drink the latter over ice as you're working, if you like, to preserve the balance, harmony, and equilibrium of the recipe's variations.) Juice ½ cup of juice from the 2 oranges. (You'll probably only need 1½ oranges, unless they're anemic.) Juice 2 Tbs. lemon juice and add to orange juice. Separate the 3 lovely farm eggs that you set out 30 minutes earlier. (Returned again to our theme of fresh, local eggs: I bought two dozen this morning from the farmer down the road. The open house was deserted except for the two dogs and one of the calico cats. I finally found him in the barn shoveling manure into a garbage can to fertilize a proposed onion patch. We agreed that summer had arrived in March and, also, that it was good to be out in the day, operating freely and without bosses on our backs. The eggs he collected from the attentive, plumed chickens while I waited were large, warm, brown and speckled, with one of them curiously elongated.)

Making the soufflé will require three mixing bowls—two large and one small (a counterful that will soon be a sinkful). In one of the large bowls, whisk together the flour, salt, and sugar. In the small bowl, whisk together the juices, zest, egg yolks, milk, and Grand Marnier (this is no extra expense, as you'll have purchased a bottle as a staple of your bar (*vide* Chapter 25). Add the melted and cooled butter and whisk until smooth. Add to the flour mixture, whisking until well combined. Don't get discouraged, now. Your back's not hurting. You're young. You're forceful. Stay the course. In the other large bowl, beat the egg whites with an electric mixer until they form soft peaks, about 2 minutes. Spoon about ¼ of the beaten whites into the soufflé batter and fold in thoroughly with a spatula. Gently fold in the remaining whites.

Turn the fluffy batter into a buttered 8"x8" baking dish, set this dish into a larger one, and pour boiling water around the sides of the soufflé, at least 1" deep. (Yes, the hot water bath is necessary.) Bake 45 minutes at 350°, until puffy and nicely darkened on top. Serve warm, theoretically to six. (*Vide ut supra*, one of the attractions of this recipe is that it isn't as fragile and finicky as a traditional, topped out, wavering soufflé. I've never had this cake fall, and it holds up reasonably well as a cold treat the next day, although that's improbable if you're serving this to four or more.)

Early Summer: Key Lime Pie with Pretzel Crust

When I was a fellow at the Helene Wurlitzer Foundation in Taos in 2001, one of my most pleasant rituals, by the end nearly every day, was to walk into town (leaving the Foundation-supplied bicycle behind, thank you) to an appropriately dilapidated coffee shop—the name eludes me—for an afternoon cup of brew and a slice of their fine Key lime pie. The day's writing complete, I relaxed outside in the courtyard or inside beneath posted offers of tarot or astrological readings, yoga instruction, past life and future life reclamations, and just general, all-purpose psychic consultancy, beneath sketches of unicorns and robe-clad desert seekers. I was more of a *dessert* seeker, spiritually speaking, but I liked the joint well enough. The astral star of the pie was its pretzel crust, which I have adapted with abandon ever since. You'll notice that the recipe below has a lot of crust in ratio to, and is a lot more work than, the filling. Well, this is what I'm saying.

1-lb. bag Key limes

1 regular Persian lime

2 farm eggs + 2 yolks

1 14-oz. can sweetened condensed milk

for the crust:

1½ cups crushed pretzel sticks

¾ cup walnuts

½ cup white sugar

10 oz.—that is correct—unsalted butter

1½ tsp. vanilla extract

pinch of sea salt

Rinse your limes and juice them, to get that job out of the way. (Yes, you can probably find a bottle of Key lime juice at Trader Joe's or the miscellaneous fancy grocer, and, yes, you can use regular limes if you prefer and really want to roll that way, but juicing the cute little limes really doesn't take very long, the fresh juice is better than the bottled, and the Key limes have a higher acidity than and a distinct aroma from regular limes. Do as ye will.) A 1-lb. bag of Key limes should yield around ⅔ cup of juice.

With a mortar and pestle, in batches, crush 1½ cups of pretzel sticks, leaving them identifiable as bits of pretzel and not brutalized into dust. In a bowl, combine pretzels, ¾ cup coarsely chopped walnuts, sugar, vanilla, melted butter, and a pinch of salt. (Look, it's a lot of butter, but those are a lot of pretzels, too, requiring a proper binder.) With your fingers, press the mixture into a 9" glass pie pan. Working the crust about halfway up the sides of the pan is sufficient. Bake the crust at 375° F for 10 minutes.

Meanwhile, in a medium bowl combine the 2 eggs, 2 egg yolks, and a can of sweetened condensed milk. Whisk well. The yolks of the farm eggs should render the filling at this point a breathtaking, almost fluorescent tangerine, which will change to a deep, citrusy yellow when you add the pale green Key lime juice. Whisk in ½ cup of the juice, test the batter for tartness to your taste, and add the rest of the juice judiciously, keeping in mind that the crust is fairly sweet. Up to ⅔ cup of juice should be fine. Pour batter over pretzel crust and bake for another 15 minutes.

Cut 4 center slices from the Persian lime and halve these. When the pie is still hot from the oven, nestle the 8 half-slices of lime, wide side down and regularly spaced, into the soft pie near the crust, demarcating a fan of 8 portions. (Demarcate 10 slices of pie with 10 half-slices of lime, if you're pretending to care about calories, gluttony, et cetera.) This is a beautiful pie, as visually attractive in color and contrast as any dish in this book. It's a knockout. Make sure to show it around for kudos before slicing. Take a photo, if you can locate where the camera's hidden. To serve, warm or cold, slice and remove with a spatula to brightly colored dessert plates and top with freshly whipped cream. (All that business and debate about a top layer of sour cream or whatnot? Forget it.) Feel the psychic convergence and be at peace.

> Even now, you raise purple sphere
> to lips, its sweaty cool, explode
> sweet skin between teeth
> in messy tribute to women young or old.
>
> Refrain for once from your labored
> meanings. Let this last plum be enough.
>
> —*from* "The Plums in the Icebox"

Late Summer: Lemon Sorbet

Here's another flower—pale yellow—extended to your lactose intolerant beloved. Actually, this bright, brutally cold summer treat is, one reluctantly admits, a refreshing *occasional* alternative to heavy cream ice cream.

4 juicy lemons

1 cup white sugar

2½ cups spring water

2 egg whites

1+ Tbs. vodka

3 + 2 sprigs mint from the garden

pinch sea salt

whipped cream

The night before, place your quart-size ice cream maker cylinder in the freezer. Also the night before, put the sugar, water, and 3 rinsed mint sprigs in a medium saucepan and bring to a boil. Stir and let simmer on medium for 1 minute. Remove from heat, steep for 5 minutes, then remove and discard mint. Cover syrup and refrigerate.

To make the sorbet, completely zest 1 rinsed lemon and reserve the zest. Slice all 4 lemons in half (they should be at room temperature, of course, for optimum liquidity) and juice with your electric juicer. Retain 2-4 of the larger, cleaner, and unblemished juiced halves for serving the sorbet, slightly slicing away the nub so that the lemon half will sit upright. Refrigerate these along with the lemon juice. Meanwhile, divide the eggs, retaining the yolks for some purpose to be determined. (Perhaps some caramel and sea salt ice cream, once the sorbet is demolished? Just a thought . . .) Set the albumen on the counter to warm.

Mix together the chilled syrup, lemon juice, zest, and vodka (to help resist over-hardening in the freezer—optional in ice cream, mandatory in the sorbet), and pour into the assembled and running ice cream maker. In 20 minutes or so, the sorbet should be fairly slushy. (It won't firm up like ice cream.) As the machine continues to run, add a pinch of salt to the room temperature egg whites and with an electric hand mixer beat whites to a soft peak consistency, around 2 minutes, and fold into the still-turning sorbet. Let the machine run for another 3-4 minutes, then remove the frozen cylinder. You may need to fold in the sorbet more with a plastic spatula. Place a spoonful into a small bowl for allowing said beloved, weary at his/her computer screen, to taste; then yourself; then the dog. After approving nods, scoop the sorbet into whatever lidded container you've earlier placed in the freezer for the purpose. Once the soft sorbet is out of the cylinder, it will melt and separate quickly, so get it right into the freezer to harden.

To serve, place 2 of the empty lemon halves into brightly colored small dessert bowls, fill each half with a scoop of sorbet, and garnish with a sprig of mint and a small spoonful of whipped cream (required, even for the lactose intolerant). Makes 1½ pints, or about 6 servings—all of which can easily be eaten by 2 in a single evening, obviously. (For a fun aperitif, place a spoonful of sorbet into flutes and top with champagne or cava. This also has the devious advantage of sneaking dessert into the meal twice—at the beginning and the end.)

Surprise Bonus Dessert for All Seasons, #1: Banoffee Pie

Banana + toffee = banoffee. Get it? I was introduced to this deadly dessert during my first residency at Hawthornden Castle in Scotland in 1996. The castle cook at the time was a sweet young woman with an accent so thick that I caught about every third word. I think. Anyway, we laughed a lot during the afternoons in the big, drafty kitchen (supposedly a *verboten* area for the writers, but, hey, an author must have ice for whisky, no?). When I returned to the castle for an encore eight years later, I looked low and high for Lorraine in Edinburgh and around greater Midlothian, discovering only after I'd returned to Tennessee that she had died of cancer at a preposterous age. (A recollection better suited to this collection, perhaps, is the Highlands wedding she took me to. Think tartan kilts, bagpipes, pageantry, dance, and just a wee spot of drink solely, understand, for the purpose of raising toasts.) Anyway, once she learned I was addicted, the pie became a staple Sunday dessert in the castle dining room. I have often vaguely yet heretically considered caramel the "thinking man's chocolate," and wherever this assertion might or might not lead us, it probably has its origin in this pie. The recipe offered here isn't especially authentic, but perhaps it's adequate to return one's thoughts to the caves of William Wallace, a peaty Islay single malt that tastes of the sea, a rousing refrain of "Scotland the Brave," and much else.

Below is a credible version based partly on distant "taste memory." It's not quite right, somehow, or maybe that's just the years intervening. No one's arguing that banoffee pie isn't too rich, too sweet, basically a young person's dessert. Still, if you're like me, you might make it anyway, just to remember. If you're like me.*

1 14-oz. can sweetened condensed milk

1 large ripe banana

10 oz. unsalted butter

1¾ cup crushed graham crackers (about ⅓ box)

¼ rounded tsp. fine sea salt

¼ tsp. vanilla

1 Tbs. sugar

½ cup heavy whipping cream

block of chocolate for shaving

In a medium pot, submerge the unopened can of sweetened condensed milk with water and bring to a simmer on the stove. Simmer for 2 hours, periodically adding more hot water from the tea kettle to make sure the tin stays covered. Otherwise, it may explode. (N.b.: Many brands of sweetened condensed milk—including the front-runner Eagle Brand—now come with pull-tab tops on the cans. If you have the temerity to attempt boiling such a can, that's your decision, but I would advise seeking out a traditionally sealed tin can. Some things don't need testing—at least not in *my* laboratory.) Dry the can and cool in the refrigerator.

Crush the graham crackers by hand into a bowl, leaving some detectable pieces. Pour the melted butter over the crackers and mix with a spoon. Add the salt and vanilla and stir again until well mixed. Pour into a glass pie pan and press and smooth across the bottom with your fingers. (A regular-sized pie pan will suffice, but if you have a slightly smaller one, that would be even better. In some ways, I've halved this recipe, but believe me it will supply calories and gooey richness aplenty.) Bake at 350° F for 8 minutes, then refrigerate. To assemble the pie, slice the banana and arrange on top of the crust. Pour and spread the toffee (i.e., the boiled can of sweetened condensed milk) over the slices. In a medium bowl, mix the heavy cream and sugar. Whip the cream into peaks and spoon over the toffee. Smooth with a spatula. Grate some dark chocolate over the top of the whipped cream. (Banoffee pie isn't fancy, so you don't need to break out the Callebaut here unless a wedge is on hand. A square of dark Baker's chocolate is good enough.)

The crust should be slightly salty to complement the toffee/caramel, but neither the crust nor the whipped cream topping should be overly sweet. The filling will take care of that. (Also, due to both the banana and the freshly whipped cream, this pie has a short shelf life. It's right and ready as soon as assembled, and will still be passable, although slightly deteriorated, by day two—adequate for leftovers on the couch, but not to serve to anyone.) Small slices, please, with coffee. Keep insulin nearby.

·

*Addendum: Long after the completion of this chapter, a rare e-mail from the person who had reported Lorraine's death casually dropped the bombshell that the latter was, um, uh, apparently alive, well, prospering, and running the Wee Bake House in Dalkeith. Great news, albeit shocking. I felt guilty having prematurely killed off my friend, but the tribute above was just too poignantly heartfelt to let subsequent facts get in the way. The photos on Facebook— which I don't do—of her shop's cakes are whimsical and fun. I've written a postal letter, a decade on, apologizing for her demise and, of course, placing blame squarely on our unnamed third party. Assemble a banoffee pie, then, not to remember, but to celebrate!

Chapter 20

·

Vita Brevis: Desserts for All Seasons
Part II—Fall & Winter

> . . . raise a final
> ripe pendulum on fingertips, take it
>
> gently, like so, as the body inhales,
> eyelids flutter, and the altar
> of the lips parts to its syrupy kiss.
>
> —*from* "Ode to the Fig"

Early Fall: Mascarpone-Stuffed Figs with Caramel Sauce

6 Brown Turkey figs or 4 Black Mission figs

4 Tbs. mascarpone cheese

½ cup white sugar

3 Tbs. spring water

½ cup heavy cream

1 tsp. brandy

¼ cup almond slivers

If you have a good local source from which to steal Brown Turkey figs in August and September (*vide* Chapter 13, sigh . . .), then apply all necessary guile to procure. Otherwise, buy these—or even better, the larger Black Mission figs—when in season at the grocer. Make sure they're ripe before you make this simple but elegant dessert of French influence (remembering, too, that they over-ripen quickly).

Toast your almonds for 4 minutes, until just browning. In a small pan, add the sugar and water. Swirl the pan over medium heat until the sugar is melted, then cook for several minutes until the resulting syrup is a light golden color. Watch carefully and don't overcook it into taffy or, worse, into rock. Cool the pan on the slab of marble where your partner kneads bread dough. Mix in the heavy cream, then return to the medium burner and stir until smooth and the consistency of a thin sauce. Remove from the burner and stir in the brandy.

On each rinsed and dried fig, make two cuts into the stem end, forming an "x" opening midway through each fruit. To serve, spoon 2 Tbs. caramel sauce onto two Fiestaware dessert plates (plum and cobalt blue), stuff each fig with an equal portion of the cheese (softened to room temperature and with a fork), arrange 2-3 figs upright on the plates, and top with the almonds. I can't imagine that an accompanying ice wine, or even a tawny port, in an attractively etched aperitif glass, would offend.

> What if the road were a metaphor
> for a road, a single curving lane of nowhere,
> and the sky for a leaden sky.
> What if, moreover, brambles represented
> brambles, barbwire a rusted steel,
> and each berry unattainable on the other side
> a dark conception of itself.

— *from* "Blackberries"

Late Fall: Berry Cobbler

This recipe is so easy to make, with a rich, buttery result that's always popular, that I've eschewed all more complicated crumbles and cobblers.

3 cups washed, frozen wild blackberries*

1 cup self-rising flour

1 cup whole milk

1 cup + 1½ Tbs. sugar

8 oz. unsalted butter

generous pinch sea salt

homemade buttermilk vanilla ice cream or whipped cream (for serving)

Combine sugar, flour, and milk in a medium bowl and whisk together. Add the melted butter in a slow stream, whisking as you go until smooth. Pour mixture into a greased 8"x8" glass or ceramic baking dish. Sprinkle the frozen berries evenly over the batter. (*The cobbler works wonderfully if you use solely your freezer blackberries. A nice mixture, though, is to substitute 1-1½ cups of blueberries, also frozen, from last summer's garden. Bear in mind that blackberries need to be washed and drained before freezing, so if they come out of the freezer in a clump, run under cold water just long enough to break them apart. Blueberries should be frozen unwashed, so don't forget to rinse them off—but not so long as to thaw them—before using. Don't ever put frozen berries on paper towels, as they will stick. Use a colander or, better still, just give each fistful a good shake. If you want to experiment with other fruits for the cobbler, peaches or raspberries in season would be my suggestion. Rhubarb, of course, requires additional prep. Cherries work swimmingly, a poor man's *clafoutis*.) Sprinkle the remaining sugar over the top of the berries and bake at 350° F for 50 minutes, until brown and bubbling. Finish the cooking with 2-3 minutes under the broiler to crisp the wonderfully unctuous crust.

That's it. So insultingly simple that apologies are very nearly required. Serve on dessert plates of any color. With a small *boule* of homemade vanilla ice cream, this can serve six, or four gluttons who'll regret it. If you don't have ice cream, add a dollop of whipped cream and likely no one will remark the peccadillo. (If you want to cut the recipe in half for some odd reason—say to serve two, our recurring theme—CorningWare makes inexpensive, small oval cooking dishes in white, in 700 ml and 450 ml. If you opt for the smaller dish, you'll have a thicker cobbler, so you might modestly adjust the cooking time. When you taste the result, though, the charge of that buttery crust, you'll wonder why you halved it.)

> Victimizing a final slice of fig tart
> and the morning's first hot cup—the best one—
> I have failed so far to banish the night . . .

—*from* "The Hunter and the Figs"

Early Winter: Gaylord's Rum Cake

I suppose, along perhaps with pecan pie (*vide* Chapter 30 for variations), this may be my signature dessert. I've certainly baked, eaten, and shared enough of them over the years. No real backstory here other than I was always disappointed with packaged rum cakes (too dry, not enough rum) so decided to make one to my own taste. No apologies for the box of cake mix, however.

I've made this cake for 20 years or more, since I was a young man who wouldn't have given a second thought to such an ostensible compromise. The cake is terrific, and I've no intention of messing with it now to restore some abstract purity of ingredients.

This can be baked in a Bundt pan, but lately I opt for a 9"-10" springform pan, as in that shape the cake seems to take the glaze more easily—even if it does droop in the middle from saturation—and there's less chance of sticking when the cake's inverted. Also, you may consider the chocolate chips optional, but I wouldn't advise it.

1 18-oz. box yellow cake mix

1 4-oz. box vanilla instant pudding mix

4 farm eggs

½ + ¼ cup cold spring water

½ cup vegetable oil

1½ cups pecans or ¾ cup pecans + ¾ cup walnuts

1 cup semisweet chocolate chips

½ + ½ cup dark rum

8 oz. unsalted butter

1 cup white sugar

pinch sea salt

Butter and flour the springform pan. Coarsely chop the nuts and sprinkle evenly on the bottom of the pan, then the chocolate chips. In a large mixing bowl, add cake mix, pudding mix, eggs, ½ cup cold water, vegetable oil, and ½ cup rum, with an extra splash for the Caribbean gods. With an electric mixer, blend the batter well. Pour/spoon over the nuts and chips and bake at 325° F for 1 hour. Let cool, then with a plastic spatula delicately loosen the edges of the cake around the springform. Invert on a large plate and expand and remove the sides of the pan. Carefully insert the spatula between the cake and the lip of the pan's bottom until the cake separates freely.

To make the glaze, melt the butter in a saucepan. Add the remaining ¼ cup water, sugar, and a pinch of salt. Bring to a boil and stir for 5 minutes. Remove from heat and allow to cool for 2-3 minutes. Add the remaining ½ cup rum. To apply the glaze, take a chopstick (forget the toothpick method) and violently attack your lovely cake, working out all the Freudian frustrations of youth, hostilities toward the workplace, et cetera, as you inflict holes all over the top and sides. Get ugly. When you thrust the chopstick into the solid layer of the nut/chips topping, you may end up with cracks and larger holes than you'd like, like a fracturing tectonic plate. Don't despair. It will look super, slovenly but sexy, as soon as it takes all that glaze love. Spoon the glaze over the cake, top and sides. Take your time, but don't fuss over the process. Keep poking and spooning until the glaze is gone and the cake is supersaturated and seemingly near collapse. (The plate will need to be large enough to accommodate a little glaze/glacial runoff.) Store in an airtight Tupperware cake holder and refrigerate.

Serve warm with a frosty glass of milk or cold with coffee (*vide* authorial eccentricities expounded upon in Chapter 9), a dollop of whipped cream on each slice in either case. This is an easy and unbeatable dessert, a perennial favorite with everyone. It also is a superb breakfast to accompany the Sunday newspaper. Lastly, individual slices, snugly sealed in plastic wrap, inverted with a second wrapped slice and then sealed in aluminum foil to form stackable packages, freeze like a rummy's dream and thaw quickly at room temperature. You may find that always having a few two-packs in the freezer bolsters confidence as you navigate the arduous day.

Late Winter: Vanilla Bean Cake

I debated what dessert should fill the last seasonal slot and was leaning toward another cake. Perhaps my modest rendition of *tres leches*, the milky goodness of which I first discovered and went crazy for a decade ago at the then-only bakery in Ciudad Colón in Costa Rica, during my first writing stay above the town. Possibly that delicious orange cornmeal cake, with its fascinating and addictive texture, that I'd forgotten all about until I was looking through my files. I rushed to the test kitchen and found the cake still delicious, not arduous to make, not too sweet and especially good when slightly underbaked. Ideal, say, for afternoon tea. How about a polenta pudding cake, with a crunchy crust and gooey-chocolately inside? Of course, there was the unredressed matter of crème brûlée, perhaps a ginger crème brûlée, especially tempting since we haven't yet played with the Williams-Sonoma mini-torch, a must-have gadget/weapon for any self-respecting home-cooking lunatic. I also had the vanilla bean cake on my mind, but hesitated due to its expense and the time it takes. I baked one up and wasn't entirely convinced by the result in relation to the effort. That is, until my companion promptly ate a second piece, then a third. Okay, here it is. On the plus side, most of the work is done the night or morning before.

8 1-oz. squares white chocolate

7 Tbs. unsalted butter

2 plump vanilla beans

5 farm eggs

⅓ cup bread flour*

⅓ cup sugar

pinch cream of tartar

pinch sea salt

powdered sugar for dusting

Butter the sides and bottom of a 10" springform pan. Line it with a circle of parchment paper and butter that as well. Chop the butter and 7 squares of the white chocolate into chunks. On a separate and smaller cutting board, slice the vanilla beans in half lengthwise and scrape out the seeds with a paring knife. (You might want to put 1 husk on top of the cake for decoration, but you might as well use the other to make vanilla. Viz., slide the latter into an attractively shaped stoppered bottle and fill to the top with 1-1½ cups of the Smirnoff vodka that you'll already have stocked [*vide* Chapter 25]. Cork the bottle, give it a good shake, and shake it again every few days for one month. The vanilla should be a dark, smoky color by then, fragrant and ready for use. Leave the pod, but don't dilute the vanilla by continuing to top it off with more vodka. A bottle of homemade vanilla makes a lovely gift. I've never seen same not receive an appreciation vastly out of proportion with the ease of its creation.) Divide the eggs—whites in a medium mixing bowl, yolks in a small bowl. Thus concludes your prep work.

If you haven't a real one, make an ersatz double boiler with a metal mixing bowl placed/held snugly in a large pot of water simmering at medium heat. In the bowl, place the butter and white chocolate and stir with a large spoon until melted. Remove the bowl from the water, add the vanilla bean seeds and pinch of salt, and whisk until well mixed. Whisk in the egg yolks. Whisk in the sifted bread flour. (*Go ahead and use all-purpose flour if you like, but with the investment in the chocolate and vanilla beans, I'm inclined to advise sticking to the bread flour. I'm not sure it makes much difference, and I know some bakers who actively dislike bread flour for the heavier texture it purportedly produces. Anyway, if you do buy a package, you'll have a good excuse to make yeast rolls—or, that is, convince your dear beloved to do so.) In the other bowl, add a pinch of cream of tartar to the albumen and with an electric hand mixer—similarly to the soufflé (*vide* Chapter 19), but with a markedly different result (*vide infra*)—beat to soft peaks, maybe 2 minutes. Continuing with the mixer, slowly add the sugar until the whites are glossy and stiff, like an angelic tide on a confectionary sea. Well, anyway: Stir a big spoonful of the whites into the batter, then fold in the rest and mix well, making sure to integrate all the batter from the bottom of the bowl. Pour the batter into the springform pan, cover with plastic wrap, and refrigerate for at least 8 hours. Nothing to it, and what else were you going to do this morning?

For decoration, place ½ of a vanilla bean on top and in center of the batter. Bake on a low rack (otherwise, the cake will overbrown) at 375° F for 30 minutes. Let the cake cool in the pan, on the counter. It should fall dramatically, like yet another demoralized soufflé, but this time by clever design. The cake will have a denseness that somehow heightens the vanilla flavor, and it's not fragile. Unless your springform pan is non-stick (in which case a blade will damage it), run a knife around the edge of the cooled cake and remove the sides. Remove from the bottom of the pan to a plate or cake holder. To finish, sift powdered sugar over the top and then with a vegetable peeler or small sharp knife cut thin curls of white chocolate over the cake with the remaining 1-oz. square. Serve at room temperature on sunflower-colored dessert plates, perhaps paired with a chilled late harvest Riesling?

Surprise Bonus Dessert for All Seasons, #2: Dark Chocolate & Chili-Pistachio Custards

No crème brûlé these days, be serious.

—*from* "Dinner Out"

As I look back over these two chapter on desserts, I think to myself what you might also be thinking: Where the hell's the chocolate?! I love chocolate, can inhale a box of Godiva with the best, and add chocolate chips to recipes with abandon. It occurs to me now, though, that it doesn't play heavily in my usual repertoire of homemade desserts. In a book already arguably light on foie gras, such a scarcity is disgraceful.

Fortuitously, as I was flying to Chicago for the annual Associated Writing Programs Conference & Bookfair (9000+ Legends In Our Own Minds and where for nearly 20 years I debuted and hustled the new number of *Poems & Plays*, the literary journal I founded in 1993), the woman sitting next to me on the plane—we got lucky and had a free seat between us—with a single word ("here") and without explanation handed me her exhausted *New York Times*. I put *Saveur* dutifully aside and began reading for signs and clues, resulting in a twofold pleasure: announcements of Wally Shawn and André Gregory's upcoming film adaptation of Ibsen's *The Master Builder* and an enticing article on *pots de crèmes*. Well played, guardian angel/stranger in the next seat who didn't look my way or speak again! Here, I freely adapt the chocolate pistachio pots the piece recommends, adding the slight but crucial chili heat, the unsweetened chocolate, and, of course, more sea salt.

This recipe takes a bit of attention, but everything looks and tastes so good all along the way that you're likely to find the undertaking a pleasure. And when it's over, you and your darling, who will be cherishing you with renewed enthusiasm over the edge of a licked-clean spoon, will be eating the best damned chocolate pudding you ever put in your mouth.

1 cup shelled chili-roasted pistachio nuts*

¼ tsp. + pinch fine sea salt

⅓ rounded cup powdered sugar

1½ cup whole milk

½ cup + splash heavy cream

1 100-gram bar Ghirardelli (or comparable) 72% cacao

1 1-oz square unsweetened baking chocolate

3 Tbs. white sugar

4 large farm egg yolks

whipped cream for garnish/serving

On a large cutting board, chop both chocolates. Shell the pistachios while you're watching your alma mater's basketball team (say, e.g., the University of Louisville Cardinals, risen in flight from 11 points down to beat Florida and return to the Final Four) or other useful diversion. I do encourage you to always shell your own pistachios, however, just as you must peel your own garlic. The principle of worth is the same. (*At least two national brands at the time of writing offer a "sweet chili" variety of pistachios, which is what I recommend for this recipe. A 7-oz. bag should be just enough, if you can resist nibbling as you shell. Of course, and otherwise, any nice pistachios will work, sprinkled with cayenne and chili powder according to personal sense and taste.) Roast nuts in the oven for 5 minutes at 325° F.

Let nuts cool, then during a full timeout in the game, add them to the Cuisinart along with the powdered sugar and ¼ tsp. sea salt. Pulse for 4-5 minutes, scraping the sides down once or twice during the process, until the mixture resembles damp sand. During the game's next timeout, in a medium saucepan combine the milk, cream, and 1 rounded cup of the pistachio mixture (reserve the rest for topping). Whisk together, bring to a low boil, turn down and let simmer for 5 minutes. Remove from heat, cover, and leave for 20 minutes.

At halftime, return the pot to the burner and bring to a simmer. It will be a thick, volcanic, voluptuous tan. Place the chopped chocolates in a medium mixing bowl and pour the cream mixture through a fine sieve over the pieces, using a spatula to push it all through and scrape off the outside of the sieve. Taste the pistachio mixture and you'll see why you want every dribble you can get. It's outrageously rich and flavorful. Whisk together until the chocolates are melted. In another bowl, whisk together the egg yolks (reserve the whites to bake a meringue later in the weekend), sugar, and a pinch of sea salt. Slowly pour the warm chocolate into the yolks, whisking all the time, until your lovely, glossy batter is fully integrated.

Fit six small, 6-oz. ramekins in a baking dish just large enough to hold them and equally and neatly distribute the batter. Yes, another blasted hot water bath is required, so gently, gently pour 1" of boiling water between the ramekins. Cover entire dish with aluminum foil, fork a few holes in the foil, and with care place in a 325° F oven. Bake for 35 minutes, no more, until firm but jiggly. By this point, the nets will have been cut down and the Cardinals, an upstart sleeper, are on the way to New Orleans—likely to get trounced by Kentucky the next Saturday, but don't let that diminish this triumphant afternoon or these lovely dark custards.

Allow ramekins to cool, then cover each with taut plastic wrap and chill in the refrigerator. Serve with a sprinkle of the remaining magic pistachio dust on top, a modest peak of whipped cream, and a cute dessert spoon. Prepare for expressions of delight, including your own. To the victors, the sweet, sweet spoils.

CHAPTER 21

.

Bonus Chapter: Gaylord Salmon Bowl

My wife and I were sitting cross-legged on the carpeting in the living room, attacking our dinner bowls on the low wooden coffee table. The windows were open to an unusually balmy March evening. I'd been working obsessively on this book throughout the late fall and winter and was sneaking up on the possibility of a complete draft, the notes and order of the last chapters in place. She pointed a chopstick. "You're including Gaylord Salmon Bowl in the cookbook, aren't you?" I was surprised. "Well, no. I mean, it's not actually *cooking*, is it, with all this prepared food? More just assembly?" replied I, doubting myself already. She gave me a pitying look before tipping back her sake cup.

Well, if my humble creation resembles more of a hunting/gathering expedition than a bravura cooking performance—although you will have a stovetop full of pots—what it *is* is a lovely collage of favorite tastes and textures and color and a meal that 2-3 times a year I crave terribly and then enjoy immensely. (Since Sakura, my favorite local Sushi joint, closed—worse, with me owing them $1.87 from when I was short of cash on a takeout—it's been a hard road. The poetry has slipped. Spirits are heavy.) So, here's my oblique but affectionate nod to *chirashi*, always with the integral addition of a generous spoonful of *ikura*, those delightful, brilliant red, explosive little pearls of salmon roe. If your squeamish partner doesn't eat raw fish, this one-dish meal solves that problem. If, moreover, he/she refuses to try the exquisite *ikura*, it won't help romance but will either save you some money or get you a double portion. Win-win. (You're likely to get both pieces of crispy salmon skin as well, as additional solace to your lonely place in a lonely world.)

Ideally, prepare this dish during the summer salmon runs—lauded exhaustively throughout this book—since the salmon fillet is the centerpiece. But when you get that hankering on a warm spring night, go ahead and use any fresh salmon that's firm, bright, and smells good.

2 8-oz. center fillets fresh salmon

1½ tsp.+ sesame oil

Emeril's Essence, Prudhomme's Seafood Magic, or similar (for dusting fish)

1 1.75-oz. jar salmon eggs

1 order squid salad (about 4 oz.)

1 order seaweed salad (about 4 oz.)

1 rounded tsp. sesame seeds

1 cup dry white basmati rice*

1 cup low-sodium chicken broth

1 tsp. rice wine vinegar (optional)

wasabi paste & pickled ginger

1 lime

8 oz. edamame in shell (for optional 1st course)

coarse sea salt (for edamame & fish skin)

1 bottle cheap sake

Once you've driven around and accumulated all the ingredients—rather like Rounding Up the Old Team—Salmon Bowl is a matter of a small amount of easy cooking and then simple and artful presentation. Sushi counters have proliferated in grocery stores, and many places now also stock small glass jars of salmon eggs, so ironically the seemingly arcane items—roe, squid, and seaweed salad—are nearly always readily available. (If not, just go to a Japanese restaurant and order a rather eccentric takeout, including the salmon eggs—I had a place that sold the latter to me by the ounce, in those small plastic soy sauce containers, before the eggs were widely available in stores. They too have closed, long since. I bought an adorable blue-striped sake set there, although in subsequent years we've moved on to larger cups.) I say ironically, because in my town at any rate, when salmon is out of season one can't always be certain that fresh salmon fillets, of a quality and freshness necessitated here, are automatically available. So hunt your salmon first, then backtrack for the more exotic ingredients. (No reason to spoon an ounce of precious *ikura* over a previously frozen, farm-raised-god-knows-where-or-how, color enhanced, curiously named slice of some fish product masquerading as a buttery cut of real salmon.)

Your errands have been successful. You've hit the mother lode of (vaguely Japanese) goodness, spent impressively and wantonly. Let's go.

Lightly toast your sesame seeds in a small pan for 4 minutes. Don't burn them. Set aside. Your salmon fillets should be thick center cuts of the same size. (8 oz. is a lot of fish for a serving, but remember this is a special day of moderate indulgence.) Move your fingers over the flesh and remove any pin bones with tweezers. Scale the skin with a vegetable peeler if your fishmonger hasn't scaled it already. With a sharp knife, gently and carefully cut the skin loose from each fillet in a single piece, as close as you can and with minimal damage to the flesh. Scrape the skins clean, rinse, dry, and set them aside. Rinse the fillets under cold running water and pat dry with paper towels. Rub the salmon all over with sesame oil, sprinkle both sides moderately with Essence, Seafood Magic, or a comparable dry blend, place on a plate, cover with plastic wrap, and refrigerate until ready to broil. That takes care of all of the prep (notwithstanding half an afternoon darting around town for the ingredients round-up if you weren't lucky at the first stop).

Combine the chicken broth, ½ cup spring water, basmati rice, and 1½ tsp. of sesame seed oil in a pot, bring to boil, stir, lower heat, cover, and simmer undisturbed for twenty minutes. (Or follow directions on your rice package if they vary slightly.) Remove from heat and let sit, covered, for at least 10 minutes. (*I do not recommend using *koshihikari*—i.e., sushi rice—for this dish, however tempting. While its adhesion—i.e., gumminess—is ideal for preparing or eating *nigiri*, the fluffy, flavorful white basmati excels for Salmon Bowl [and is more amenable to chopsticks]. If you want to insinuate sushi rice a bit more, add the optional 1 tsp. of rice wine vinegar to the basmati when you stir it up for plating. I used to, but lately prefer—by a nose, so to speak—the rice sans the vinegar.)

Set out the seaweed and squid salads so they are not overly cold at the time of serving. Place your uncapped bottle of cheap sake in a pot of cold water and heat gradually. Raise your oven shelf, turn the broiler on high, and place your salmon—nice side up, skinned side down—in a baking dish. Stretch the oiled strips of skin flat between them. (Okay, let's stop here for a moment. If you're going to have the edamame—and the beans are a lot more fun and interactive to eat in shell than shelled—I highly recommend you go ahead now and prepare, serve, and eat them, then have a brief respite in the proceedings while you broil the salmon. That way, you can relax, enjoy, and not overcook your fish. Place the frozen edamame in a small pot of boiling water, boil for 4-5 minutes, drain in a colander, divide on two small plates, sprinkle with coarse sea salt, and serve with a bowl for the shells. Pour a little sake to ensure your enthusiasm. If you prefer, you can complicate this simple dish by, after draining the edamame, adding them to a skillet where you've cooked 1 minced garlic clove, 1 minced and deseeded chipotle in adobo, and a large pinch of ground cumin. Stir pods over medium heat for a minute or so, sprinkle with sea salt and ground pepper, and serve as above. They're excellent, too, but are they "better enough" to warrant the extra rigmarole for an otherwise effortless and perfectly enjoyable dish? *Tabun.* A perpetual debate. My vote this time: boil, drain, salt, and serve. Words to live by.)

After you've enjoyed playing with your edamame, cleared the coffee table, and poured another fortifying cup of sake for both you and your date (always returning the bottle to the very warm water on the burner until you're serving the bowls), place your salmon and skin under the broiler. Let's stop again. Here, you need some common sense. I absolutely require, and strongly recommend the same to you, that my salmon for this dish be extremely rare. Broil a thick 1"-1½" fillet 3-4 minutes close under a high broiler, and that's it. The top is slightly seared, but as soon as you flake the fish it should be firm and bright red inside. *Never* turn it over under the broiler. If your date prefers the fillet further cooked—e.g., medium; i.e., ruined—and you deign to allow such contravention, hold your piece out for 5 minutes and then add it along with the strips of skin.

Assemble the salmon bowl in large, colorful bowls. (Not to be tediously redundant here, as I'm not on their payroll, but Fiestaware makes a one-quart serving bowl, 8"+ wide including the lip and 2"+ deep, that's ideal. I serve one Salmon Bowl in peacock blue, to suggest the sea, and another in tangerine or persimmon to highlight the bright hues of the salmon and eggs. Anyway, use bold and colorful bowls and not, please, pasta bowls illustrated with vegetables.) So, at last, fluff the rice and distribute, tamping it down in an even layer across the bottom of the bowls. Sprinkle the toasted sesame seeds over the rice. Place the rare salmon fillets in the center, and around these artfully and symmetrically divide the seaweed and squid salad. You are creating a work of edible art here. Add small dollops of the potent wasabi, generous clumps of pickled ginger, a wedge of lime, and spoon the *ikura* over the tops of the fillets. (One small jar of *ikura* will supply a generous, luxurious serving for two. And just wait until the tiny, glowing eggs start falling into the rice and warming. My god!) Finish each bowl with an angled strip of crispy, salted salmon skin.

Have you every seen a dish more beautiful? It tastes just as good. (By the way, and I mean this, every ingredient listed here is necessary for the full, uncompromised, umami explosion you've paid and labored for. If you can't locate everything, grill the fish and attempt Salmon Bowl another time. Trust me.) Dry off the bottom of the sake bottle. Serve the bowls with decorative, quality chopsticks. Sit on the floor on pillows or plush carpeting. Eat. No recordings of cascading waterfalls, wind chimes, or wooden flutes required, just the chorus of the night locust through open windows.

CHAPTER 22

.

On Drink: At Last, the Martini Chapter!

> But even they, the doubters,
> league of unwilling, unable, uncool,
> acknowledge sexy stiletto neck, cold allure
> like nothing else in life between trembling fingers.

—from "Apologia for the Martini Glass"

Today is my birthday, a date I share with Marlon Brando and Washington Irving, both of whom I'm certain would have made memorable drinking companions. As a result, I'm banished from the kitchen. I believe a strawberry cheesecake (requested) is in the works, and prior to that some sort of mystery duck. Since birthdays tend to be reflective events—squinting forward, peering back—this is as good a time as any to wax philosophically and practically on the Martini, the most elegant and powerful of drinks, and indisputably, as H. L. Mencken recognized, "the only American invention as perfect as the sonnet." What civilized person would disagree?

Let's proceed with the recipe for a single Martini, then list a few commands and warnings for the novice. (If you want to make 2 Martinis at once, simply chill your larger shaker—*vide* Chapter 25—and adapt accordingly.)

> He will reach
> a hand through chains securing him
> in space, reach for a stem of crystal,
> cold clarity.

—from "Apologia for Private Drinking"

The Martini

4 oz. premium gin*

4-5 drops dry vermouth

1 olive or, occasionally, a lemon twist

A proper Martini, despite (or arguably because of) the apparent simplicity of its preparation, is deucedly difficult to make. It will take you several years to master, and this dedicated time will be well spent. Your small 8-oz. metal shaker, Martini glass, and bottle of gin should be kept in the freezer *at all times.* We'll further discuss brands of gin, but in the meantime as soon as your finances afford the opportunity, upgrade to a premium product (*Bombay, Bombay Sapphire, Beefeater, or Tanqueray). You won't ever return to Gilbey's, Gordon's, or worse. In fact, come to think of it, don't even bother to begin until you can afford to have a bottle of good gin consistently in the freezer. Recently, Beefeater is my daily gin, because I can get the best deal for it at my local store. On special occasions, or when I'm feeling unusually flush, I'll opt for Bombay or on holidays Bombay Sapphire or Hendrick's—*vide infra.* For the vermouth, stick with Martini & Rossi or Noilly Prat. A bottle lasts for months, so the cost is negligible.

To make the Martini, fill your cold shaker with medium-sized ice cubes and top with the cold gin, about 4 oz. Add 4-5 drops dry vermouth, cap the shaker, and shake vigorously 10-12 times. Don't shake it to death. (If you're attempting to use warm gin, then of course you'll need to shake more to achieve your diluted and inferior result. Also, I've no intention of getting into some rhubarb about stirring gin to avoid "bruising" or "over chilling" it. Please.) Pour/shake into a chilled Martini glass into which you have already placed a single speared olive or squeezed twist of lemon. If you have a top freezer with a wide lip when the door's open, I recommend making and pouring the Martini right there, to keep the ingredients as cold as possible. This may not seem energy efficient, but as your skill level increases so will your speed.

(Let's talk vermouth: Lots of jokes circulate about merely "waving the capped bottle" over the shaker, raising the shaker in the general direction of Italy, et cetera, but if you do find you have a heavy hand with the drops—it takes a decade of practice for the muscle memory to do it effortlessly—try the "thumb over the top" technique, letting just a bit of vermouth escape. Obviously, a Martini should be crystal clear and never discolored. If you can even taste the vermouth distinct from the gin, you've botched it and the shame is yours. If you're still having trouble, Williams-Sonoma makes, or anyway used to, a miniature cocktail mister—just a shade larger than a tube of lipstick and accompanied by an adorable tiny funnel—that is, in actuality, a vermouth atomizer. I use mine only when traveling, but you could integrate it permanently if you remain "vermouth challenged." It really is a cute little thing, always a conversation starter when it emerges from the pocket, and 2-3 sprays admirably do the job. If you can't locate this invaluable little device, adapt a small cologne dispenser.)

Raise the frosted glass by the stem. (Invest in thin and graceful Martini glasses, with seductively long and narrow stems, and always in clear glass.) Admire, wide-eyed, smiling, aroused and anticipatory, the gentle shards of floating ice. Bow your head slightly and bring lips to the glass. There is no other sensation in the world like that first sip. You will feel and know its transformative power immediately. (I make the second-best Martini I have ever tasted. I am surpassed only by one of my two original sensei, who insisted on keeping several glasses—and of different sizes—in his freezer. Each subsequent Martini received a new chilled glass. While I always marveled at the vision and obsessive dedication of this, I could never, somehow, quite bring myself to do it. Plus, if I may, my freezer is usually loaded with duck breasts, calamari, cut corn, homemade pesto, wild berries, and so on, while the Master's tended to be, um, dedicated exclusively to ice, bottles, and glasses. He was a hardcore specialist.)

> Commit to the diet. Once you've selected gin,
> give it a chance, even a lifetime.
>
> —*from* "The Martini Diet"

Now a few self-evident truths:

1. Martinis are made with gin and only gin. Try to intervene the "gin or vodka" question by the naïf waiter, but when confronted with such an insulting and preposterous inquiry, maintain your good humor. The poor kid was raised wrong and doesn't know any better. Nature/ nurture. And no apologies whatsoever to Mr. Bond. He *should* know better.

2. Drink a Martini on the rocks only in hostile and remote areas and when you can't control the conditions. Otherwise, always up and always icy cold. Here, 007 recovers a bit of street cred.

3. There is no such thing as a dirty Martini. If a guest (invariably a young guest) asks for or even insinuates such a thing, simply and politely pretend not to have heard. (You're the accommodating host, after all.) If

said individual persists with such misguided heresy/idiocy, back slowly away. Protect yourself.

4. On a similar note, there is no such thing as an "appletini," a "chocolatini," or any other damned absurdity in similar vein. This requires no further comment.

5. At some point in your learning curve, experiment with replacing the olive with a cocktail onion (in which case the Martini becomes a Gibson) and, at another point, leaving out the vermouth entirely (and the Martini becomes a Silver Bullet). Then return to doing things properly. The few drops of vermouth are a subtle, precious part of the alchemy. They are necessary. Also, while I was tempted in the ingredients list above to make the olive or twist optional, actually I believe one or other is also necessary, if primarily for aesthetics. The olive should be a simple green olive, pitted, and without pimento. (*Vide* Chapter 16 for brand suggestion.) On special occasions, or when you're feeling spirited, you may use a black olive you've stuffed yourself with a quality blue cheese, or a green olive you've stuffed with a sliver of jalapeño or other fiery pepper. There's no need to be fascistic here, and a change of pace and taste can be rejuvenating, if only, ultimately, to adjudicate the classic quality and superiority of the simple, unadorned olive. (Eating the olive, by the way, is optional, although attitudes vary on this. It's optional.)

6. There's been a recent proliferation in designer gins, and if your wallet allows some experimentation and you're inclined to "drink around," these can be fun and sometimes enlightening to sample. *Vide ut supra*, a favorite special occasion alternative is the popular Hendrick's, a Scottish gin made with cucumbers and rose petals that comes in a sturdy and attractive crock. It's surprisingly good and refreshing. In place of an olive, float a thin slice of cucumber in the glass. For those who never recovered from the disheartening revelation that Bombay Sapphire isn't, regardless of quality, actually blue, there's the French offering Magellan, made with iris flowers and a lovely pale blue in color. (No olive with it, please—twist only.) I recently enjoyed a bottle of Blackwood's made with "wild water mint" and a Viking theme on the Shetland Islands. On the other hand, a return to Broker's (the award-winning London product that comes with the little derby hat atop the

bottle), a gin I've appreciated in the past, was a disappointment. I've inexplicably, at least for the moment, lost my taste for it, and in the meantime have been beguiled by the spiciness of 209, distilled in Napa. Another California producer, St. George Spirits, has released three distinct pot-distilled gins, all with bold, distinct flavors (and charming labels). I give a slight nod in preference to the Terroir offering, with its fresh and radical overture of Douglas fir, above their Dry Rye and Botanivore. (I think. I may need to continue my research.) Corsair, an experimental Nashville-based distillery, recently produced a limited edition gin barrel-aged in the same charred casks they'd used for their spiced rum. The result, slightly smoky/cloudy and the color of pale iced tea, on the tongue was indisputably gin, but with a peculiar, suprisingly subtle, and not quite distinguishable alchemy of flavors. Drinking it seemed risqué. I enjoyed the bottle. Returning to the subject of my birthday, I've just been presented three special order bottles—a leap of faith—of the peculiarly named The Botanist, an Islay gin (home of the heavily peated, ocean-scented, single malt whiskies that are my favorites) that I read a review of somewhere or other, a gin where the classic botanicals are, according to the raised lettering, augmented "with a heady harvest of 22 wild native island botanicals, hand-picked by our foraging team from the windswept hills, peat bogs and Atlantic shores of Islay." Sounds dangerous. Well, we'll see how it tastes.

Postscript and final note on the subject: I'm currently drinking a bottle of saffron gin I bought at the duty-free in Toulouse returning from France [*vide* Preface]. The spirit was distilled by Gabriel Boudier in Dijon, and the taste fascinates, with the saffron flavor much more pronounced and forward among the botanicals than I expected. I remain unconvinced that gin should taste like saffron, however, and surely one of the unassailable tenets of civilization is that a Martini should not be *orange*. Very disconcerting.

7. After even a successfully pleasant detour into several of the eccentric and exotic recipes above, you'll be happy to return to the perennials: Beefeater and Bombay. A word of caution about artisanal gins from smaller distilleries, especially domestic ones (which are the ones you're likely to serendipitously come across): You buy the attractive bottle littered with superlatives, and you take your chances. The potential and ironic problem lies, I believe, in the maker's enthusiasm and

good intentions. A small, hand-crafted batch of gin, pot-distilled or whatnot, by definition needs to be bold and eccentric in its botanicals and methodology in order to distinguish a unique, even shocking, flavor. Otherwise, what's the point or the temptation? I was recently vacationing in Washington and rather impulsively at a shop in Walla Walla bought three small-batch gins made in the northwest: two in Washington and one in Oregon, I believe. Two were quite interesting, but the third and last I opened was horrendous, those good intentions gone badly awry in the laboratory. Unfortunately, I was by that point sequestered in a remote cabin near Mount Rainier, with no possibility of other provisions for several days, so I drank it anyway, although each sip conjured the image of something bubbling and odious in a washtub out in the shed. You didn't quite have to hold your nose to get it down, but close. "If it hurts, it works," I suppose, as we wheezed in the college gym. Or more to the point: "Let the gin drinker beware"?

8. Wherever you stand on the debated provenance of the Martini, to this author's mind (and in his experience) the drink remains very much an American libation. Even the staunchest Martini enthusiast has to change his habits and his tune when traveling in Europe (and, if even farther afield, surrender completely), where ordering a Martini, along with hand gestures and faltering instruction (in pidgin French, pidgin Italian, et cetera), will yield you a noxious and undrinkable yellow result more suitable for cleaning drains than for drinking. However, if you order a Martini without explanation, you will likely be brought an inch or so, on the rocks, of a light, straw-colored, slightly sweet spirit. This is Martini Bianco, an Italian vermouth that's actually pleasant as an aperitif, so try it before you send it back in a rage. It's not a Martini *qua* Martini, of course (and Martini Bianco cannot be substituted for the dry vermouth used in a proper Martini, however much the name might suggest otherwise), but I'd suggest you sip, enjoy the parade of passersby, and wait until you get home for the real thing. The error (of judgment) was yours, after all. (Martini also produces a Rojo— addictive on the rocks with a thin slice of lemon—and more recently a Rosé, neither of which has a thing to do with the Martini under our discussion.)

9. Years ago, on *A Prairie Home Companion*, the late and legendary curmudgeon Studs Terkel was being grilled by a deadpan Garrison Keillor about holiday etiquette. In answer to the question of a proper wine to serve, Mr. Terkel paused a beat and growled this response, which I paraphrase: "Proper wine for the holidays? A dry Beefeater Martini, straight up." He was kidding precisely as much as I am in agreeing.

CHAPTER 23

•

On Drink: Home Winemaking

Don't. Just don't.

What did family, friends, neighbors, guests, or peers ever do to you?

There's a fellow who sometimes helps me with maintenance and restoration of my log house. He and I were rebuilding the front porch several years ago. We've occasionally exchanged samples of the odd home canning or brewing experiment, maybe a lily or iris. On this anecdote's morning in question, C____, with a mischievous but distinctly prideful grin, presented me with a bottle of his latest homemade wine, its appropriate name, "Man Down," scrawled in marker directly onto the glass. Although appreciative of the gesture, I withhold his name to protect the guilty. Whatever the indeterminate lineage of its grapes and vintage, the wine was dark red, but instinct told me get it cold, very cold. That bottle lived in the refrigerator for a long, long time, sort of . . . lagering?

Still, in the spirit of adventure, conviviality, and literary history, let me introduce you to poet Robinson Jeffers' Prohibition recipe, which I made 3-4 times 18-20 years ago when I was a tenure track and in debt assistant professor. There's a relevance to this correlation, I'm certain. The poet's son, Garth Jeffers, recalled "beginning perhaps in 1927 or '28, a quite palatable wine concocted from rice and oranges and raisins and other items. Mother christened it 'Cairngorm' after the Scottish mountains that display crystals of the same color. When Father arose in the morning after putting on the coffee, he would stir the wine in the crock, where it fermented for several weeks." The recipe was discovered on a typed carbon. Here's my adaptation.

> Two hours hard up the mountain,
> we broke fast at shared tables—
> eggs and raw onion, bacon, cheese,
>
> bread. Always wine for blood.
>
> —*from* "The Walk"

"Cairngorm"

2 lbs. white rice

3 lbs. white sugar

3 lbs. golden raisins*

1 lemon

1 orange

1 cake Fleischman's yeast

1 gallon spring water, slightly warmed

In a large stock or canning pot, add the rice, sugar, golden (*my revision) raisins, several slices of lemon and orange, the cake of yeast dissolved in a bit of tepid (70-90° F) water, and a gallon of just slightly warm water. Stir well. Cover the pot and leave on an unheated stovetop burner. Allow to "cook" for two weeks. Faithfully stir the pot every morning and evening. The house will begin to smell wonderful.

After two weeks, strain the liquid first through a colander, then through multiple layers of clean cheesecloth, and finally through a coffee filter if you can manage it and have the patience. Using a funnel, distribute to clean wine bottles, cork, wrap the tops of the bottles tightly with duct tape (which offers both a reasonable facsimile of a wine seal and a bit more protection in the odd, unfortunate chance a bottle wants to explode, *vide infra*). Store the bottles away for several weeks as the wine, the carbon copy optimistically predicts, "mellows beautifully and becomes smooth and warm and rich." Well, let's not overreach here. It *is* potable, albeit sweet, and has a lovely golden hue, and folks are curious for a sip (and not only for its pedigree). I did have a bottle blow once (in the middle of the night, with a sound like no other to awaken to). I'll spare you the gory (and sticky) details, but clearly the use of the yeast here isn't an exact science. The other side of the coin, though, is that the best batch I made had a nice, slight—if I may presume—*frizzante* quality out of the bottle. (Another time, however, it was flat.)

Anyway, students always seemed to like it, or anyway drink it, and assistant profs seem to have students over to their (rented) houses more often than their more-litigiously-cautious-if-not-necessarily-wiser older colleagues, so this is all from memory. I'm not going to concoct any *now*, for goodness' sake, to test my feeble précis, but the warming, yeasty smell alone makes the recipe worth a try once, and the ritual of daily stirring instills a pleasing "witch's cauldron" quality. Make an autumn batch, just for fun. I can bring over a nice Cabernet and cheer you on. We'll be reciting "Hurt Hawks" in no time.

CHAPTER 24

.

On Drink: Mary Bloodied Two Ways; or, Uncle Sam vs. John Bull

Always *yo requiero,*
yo requiero, so many earthly desires.
And always, it seems, the next day
Sunday, these hours too vanished
as if in dream or prayer or sorrow.

—*from* "What Is It You Would Seek?"

I just returned at 1:00 a.m. from giving two poetry readings in California, so I missed five days of writing time and am anxious to get back into the kitchen with a couple of ideas. Apparently, legislation just passed in that state that foie gras can't be served on menus beginning summer 2012. I'll reserve comment on that—despite this chapter's patriotic slant—except to note that at dinner at Mulvanie's Building and Loan, an intimate spot in Sacramento, we tried to make the most of the window remaining: to begin, for each of us an *amuse bouche* of foie gras mousse on a just-in-season local strawberry. For the first course, seared foie gras on toast points with a dicing of more strawberries, and then on to—seriously?—tortellini stuffed with marrow, foie gras, and sweetbreads. Wild-eyed, threateningly, I took over the ordering— begrudgingly agreeing to the odd concept of sharing—for which the visiting writer entertains enough, just enough, short-lived cachet. For drinks, the chef-owner (it was early and he wasn't cooking yet) had given us samples of a single malt Irish whiskey of which we'd never heard (Redbreast 12-year-old— excellent), then, when I sniffed out a covert bottle with a hand-drawn skull and crossbones label, a sip of house-made absinthe, which would peel the porcelain off your teeth. It was delicious. We moved on to a bottle of Tempranillo made down the road by a friend of one of my hosts, this to accompany, I say without hyperbole, a medium-rare rib rack of local, organic lamb that was as tender and flavorful as any I've ever had. Review complete.

The lamb made me think back to the shanks I braised for Easter last Sunday. I'd intended to write about Bloody Marys that day, but cooking and packing consumed the hours. Now I am back in Tennessee, the irises full in bloom, and it is, low and behold, Sunday yet again. Sunday, of course, more specifically Sunday afternoon, is quantifiably, indisputably, internationally, transcendentally, and wonderfully, Bloody Mary Time. Mimosas or Screwdrivers in the morning, if occasion or weather or disposition or all three incline, but only the affections of Mary in the afternoon. But then, you already knew that.

I've never understood or given much credence to the advice of the Bloody Mary as a cure for hangovers, which relegates an inestimably fine potion—one of only two in this book to warrant its own chapter—to a dubious goal that, frankly, it doesn't accomplish anyway. (Granted, I make my BMs strong—the measurements that follow are not typos—because a] that's how I like them, and b] I find them far too filling otherwise. Anyway, this girl certainly won't sober you up. She'll go right to your head. If you find my proportions too aggressive for your taste, adjust accordingly.) I know proponents, too, of the belief that BMs should be made and stirred by the pitcher. A pleasing concept, but as a) I often just want one myself when the siren of Sunday afternoon calls, and b) this book proceeds on the general premise of eating and drinking for two, let's just make them individually.

You're correct, too, that that's quite enough with the "a) and b)" folderol. I propose a taste test of two radically different approaches to our subject, ideologies divided by an ocean. The first version below is a loose but, I believe, faithful in spirit variation of Kingsley Amis's presentation in his brilliant and indispensible *Everyday Drinking* (a collection of his three short volumes on booze—its culture and etiquette in a life committed to its mastery). The second is the humble submission of your American author, based on a couple of decades or so of inquiry.

<u>A Note on Glassware</u>. In part simply to further separate the following recipes and give them even more distinct personalities—and genders?—I'm presenting my version of Sir Kingley's BM in a highball glass. I recently bought a very attractive model with an alluring curve of hip in its design. My own BM I make in a standard, sturdy—but not overly heavy or thick at the base—lowball glass that I like for just about any kind of cocktail. It's easy to stir and to hold. Both glasses in question are 10 oz., so they may proceed as equal partners. If you want to get fancy, you can use a Martini glass with a lip of celery salt, although I discourage this on the general principle that Martini glasses are for, you know, Martinis. In any case, whatever glassware you select should be properly chilled in the freezer for at least an hour beforehand. Sunday afternoon always arrives. Think ahead.

<u>A Note on Measuring</u>. Let's not indulge here a bunch of distractions about the proper size of a shot glass, how it might or might not differ traditionally from a jigger, et cetera. (*Vide* Chapter 25 to hash this around further.) To make cocktails, I use a professional steel double shot/jigger. Mine's 1.2 oz. on the big/top end, .8 oz. on the small/bottom end. You need to get one, but whatever measure you're using in the meantime, just make sure it's reasonably accurate and employ consistently.

<u>A Note on Garnish</u>. A cleaned and trimmed stalk of celery is fine, if you like celery and want to commit that much volume of your glass to it. Personally, I don't especially enjoy celery hitting me in the face and forehead when I'm trying to drink, so I might suggest this: Spread your crisp stalk of celery with peanut butter and crunch on it as you assemble the several ingredients acquired to create the BM. An ideal compromise. If you don't like celery and don't eat the stalk anyway, then why are we even talking about this? Another briefly popularized/polarizing option, the pickled caperberry—not to be confused with capers—is attractive but doesn't taste like much (and for god's sake, or at least for mine, please don't *ever* put one in a Martini). I do like a crisp dilly bean—a pickled green bean—in a BM but usually can't be bothered to keep a jar around. A wedge of juicy lime (or lemon, depending on your fealty) is all you need.

<u>A Note on Vodka</u>. Expensive, trendy, designer, and flavored vodkas constitute a very profitable marketing scheme (i.e., scam). Apologies to my brother-in-law. Use Smirnoff, which is ubiquitous in stores, affordable, and works swimmingly in a BM. You won't be able to tell the difference, nor will any vodka snob who claims he/she can.

<u>A Note on Tomato Juice and Then No Further Notes</u>. Obviously, the quality of your tomato juice is crucial to the quality of your BM. A long-time friend of mine disappears into the woods every late summer, when our local tomatoes are most succulent, and with his like-minded compatriots cans several hundred one-quart Mason jars of the best tomato juice, hands down, that I have ever tasted: sweet, rich, not at all viscous like home-squeezed tomato juice can be (they've perfected some secret filtering process—I don't ask), and with low acidity. I could live on the stuff, icy cold and straight from the jar. I would recommend locating a similar source and exploiting the hell out of it. Don't be proud. (Unfortunately, my old friend and I are now slightly

estranged, just enough so that I'm no longer in *la familia tomate* to receive my 4-6 quarts from each seasonal session. It's been difficult, a hard and humbling fall to earth.) Otherwise, buy the best organic tomato juice you can get at the grocer and get on with your life. No V-8 juice, *ever.*

Brewer Bloody Mary (American)

4 oz. vodka (*vide ut supra*)

2 oz. tomato juice hand-pressed and jarred by a friend (*vide ut supra*)

1 tsp. + Worcestershire sauce

¼ tsp. + Tabasco sauce

large pinch prepared horseradish

1 juicy lime (firm and green, not shrunken and mottled), room temperature

5 turns freshly ground black pepper

2 shakes celery salt (+ that frozen on the rim of the glass)

½ tsp. + clam juice—a good one (optional)

1 dilly bean (optional)

Stars & Stripes on toothpick (optional garnish)

    Run a wedge of lime around the outer rim of a lowball glass and then shake celery salt over the rim to adhere to the juice. Pour the salt over a plate so you can return any excess to the jar, thereby neither wasting any nor conjuring bad luck. (During a recent getaway in Savannah, at a new favorite shop called The Spice and Tea Exchange, I loaded up on various salts. The devilishly hot ghost pepper sea salt, blended with Naga Jolokia, purportedly the hottest pepper in the world, makes a nice rimming salt for BMs, but adhere only a few crystals on one side of the glass, unless you like to suffer. By the way, however silly the recent salt craze has been, I must admit it's an enjoyable fetish, perusing the various blends, types, and flakes. These are mostly finishing salts, to my mind, and I indulged in about ten from the shop, from chocolate sea salt to applewood-smoked sea salt, from a lovely russet Hawaiian red sea salt to replenishing tested favorites like Himalayan mineral salt and Cyprus black lava sea salt, the latter indispensable for sprinkling on ice cream. *Vide* Chapter 9.)

    Freeze glass for at least 1 hour. Into the frosted glass, add 4-5 medium-sized ice cubes (not large and not crushed), then, in order: an initial splash of the Worcestershire, the vodka, the tomato juice, the Tabasco, and a squeeze of ⅓-½ of the lime (depending upon its size). Add the pinch of horseradish, the ground pepper, the celery salt, and a finishing splash of Worcestershire. (The clam juice is optional. It's an enjoyable occasional variation, but be sure to find an aromatic juice redolent of the sea. Some bottled clam juices are quite unpleasant in both smell and briny taste. Bar Harbor is the brand I recommend.) Mix well with a glass—not plastic—stirrer, sip, adjust heat and spiciness according to taste, mix again, and top off with additional ice cubes and a wedge of lime. If you want to nibble on the side, I suggest Triscuit wheat crackers (cracked pepper and olive oil flavor or original) or their equivalent, something salty and crunchy. (Or perhaps, *vide* Chapter 14, deviled eggs, blue cheese crackers, or cheddar cheese straws?)

Amis Bloody Mary (British, Freely Corrupted)

4 oz. vodka

2 oz. tomato juice

1 tsp. + Worcestershire sauce

¼ tsp. + Tabasco sauce

2 shakes celery salt

peculiar UK elements:

1 juicy lemon

1 Tbs. + orange juice (or approximately ¼ of fruit hand-squeezed)

¼ tsp. + ketchup*

Union Jack on toothpick (optional garnish)

At times I have greatly enjoyed this odd—to my palate and experience—amalgamation of BM, and once was enthusiastically committed to her for weeks. Then, just as suddenly, it tasted unpleasing to me and I went home to my recipe. (Since then, I've periodically enjoyed the latter version again.) Fickle? Promiscuous? Or merely needful and appreciative of variety? Try it.

In a chilled highball glass of attractive contour—again, just to arbitrarily differentiate the two versions of BM discussed here, I don't generally rim the glass with celery salt on this version, an innovation that I sense would offend Sir Kingsley—add 4-5 medium-sized ice cubes and assemble as above with the appropriate substitutions (including lemon for lime). *I realize that British ketchup is a different animal from ours, but the variation still intrigues. (Amis argues that the "ketchup is the secret of the whole thing: I am not at all clear on what it does, but it does something considerable.") Stir, sip, adjust, stir, and garnish with a wedge of lemon. Cheers.

N.b.: In the case of both recipes above, it should go without appending that you need have on hand sufficient quantities of ingredients to make at least two rounds of BMs for however many parties are participating. Possibly three rounds. For testing purposes.

CHAPTER 25

•

On Drink, Stocking the Bar:
Quiddities, Bon Mots, Sins, & Perversions

... the Himalayan ridge
snags you on its jagged smile—
who may blame the traveler for his thirst?

—from "The Whiskies of Nainital"

Let's get right to business with the bare bones essentials of this important subject, stripping all to the absolutely necessary philosophically. (I mean, you can chug from a warm bottle of Jäger in a brown paper bag for all I care, but I'm proceeding on the assumption that we're conversing here as serious, like-minded adults dedicated to and fully appreciative of the crucial matter of properly plied libations.)

General Equipment:

1. several bottle openers (so you can find one)

2. servers corkscrew (for when you can't find the butterfly corkscrew; please learn how to use it, even if your server can't)

3. butterfly (or winged) corkscrew (for when you can't find the servers corkscrew)

4. a sharp paring knife

5. several glass stirring/swizzle sticks (so you can find one)

6. sturdy toothpicks (preferably turned at the end and attractive)

7. small wooden or (better) marble mortar and pestle (for muddling; optional but useful)

8. double-cupped metal jigger (with a small shot on one end and a large one on the other, marked to accurately measure 1 oz. and ½ oz. pours until, after a decade or two, you can do this instinctively)

9. a small, handled steel mesh strainer (for retaining seeds and excessive pulp when juicing citrus by hand, the preferred method, into a glass or shaker; optional but useful)

10. ice bucket and tongs (entirely optional except for parties—especially student parties—then necessary)

11. 8-oz. metal shaker for single Martinis, et cetera (kept *always* in freezer)

12. 24-oz. metal shaker for 2-3 Martinis (placed in freezer when unavoidably expecting dinner guests)

> Only your worst skeptics, in wounded dream,
> denigrate the questing, open mouth
> so willing of that first sublime frothing splash.

> —*from* "Apologia for the Martini Glass"

Glassware:

1. several shot glasses (preferably without Las Vegas logos, company insignias, or pithy—i.e., imbecilic—sayings)

2. highball glasses (in a pinch, can be used for Collins glasses)

3. Collins glasses (optional if budget and space are tight, but nice to have)

4. Old-Fashioned glasses (i.e., lowball or rocks glasses)

5. Martini glasses (1-2 kept in freezer *at all times*)

6. smaller Martini glasses (optional, but useful for various mixological creations and also shrimp cocktails)

7. brandy snifters

8. large red wine glasses (one design with a delicate stem to accommodate all styles; we're not snobs)

9. white wine glasses (*ibid.*)

10. sherry glasses

11. champagne flutes

12. Margarita glasses (optional, believe it or not; since margaritas should be drunk on the rocks, rather than blended/frozen, it seems to me perfectly acceptable socially to serve in either a highball or rocks glass, according to aesthetic preference)

13. various attractive and decorative small cordial glasses (for aperitifs, digestifs, Calvados, port, and miscellaneous occasional oddities)

Just a few simple cherries
in a bowl on a table by a window,
beside a pink rose dying
in a bottle from Châteauneuf-du-Pape,
beautiful as it dies.

—*from* "Provisions"

Set-Ups & Mixers:

1. an abundance of fresh, mid-sized ice cubes

2. fresh, juicy lemons (for twists and for juicing)

3. fresh, juicy limes (*ibid.*)

4. fresh, juicy oranges (*ibid.*)

5. Maraschino cherries with stems

6. English cucumber (optional/seasonal, for Hendrick's Martini and, *vide infra,* surprise recipe)

7. unadorned, unstuffed, minimally processed green and black olives

8. lots of mint from the garden

9. small, chilled bottles soda water

10. small, chilled bottles tonic water

11. spring water

12. grapefruit juice

13. cranberry juice

14. simple syrup (1 cup spring water + 1 cup white sugar, boiled for 1 minute, stored in a glass Mason jar in the refrigerator; lasts for a month or more and useful to have on hand at all times)

15. Margarita salt (for rimming glasses)

16. Coca-Cola (optional, except in summer)

17. additional Bloody Mary ingredients, *vide* Chapter 24 (organic tomato juice, celery salt, pepper, Tabasco, et cetera)

But where the sturdy inch
of scotch obviously required, its muscles

of peat, salty North Sea solitude?

—*from* "Apologia for a Martini in Winter"

The Actual Booze (with Recommended Brands, Tested, & Mostly Traditional):

1. gin (Beefeater, Bombay, Bombay Sapphire, or, optionally, Hendrick's; the bottle is kept in the freezer *at all times*)

2. vodka (Smirnoff)

3. bourbon* (Jim Beam 7-year or Maker's Mark; if you prefer a Tennessee whiskey and for some reason can't maintain a bottle in addition to bourbon, then George Dickel yellow label, which is superior to Jack)

4. rum (Bacardi dark)

5. tequila (optional, except in the summer)

6. dry vermouth (Martini & Rossi or Noilly Prat; kept in the refrigerator)

7. sweet vermouth (Martini & Rossi or Noilly Prat)

8. Campari

9. Cointreau

10. Angostura bitters (a bottle lasts for years)

11. crème de cassis (or any quality blackcurrant liqueur [avoid anything conspicuously inexpensive] either French or domestic; Clear Creek Distillery in Portland, Oregon—of which I'm a big and long-standing fan—makes a dark, lovely cassis as well as several other excellent fruit-based liqueurs)

12. mid-level brandy/Cognac (for sipping)

13. cheap brandy (E & J or Christian Bros., for mixing)

14. pastis (Pernod-Ricard or Pastis 51; mandatory in the summer—even if it doesn't taste at home like it does in the sunshine of Provence—optional the rest of the year)

15. various additional liqueurs according to taste for entertaining yourself and others (Chambord and Galliano highly recommended)**

16. various additional after-dinner and dessert drinks (Calvados—Clear Creek Distillery, mentioned above, bottles an aged apple brandy that rivals or surpasses top-shelf Calvados—a tawny port, late harvest and ice wines)

17. a modest but flexible (4-5 cases) selection of red and white wines (mostly red)

18. several bottles of sparkling wine: brut both in white and rosé, as well as cava, Lambrusco, and sparking Pinot (there are lots of delightful options under $20; let someone else mortgage the farm for the Cristal, Moët & Chandon, and Dom Pérignon)

19. beers and hard ciders (selected according to season, taste, and menu)

20. lastly, a bottle of Islay single malt scotch (Ardbeg or Laphroaig; for sipping on the rocks with a splash of spring water or soda at Thanksgiving, Christmas, and during times of stress, celebration, or boredom)

With the first 11 alcoholic items listed above, and the appropriate mixers, you are ready (and with 20 years of training, able) to make the entire pantheon of staple drinks: Martinis, gin & tonics, Tom Collinses, Greyhounds, vodka & tonics, Blood Marys, Cosmopolitans, Cape Codders, Sea Breezes, Salty Dogs, Screwdrivers, Manhattans, Whiskey Sours, Highballs, Old-Fashioneds, Mint Juleps, Cuba Libres, Mojitos, Margaritas, Campari & sodas, Negronis, and (with the addition of white wines calm and bubbly) Mimosas, Kirs, and Kirs Royales.

Invest in a thorough bartender's guide. Not one of those big, glossy cocktail guides full of grotesqueries—which are, granted, fun to look through—but a stodgy, picayune, old-school bartender's guide (such as *Mr. Boston*). Then, practice. The Big Three, I suppose—remembering, *vide* Chapter 24, that Bloody Marys are daytime drinks—are the Martini, the Cosmopolitan, and the Manhattan, in the sense that they cover a range of flavors and sweet/savory profiles and one of them should strike a chord with any but the most finicky drinking visitor. You could argue the selection, but in any case master the proven perennials first, then move on according to temperament and temperature. (E.g., you're likely to drink more tequila and pastis in the summer, more brandy in the winter, et cetera, so there will be some seasonal flux to mediate individual tastes. Bear in mind, though, that your goal is not only to accommodate your own lascivious thirsts, but of course to anticipate and be prepared to satisfy those of your companion and any additional guests.) Also, over time, you'll naturally accrue much of what you need. The Angosturas bitters last forever, since you never use more than a few drops. Ditto a bottle of dry vermouth, which even for a dedicated Martini drinker will last for months. Unless you become temporarily fixated on Negronis (easy to do in July-August), that bottle of Campari will last a while. You can gradually build up a modest but varied collection of white and red wines. And so on. If you've a weakness for, say, White Russians (really, grandma?), then add a bottle of Kahlua to your stock. And always: Practice, practice, remembering the "10,000 hours" rule for mastery of any art. You'll find your way.

*A Note on Kentucky Bourbon vs. Tennessee Whiskey: I'm a Kentucky native (*vide* Chapter 30) who has, to his surprise, lived in rural Tennessee for 20+ years, so I'm of two minds here about preferences and what is or is not interchangeable. I wouldn't indict you for using Dickel in a Manhattan or Mint Julep, but neither would I necessarily or publicly condone the practice. I don't agree with many that the suggestion of such a substitution constitutes fightin' words worthy of lifting the feudal muskets or drawing swords, but hey, how often do you make a Mint Julep? You can't spring for a bottle of Maker's Mark on Derby Day (again, *vide* Chapter 30)? Meanwhile, Dickel is a good sipping whiskey and has many laudable uses. (And remember, "If you only know Jack, you don't know Dickel," a million dollar slogan I'd have happily given the marketers for free.) I mean, can't we all just get along? (And those of you who are chafing about my inclusion of an Islay malt as the perceived exclusion of your beloved Irish distillation, Jameson or Tullamore Dew or whatnot, relax. I'm happy to share a peace-abiding tipple.)

Having Appeased the Irish, a Note on Further Exclusions: If you're just crazy for a Mudslide, go right ahead and blend up a pitcher (but at least stiffen the goop up with some rum, so we know we've been somewhere and aren't just drinking dessert). That doesn't mean you have to be proud about it, however, or keep the bottle of mixer around. You may have noticed that the lists and notations above include no mention of Red-Headed Sluts, Sex on the Beaches (or anywhere else), Kinky Witches, Oyster Shots (ahhg!), Black Widows, White Zombies, any "drinks" with names involving animal parts, sexual puns, self-referential allusions to hangovers, and any sort of daiquiri or concoction involving whipped cream. That is correct. We abrogate all.

I perpetually "mess around" with new drink recipes, either riffing on something I read or tasted or just diving in like a frenzied but dutiful Dr. Drinkenstein. The results can be good, bad, surprising, disappointing, curious, or just plain what-in-the-world-was-I-thinking dreadful. (I was recently quite enjoying my brandy and orange juice before bed—until I suddenly wasn't. Things change. Relationships bloom and fade. Sometimes they never were in the first place. On the other hand, Nashville mixologist Pat Hallorn's blend of gin, smoked paprika simple syrup [half of what he recommends], lime juice, and bitters, garnished with a sprig of mint doused with rose water, is an eccentric winner. Go figure.) Anyway, like any other flings and flirtations in your life, however unexpected, ill-advised, and/or briefly titillating, you'll soon forgive yourself and just go back to the one who understands you best—the Martini you married. In a spirit of camaraderie and attempted hipness, however, I'll offer my version of a Gordon's Cup, which according to my notes originated at Comme Ça in Los Angeles before somehow morphing and migrating into the Southern sticks. It's weird and salty, an odd and refreshing change in the summer, and you already have the English cucumber on hand—ah *ha!*—that you bought to float wafer-thin in that special occasion Hendrick's Martini. Here's what you can do with the rest of the thing. The name, I assume, is an oblique nod to the Pimm's Cup—and by extension a play on Poe's *The Narrative of Arthur Gordon Pym?*—the fruity, refreshing drink that's an English cousin of sorts to Sangria. Cheerio, I say.

Gordon's Cup

1 English seedless cucumber

1 lime

4 oz. gin

1 Tbs. simple syrup

pinch sea salt

In your muddler, mash up 3 ⅓" slices of peeled cucumber and about ⅔ of a lime cut into wedges. Partially fill your chilled small shaker with ice, add the cucumber-lime muddle, 4 oz. gin, and 1 Tbs. simple syrup. (As you've discovered by now, I prefer drinks strong and even "sweet" drinks not overly sweet. Adjust ratios of gin and simple syrup as you prefer.) Cover and shake it like you mean it.

Pour contents into a rocks glass, add another ice cube if there's room, and sprinkle a pinch of sea salt over the top. Strange, eh? But a pretty color, a nice tang, and, quite possibly, sufficiently engaging to require a second test batch.

A Word on Homemade Infused Vodkas: And that word is: No. *Vide* Chapter 23's advice on homemade wine and reaffirm the commitment. Just don't do it. What might seem adventurous and fun at the beginning will come to a rank and undrinkable end involving horseradish or beets or something even more execrable. The only potable infused vodka I ever produced involved lemon verbena, that seductive smelling but largely useless plant towering over the garden. If you want to try a quart of same, dramatically reduce the sugar, by ⅔-¾, from whatever any online recipe suggests.

A better idea, if you simply can't rest until you infuse some vodka, is to locate a fleshy vanilla bean and a small, decorative bottle and, *vide* Chapter 20, make homemade vanilla. (Reserve the scraped vanilla bean seeds for ice cream or a vanilla bean cake, obviously.) In the meantime, if you want a shot of spicy horseradish vodka that's actually commendable, go to Russian Tea Time on East Adams Street in Chicago. My Red Hen Press publishers and I have a tradition of clandestine dinners there when we're all in town—at which, of course, all we do is gossip. The restaurant has a wide and fascinating array of in-house infused vodka—ranging from the curious (cinnamon) to the inspired (yes, the horseradish), but all more than palatable—served in flights in frosty over-sized shot glasses.

**Finally, an Extended Note on Liqueurs and Personal Eccentricities: The array of odd and whimsical liqueurs on display in a well-stocked liquor store are a delight to study but can overwhelm when making a selection. There's real risk and danger, too, as liqueurs are a fairly expensive investment, and any overly quirky purchase can prove undrinkable. (In case you've wondered, Cynar, the dark and bitter Italian liqueur made from artichokes, is actually rather beguiling but a shade obscure for stocking the home bar. Try a sip neat at a sunny outside table in Umbria or on the Amalfi Coast. It has a small but deadly loyal cabal of underground supporters, so watch what you say aloud even in English.) I recommend two: the raspberry-based French Chambord and the herb-infused Italian Galliano—its more than century-old recipe top secret, of course. They complement each other winningly: rich and different flavors, beautiful colors of deep red and yellow, and packaged in a pair of the most eccentric and dramatically shaped bottles on the market. This latter—the svelte or droll bottle body shape—is integral to the true liqueur experience, as, late in the evening, bottles are retrieved from deep within the sideboard and the tray of exquisitely etched cordial glasses is presented.

Bonus recommendations: If you like cream-based liqueur, try ice cold the fairly new Coole Swan, with its dreamy blend of cream, vanilla, cocoa, and single malt Irish whiskey, and you'll shudder if you ever again even hear the name "Bailey's." On an entirely different note, I share the ubiquitous enthusiasm for the subtly floral, elderberry-based St. Germain, which also has a beautiful art deco bottle. It's been over-hyped and over-endorsed but is a treat to have on hand even if all you do is add a splash of it (and grapefruit juice?) to champagne. (Too, try St. Germain shaken with vodka and lime juice, up and icy in a small Martini glass.) I believe the same company also produces the even newer entry Domaine de Canton, a ginger liqueur lighter than you'd expect and entertaining to experiment with. These are three products I hope stay available on the store shelf, so please help the cause. (Of course, absinthe—purportedly with the original recipe including wormwood—has recently returned to the market with a pricy vengeance. I suppose we're all obligated to replicate the whole ordeal of the spoon and sugar cube and whatnot, but I find the drink no more dramatic—or dangerous—than a super-charged pastis. I was seeking Parisian dementia but just ended up with a headache. Suit yourself. It's an entertaining show for guests.)

Chambord and Galliano are also both widely available, which is advantageous. One of the dangers of travelling a lot is developing fixations hard to maintain when again stateside. Two current cases in point: Teaching during an uncustomarily hot summer in Prague, I discovered and came under the sway of the Czech liquor Becherovka, a bitters of sort made with anise, cinnamon, and a reported 32 additional herbs. The taste is unique, and during weekly afternoon screenings in the small, muggy cinema, a large Becherovka & tonic (they serve drinks at the movie theatres, which beats all hell out of Raisinets) was salvation. I now much prefer a "beton" to a gin & tonic, heresy if that be, and it's a habit that has translated swimmingly to the sweltering Tennessee summer. Unfortunately, Becherovka has grown harder to find here, rather than easier, and some kind of recent embargo from our state liquor distributor apparently means I'll have to broaden my search. (Afternote to the worried reader: I found bottles in Kentucky!) If that weren't enough to dishearten a man, my stash of Salmaikki—the salty and black licorice-based drink that I smuggled back from Finland last summer—is running dangerously low. (Afternote to the worried reader: Now gone . . .) Imbibed late at night, in a double shot glass over a single ice cube, preferably by an outdoor fire, Salmaikki is an incomparable companion, well worth risking the ire or worse of the border police. But Helsinki's a long flight.

CHAPTER 26

.

A Brief, Necessary Word on Caviar

Somewhere in the spiral,
think fortieth birthday.
Claudia on pins all day to avoid
The Wrath, lavishing me with smoked salmon,
truffle butter, caviar from
two types of domestic sturgeon,
good things of the earth
echoing vaguely back to some
comically pampered life, echoes awkward
in my hands and foreign in my mouth.

—*from* "Men, Building"

I hesitated to include this final happy hour indulgence due to the small amount of actual cooking involved but decided that the delicate preparation makes up for that. I'm assuming you've better sense than to shell out for the increasingly rare, endangered, and costly Iranian beluga (Russian's illegal in America) or even sevruga, but there are alternatives. The American paddlefish, a slumming cousin of sorts to Caspian and Black Sea sturgeon, has become widely available. It's not cheap, but you won't have to trade your firstborn for an ounce—an enjoyable substitution for the "real thing" unless you're a caviar snob. (Does such a being still exist?) More widely, we're using caviar here to mean any sort of fish roe. (I used to fight the corruption of the term, having taught in Russia, where I guiltily slurped down black market beluga supplied by a student's girlfriend. I vividly remember us standing in my dingy St. Petersburg dorm room, devouring the eggs with plastic spoons and washing them down with a bottle of cold vodka—which bore a bear on the label, or maybe a Viking or a red hammer—I supplied from the tiny refrigerator. I really did feel guilty as hell, having recently read Inga Saffron's thoroughly depressing exposé *Caviar*, but this was "my moment" of exploitation and historical decadence. What could I do? There were hundreds of dollars of eggs in that plastic tub.) Anyway, for expedience please allow my erosion of the term "caviar" for the purposes and duration of this chapter.

Employing our broader definition, your best option for this wonderful "occasion" snack is probably to forget about sturgeon entirely. Try to do a bit better for yourself, however, than the generic little jars of artificially colored black and red capelin and lumpfish roe every grocery chain now seems to stock. (The latter's sole purpose that I can fathom is for striping cream cheese "candy canes" for the office holiday party.) Salmon roe works alright, and hardwood smoked salmon roe is an even better option. (C.f.: A water cracker spread with a bit of soft cream cheese, then topped with a flaky portion of hot-smoked salmon and a small spoonful of *ikura* is delightful, of course, and much simpler and less expensive than what follows.) However, oddly enough, it is through our local butcher that I've discovered my caviar of choice for this snack: smoked trout roe. The eggs are about half the size of salmon eggs and a beautiful glowing orange, they have a delightful, resistant pop, and their smokiness is rich and pronounced. A small jar's an expense—around $30 the last time we ordered—but nothing in the hemisphere of sturgeon, and 2 oz. accommodate the happiest of happy hours for two, with a blini's worth left for tomorrow. Go Dutch?

Blini with Caviar

<u>for the blini</u>:

⅓ cup whole milk

½ tsp. yeast

1 Tbs. sugar

½ cup, less 2 rounded Tbs., all-purpose flour

2 rounded Tbs. buckwheat flour

1 farm egg

1½ Tbs. unsalted butter

pinch sea salt

½ tsp. vegetable oil for frying

<u>condiments</u>:

2 oz. smoked trout eggs or similar (*vide supra*)

4 oz. hot-smoked trout (optional, I suppose)

1 large farm egg

¼ red onion

3-4 spears chives

crème fraîche*

mother-of-pearl spoon with silver handle (for serving)**

To Prepare the Blini. Melt the butter and set aside to cool. Slightly warm the milk and stir in the yeast until dissolved. Separate the egg. To the milk, add the yolk, sugar, and flours, and whisk together. Set in a warm place—the stovetop? Leave the albumen, in a small mixing bowl, on the counter. After 30 minutes, add a pinch of sea salt to the egg white and beat with an electric hand mixer until soft peaks form, around 2 minutes. Add the cooled butter to the yeast-flour mixture, then gently stir in the whipped egg whites to complete the dough.

Heat the oil in a nonstick skillet. You don't need much oil, just enough to barely coat the cooking surface—really, a generous spray is good enough—and you won't need to add any more for subsequent batches of blini. In the medium skillet, spoon in enough batter to make blini about 1½" in diameter (you want them small). This recipe will make approximately 20, more than you need for a 2-oz. jar of eggs, but some will finish/brown superiorly to others, and anyway they're easy to eat. They also freeze well. In four batches of 5 blini, brown for 1-2 minutes on each side. They'll be a bit puffy, which is good—resist pressing them with the spatula. You want them cooked through and browned, but not overly browned, so be careful. (In the mystical tradition of all flapjacks, crêpes, tortillas, et cetera, the subsequent batches of mini blini will tend to cook better than the first, and also faster.) Keep the finished blini in foil in a 190° F oven. (N.b.: Serve warm to the touch, but not overly so or the crème fraîche will melt.)

To Prepare the Condiments. Hard-boil the egg, allow it to cool, and then separate the yolk and white. If residue of the yolk remains on the albumen, gently rinse and pat dry. Finely dice both, separately. Fill five small, decorative bowls with the following: diced yolk; diced egg white; 1-2 Tbs. finely chopped red onion; several cleaned, chopped spears of chives; and crème fraîche. (Serve the crème fraîche out of its plastic tub if you like, but you're going to a lot of effort here to be fancy and enjoy it, so washing an extra bowl is beside the point. *In either case, do make the effort of seeking out the latter, which is far superior to sour cream and adds an appropriate luxuriousness to the hedonistic proceedings.) Place the smoked trout—it really is a nice addition to both taste and texture—on a small wooden cutting board. Set out four small decorative serving spoons, a spreader (for the crème fraîche), and a small knife for the fish. Fill a small glass bowl with crushed ice or small cubes and nestle the opened jar of smoked trout eggs in the ice. Place the blini on a plate. Arrange the bowls attractively, but in a logical sequence, on the table, with of course the caviar as the centerpiece of this little world. Retrieve your mother-of-pearl spoon and brandish it in the air as the Czar would have in his heyday of carnage, repression, and victory. (**Tradition has it that only this iridescent implement will not alter or damage the incredibly subtle flavor of fine caviar. Whether true or hogwash, this hardly constitutes a pressing concern for our little jar of smoky trout eggs. Nevertheless, I was given just such a lovely spoon many years ago. I wield it proudly and precisely and maintain that in fact, to me at least, it *does* makes the eggs taste even better, if for no other reason than that I own a mother-of-pearl spoon and you probably don't. One of my great, lingering regrets, by the way, is that when the Soviet Union collapsed I didn't buy a silver caviar bowl that had been in actual dinner service in the Kremlin. Perhaps you too, comrade, still feel the pang of opportunity wasted.)

You serve yourself, according to the subtleties of personal style. My assembly, the correct method, proceeds thusly: Spread a blini with crème fraîche, position a piece of smoked trout, top with a small dollop of glowing eggs, then sprinkle over with chopped yolks, whites, onion, and chives. How lovely! (My wife puts the trout eggs on last, which philosophically confounds me, but I do credit her enthusiasm.) Each mini blini offers two smile-inducing bites, and you can probably spread the little jar out for 10 blini, so with a modicum of restraint you will have a taste remaining for a second day's 5:00 p.m. Drink with shots of icy vodka if you prefer, but that's more authenticity than I really need in the Tennessee woods. I'll stick with a properly made Martini—up, dry, and frigid as the Baltic. *Za vas.*

Chapter 27

·

Deux Cailles, pour Deux:
A Mix & Match Quail Dinner

Brown one side quickly, turn, brown again.
Lower heat, douse liberally with local
vin blanc, cover and simmer one hour.
Pour another drink. This is crucial to season
appetite, introduce music to private thoughts.
Stare into sunset, appreciate the magpie's
melancholy.

—*from* "Why Eating Alone Is Fortunate"

You've got the itch again, right? You're overdue for another date dinner for two on which you can waste a prodigious amount of time and attention. Actually, the level of effort here has a lot to do with how you decide to use this chapter. I don't know why quail are so engaging to poke, prod, animate, marinate, stuff, sauté, roast, and grill, but they are. (An additional benefit is that the resulting meal here needn't be overly heavy, so you can sweat over this dinner in the spring and summer, after you've put aside winter pursuits.) Also, I've found that finicky American eaters will tend to give quail a try—much more often than they will, say, rabbit—as long as you're not constantly announcing how cute they are (the birds, not the companions). So, do a nice preparation (or two, *vide infra*) and try to be quiet.

Actually, a basic rubbed or sauced quail on the grill is easy to effect, although, like all things, you can complicate the matter exponentially if that's your preference. The idea of this chapter—an expansive, slightly whimsical (and moderately expensive, according to choice) riff on André Daguin's "Two Quails, Two Sauces" recipe—is to offer you several different preparations, both in ingredients and cooking methods, and have you select two to prepare for your dinner: a quail for each of you in two styles. (You could serve as consecutive courses, but I recommend plating the dishes side by side so you can sit down, enjoy your wine, and take an earned breath.)

So, the recipes that follow are each for 2 dressed out and butterflied quail, either wild—if you have a connection and/or predilection—or bought frozen at the grocer. Packages of 4 are fairly easy to locate, and that's precisely what you need, isn't it, to be on your romantic and culinary way? (If purchasing at the store, try to find birds that aren't shot full of sodium and worse—the common "turkey treatment." These will still work for the ideas below, but be sparing with the salt. Ideally, you'd rather have a clean slate.) Here are a few options and variations, roughly in ascending order of difficulty/commitment. I've tried to simplify the French techniques and influences as much as possible while retaining depth of flavor. Remember, you're looking for two recipes to mix and match, with appropriate red and/or white wine pairings, side starches and vegetables as sensible and complementary, and perhaps a customary simple green salad.

Grilled Quail with Pomegranate Molasses

2 quail

pomegranate molasses

sea salt & freshly ground black pepper

Don't worry. We're starting easy, but I guarantee matters will grow vexing soon enough. Pomegranate molasses is a useful, rich, fairly exotic item to keep on hand. A bottle should be available at any worthwhile Middle Eastern grocery and will last a long time. (If you discover a half-empty bottle in the back of the refrigerator and its contents have crystalized, simply heat and dissolve in a pot of water, as you would honey.) If you can't find or can't be bothered—why can't you be?—with the pomegranate variety, then standard molasses, or even maple syrup, is a viable option. The main idea of this one is to keep it simple.

Position the quail on a plate and dribble with the molasses. Rub it into the birds inside and out, then salt and pepper. Spray a hot grill with canola oil to avoid sticking and, with metal tongs, place the butterflied quail split side down on the rack and lower the lid. Grill for 4 minutes, turn the quail once, and grill, lid open, for another 4 minutes, or until nicely browned but still succulent and juicy. Serve at once, with couscous.

Grilled Quail with Mustard & Herb Coating

2 quail

1 Tbs. olive oil

1 rounded tsp. Dijon mustard

½ Tbs. unsalted butter

1 tsp. fresh thyme

1 tsp. fresh rosemary

wedge lemon

sea salt & freshly ground black pepper

Rub the quail all over with the olive oil and allow them to sit out while you prepare the coating. In a small bowl, combine the mustard, the room temperature butter, the cleaned and finely chopped fresh herbs, a squeeze of lemon juice, a generous pinch of salt, and a few turns of pepper. Mix well with a fork and spread equally over the quail on both sides. Grill as above. Serve immediately, with buttery mashed potatoes or white basmati rice. (Both grilling recipes above can also be prepared in the oven, if the gas tank goes empty or the storm arrives. Place the oven rack at medium-high and broil the birds for 8-10 minutes.)

Fried Buttermilk Quail

2 quail

1 cup whole buttermilk

1 tsp. + 1 shake Tabasco

¾ cup locally milled coarse white organic cornmeal*

¾ cup white all-purpose flour

⅛ tsp.+ sea salt

several turns freshly ground ground pepper.

Okay, this option returns us to familiar passions, themes, and cultural dispositions: frying and buttermilk. I trust you have no problem with that. Mix the buttermilk and Tabasco. Pour over the quail in a small Tupperware container, coating the birds thoroughly. Cover and refrigerate for 4-6 hours (or longer if you like). In a wide bowl, combine the cornmeal—*alright, alright, do your best regarding the organic cornmeal, and use yellow if you must, but I'll continue to advocate local milling—flour, and salt and pepper. When you're ready to cook, shake off the quail and dredge them all over with the cornmeal-flour, making sure you coat beneath the wings and other miscellaneous tiny recesses. Over the sink, add the birds to the fryer basket, give it a good shake, and deep-fry (in corn oil) at 350° F for 5 minutes, turning the quail once with tongs. Place on paper towels, season with a pinch more salt and pepper, and serve immediately atop creamed spinach, kale, or collard greens.

Quail Stuffed with Cornbread Dressing, Walnuts, & Apples, Wrapped in Smoky Bacon, in a Sauce of Grapes, White Wine, & Cream

How's that for a recipe name? The book's award for longest? Okay, enough already with the stretching exercises, the kid gloves, and the facile preps. My friend, if not now, when? If not here, where? If not us, et cetera. Let's start gratuitously stuffing and saucing!

2 quail

3-4 oz. cornbread dressing from your freezer*

¼ cup diced Granny Smith apple

¼ cup shelled walnuts

2-4 slices of thick, smoky bacon**

sea salt & freshly ground black pepper

thin bamboo skewers

for the sauce:

8 seedless white grapes & 8 seedless red grapes

⅓ cup white wine

¼ cup low-sodium chicken broth

¼ cup heavy cream

(*You didn't freeze any dressing after Thanksgiving? You should have and may do so the next happy thankful season, both the cornbread dressing [with sausage, your cut corn from summer, and the last of the season's sage from the garden] and your oyster dressing [brimming with mollusks, pine nuts, and plenty of oregano, thyme, and parsley]. You're going to all that effort, anyway, and it's useful and relaxing to have packages of each in the freezer. So you can stuff some quail, for one good reason. However, for the time being and in a pinch you may have to substitute some baked Stove Top with sautéed celery and onions and chicken broth mixed in. Come November, though, no excuses.)

Stuff your quail with the divided cornbread dressing and chopped walnuts and apple. Wrap each bird in 2 slices of thick, smoky, perhaps peppery bacon— **if the bacon is a long cut, 1 slice may suffice—surrounding the bodies snugly and tucking the slices in under the wings and around the legs. Break the ends off bamboo skewers at 2"-3"—long enough to secure the quail around the stuffing but short enough to allow browning the birds in a skillet—and insert through the bacon to close the body cavity. Salt and pepper the quail lightly on both sides. Heat your best copper-lined sauté pan to medium-high and brown the bacon/quail on both sides, 2 minutes per side. (At this point, you can either finish the birds in the pan—turn the heat down to medium, cover, and cook for about 12 minutes, turning the quail once—or, my preference, complete them in the oven. The advantage of the latter is that while they're baking you can immediately proceed with your sauce. Let's do that.) Move the quail to a medium enamel dish and a 350° F oven for 15 minutes.

As the quail are baking, add the grapes to the medium-hot pan. Deglaze the pan's bacon grease and stickings with the white wine and then reduce by half. Add the chicken stock, again reduce by half, and add the cream and reduce a bit further. These reductions won't take long, perhaps 10 minutes. Stir the sauce regularly with a spatula. (If it reduces too much to be a generous serving for two, simply add a splash more each of wine, broth, and cream.)

To serve (immediately), place the quail—onto two plates, with whatever other version of the bird you're presenting—over brown basmati rice, beside a mix of spring greens, and spoon the grapes and sauce over the quail.

There's certainly some flexibility here in terms of taste and effort. This same dish could be prepared without the bacon—why?—by browning the quail in either 1 Tbs. of duck fat (from the freezer) or 1 tsp. of olive oil and 1 tsp. of unsalted butter, then proceeding (*vide ut supra*). A second variation could leave out the stuffing entirely. You'd sacrifice a lot a lot of flavor, obviously, but it would ease preparation considerably, and the sauce is delightful. A final option would be to stuff and wrap the birds, then brown and bake them and forget the sauce. The wine and cream sauce, however, is actually the easy part and is rich and delicious, so unless the ugly, recurring specter of lactose intolerance raises its unforgiving head, go ahead and make the sauce. It's ideal for the birds and perfect with the rice. (Actually, make the sauce regardless. You can eat it all yourself, if necessary.)

Quail Stuffed with Foie Gras & Chanterelles in Red Wine Sauce

In terms of luxurious taste and self-pleasing excess, this recipe can hold its own with any in the book. On the other hand, it is time consuming and even arduous to pull together. One advantage is that the sublime sauce (nobody will believe you made it without a veal or beef demi-glace) can be prepared the day before and reheated, which I highly recommend. Honestly, both stuffed recipes on offer here (if the one above is prepared with all components), and especially this one, require enough time and effort that an exemption to our chapter's jovial mix & match premise should probably be offered: While you're in battle reducing your beef stock, cubing your foie gras, and sautéing your pricey fresh chanterelles, you might just go ahead and prepare 4 quail with this single recipe. Your beloved won't complain if served 2 of these birds, I guarantee. In either case, make the sauce here a day ahead and relieve a little stress.

2 quail

2 1-oz.+ squares foie gras

½ tsp. + 1 tsp. olive oil reserved from duck confit (*vide* Chapter 2)

½ tsp. black truffle butter*

3-4 oz. fresh chanterelle mushrooms**

thin bamboo skewers

for the Sauce Divine:

1 tsp. olive oil

1 tsp. unsalted butter

1 tsp. all-purpose flour

½ cup red wine

1 cup beef stock

pinch of anise seeds

1 medium shallot

sea salt & freshly ground black pepper

to reheat sauce:
2 slivers foie gras from squares above
½ oz. black truffle butter

A Day Ahead, Preparing the Sauce. Heat the olive oil and unsalted butter in a small sauce pot. Add the thinly sliced shallot to medium heat and brown and caramelize for 5 minutes, stirring regularly with a wooden spoon. Deglaze the pot with half the red wine, whisk in the flour, and add the remaining wine. Stir in the pinch of anise seeds, lower the heat just a bit, and cook down for 5 minutes. Add beef stock (not broth), a pinch of salt, and 5-6 grinds black pepper, stir, and cook down at medium-low heat for 30 minutes, until thickened and beautiful. Strain the sauce through a fine sieve into a jar, pressing the spoon over the soft shallots to get every bit of liquid. Dip in your pinkie and taste the result. Be impressed with yourself and think kindly of the author. Close jar and store in the refrigerator. To reheat the sauce the next day, return it to the sauce pot, warm it slowly, then whisk in diced slivers removed from the squares of foie gras and ½ oz. black truffle butter. (*If I've really not convinced you by now that there is no fully lived life or fully realized poetry without a tub of black truffle butter always on hand in the freezer, I humbly surrender. Use regular butter and be damned.) The foie gras will mostly melt in the warm sauce, but if some bits remain, that's good news, too. Over medium heat, cook down the sauce again for maybe 5 minutes, until it looks right to you, thick and dark and irresistible. Cover the pot and keep warm.

Gently brush any dirt from your chanterelles—wiping lightly with a damp paper towel if you must—then scissor them into small pieces. (Yes, foie gras and fresh chanterelles/girolles, and to some extent the quail, are all high-end ingredients, but the small amount of the first two you're using make the expense manageable. Even if the mushrooms are some absurd king's ransom of $30+ per lb., bear in mind that 3 oz. really will suffice if they're firm and nice, and their earthiness is integral here. Don't be embarrassed at the checkout, and don't evade questions if some young nerd asks their use. If you can't find chanterelles, good alternatives are porcinis or lordly morels. Among less expensive and more accessible options, do your best with oyster mushrooms or, last choice, criminis. I wouldn't advise shitakes.) In a small skillet, heat the ½ tsp. of reserved duck confit olive oil (that you've come to love and depend upon) and black truffle butter—regular olive oil and unsalted butter if you refuse to play the game by the rules. Add the chanterelle pieces, coat them in the oil and butter with your trusty wooden spoon, and sauté at medium heat, about 2 minutes, until they cook down a bit and lose their water. Spoon them into a bowl and cool in the fridge.

To stuff, salt and pepper the cubes of foie gras, place them inside the butterflied quail, and divide the chanterelles over the cubes. Close each bird with the end of a bamboo skewer, *vide ut supra.* Add the remaining 1 tsp. confit oil to your copper-lined skillet and at medium heat brown for 2-3 minutes on each side and 1 minute each "standing up" on the top and bottom. On a rack slightly above the middle of the oven, finish the birds at 350° F for 10 minutes (preferably in the heavy skillet, if it allows such use).

Accompany with creamy polenta, made from, of course, organic and locally sourced coarse white cornmeal. (Here's a little trick I just learned, and it complements this quail nicely: When you put your chicken broth on to heat, throw in 2 peeled, whole garlic cloves and a large sprig of thyme from the garden. When the broth boils, remove the garlic and thyme before you add the cornmeal. You'll detect a fragrant and subtle redolence of both in the finished polenta. Don't forget to stir in a little cream at the end, even if you have to lie about it, and always make extra. If lush and creamy, the polenta will probably all be eaten anyway by dinner's end, and otherwise it's excellent and expedient for grilled or skillet-browned slices in the days following.) The serving's simplest of all: Distribute servings of polenta onto two attractive plates (pick your own colors this time)—beside your second preparation of quail, or not—top with a browned bird, and divide and drizzle all of the dark, warm sauce over and around. Probably best without music, so to appreciate the insuppressible groans of approval.

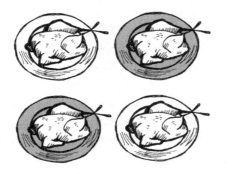

CHAPTER 28

·

Lamb Two Ways,
as from Winter Spring Emerges

He gathers meat. Stuffs cold shelves
with duck breast and rabbit, lamb
shank, head cheeses, shuddering livers,
bowls of heart and kidney.
Buries a room under the hirsute
red of the herd,
half-feathered legs,
testes and brains
and black sausage.
Lines up encrusted pâtés and fine, lard-white
terrine. Snouts, ears,
soft fatted chops of veal and wild hog.

—*from* "Man's War against Depression"

As mentioned, I began writing this book and determining its content in
the fall, then cooked and wrote fairly intensely throughout winter, which may
account in part for the volume's preponderance of heavy dishes, if indeed you
feel such a preponderance exists. The personal taste of the author is, of course,
another central factor. Looking over these pages, I can't help but lament, just
a bit, a few hearty entries that remain missing: no roast leg of lamb inserted
with whole garlic cloves and coated in spring herbs, no osso buco with its
heavenly pudding of marrow in the center. I have a delicious—surprisingly
so—entrée of braised turkey legs, cooked down in a dark wine sauce with
prunes and small onions, that there's simply no practical spot for. We'll lead off
the reader-demanded sequel with it. (We've plenty of poultry dishes already,
with the flurry of duck activity early in the book and the quail enthusiasms
later on.) Perhaps, however, you'll indulge the humble poet slipping in one
more irresistible hunk of meat. We genuflect to braised lamb shanks, and here's
a version I made for Easter dinner last year. So, an homage, if you will, to
the change of seasons, as we indulge in a last, for now, hearty repast even
while stepping happily into the lengthening, fragrant nights of spring and an
anticipated bounty of vegetables and fruits and grilled fish.

The second lamb recipe offered below is, by design, fundamentally different from the first, a spicy and delightful savory dish with sweet underpinnings from the coconut milk and potatoes. It perfectly accompanies a warm spring night and dinner out on the deck. To be sure, we tested and confirmed the hypothesis just last night.

> Joint crack,
> quick serrated edge, thieved shank
> free in your hand. Ghost at the head of the meal—
> blessing potatoes lathered in gravy fat,
> crossing with a fistful of the lamb of Christ
> —whatever—all over your sticky smile.

> —*from* "Ghost Holds His Vow of Fasting
> for Nearly Twelve Hours"

Lamb Shanks with Orzo & Feta Cheese

2 1-lb. lamb shanks

1 medium white onion

4 large cloves garlic

2 Tbs. olive oil

1½ cups white wine*

1½ cups low-sodium chicken stock

1 cup fresh or canned tomatoes**

1 Tbs.+ (about 3 nice sprigs) oregano, plus other herbs***

¼ cup Italian parsley

1 Tbs. Worcestershire sauce

1 cup orzo****

⅔ cup feta cheese*****

flour for dusting

sea salt & freshly ground black pepper

mint jelly for serving (optional, unless you're the author)

Rinse and pat dry the shanks. Dust with flour. Add 1 Tbs. of the olive oil to your Dutch oven and brown shanks on both sides over medium-high heat, about 3 minutes each side. Salt and pepper as you're browning. With tongs, remove to a plate.

Heat the remaining 1 Tbs. of olive oil in the Dutch oven. Over medium heat, brown the peeled and chopped onion for 2 minutes, stirring occasionally with a plastic spatula, then add the finely chopped garlic and brown for 2 minutes more. (Obviously, you could prepare and brown a traditional *mirepoix* of onion, carrot, and celery here if you like. This time around, I preferred the moiety of the simple onion.) Remove from the heat and deglaze with ½ cup of the wine. (*Use red wine, if you prefer—it changes the color and flavor as you'd expect. Here, I'm hoping to invoke "spring-like" rather than "wintry"; ergo, white wine.) Return pot to heat and shanks to pot (including any drippings or blood on the plate). Add the rest of the wine, chicken broth, tomatoes, chopped oregano, Worcestershire sauce, and salt and ground pepper to taste. (**My rule of thumb is that if tomatoes aren't in season locally—i.e., when cooking throughout the winter—you're just as well off or better with good, organic, minimally processed canned tomatoes, whole or already diced. If using fresh tomatoes, I suggest adding 1 rounded tsp. ketchup. If using canned tomatoes, I recommend 1 cup here. If you don't mind the result being more "tomatoey" and likely soupier—a personal choice no one should denounce you for—go ahead and dump in the entire 14.5-oz. can, but be sparing with the juice. ***Meanwhile, if spring has sprung and the thyme in your garden is again green and sweet, feel free to add some sprigs along with the oregano. I'm obsessed with thyme lately and use it in everything. For that matter, as far as herbs go, lamb and rosemary pair so naturally and winningly, scissor off a sprig as well from the rosemary bush as you walk by, if it looks good and smells fragrant to the touch.)

Stir everything well, bring to a boil, cover, reduce heat to medium-low, and cook for approximately 3 hours, occasionally stirring and checking that there's sufficient liquid (there should be). Slow cooking to fall-off-the-bone tenderness is the key here, and the shanks probably will need the full 3 hours, so get this recipe on no later than mid-afternoon. (You don't want to look up at the clock, find yourself furiously mincing garlic at 5:00 p.m. and then having to try to rush—i.e., undermine—the entire braising philosophy. Plus, your happy hour will be sabotaged, a disagreeable sequence of events all around.)

When the shanks are tender, take a look at how much liquid remains and estimate whether or not there's too much for cooking the orzo. (Orzo is practically invincible, so you're not worrying so much about overcooking the pasta as how soupy you want the finished dish.) If you've too much liquid, remove the lid and cook down on a higher heat for 10-15 minutes. If you're not sure, err on the side of soupy.

On medium heat, add the cup of orzo directly to the shanks and Dutch oven. Stir it in well, cover, and cook for 10 minutes or until soft. Keep an eye on the orzo, don't let it stick, and make sure it is all in the liquid. Stir 2-3 times and adjust the heat if necessary. (****A delightful alternative to the orzo, which I like just as well, is cannellini beans. Empty a can into a colander, rinse well, shake, add to the Dutch oven in place of the orzo, and heat for 8-10 minutes. If you use the amount of liquids indicated, the result will be more of a stew than with the orzo. Delete the feta cheese, but otherwise plate the same, *vide infra*.)

Ladle the orzo into two wide dinner/pasta bowls, with tongs place the glorious, falling apart shanks—the smell of which has tortured the house for 3 hours—over the orzo, and top with the crumbled feta cheese and chopped parsley. (*****A proper Greek feta poses no intolerance problem, as it's crafted from sheep or goat's milk. Hoo-rah!) Serve with hot, crusty bread, a small bowl of mint jelly nearby (just in case), and a sassy bottle of Mourvedre, Zinfandel, or whatever you like, and raise a cheer to Holy Week, the Blood of the Lamb, or your beliefs of choice. How *does* a rabbit lay eggs, anyway?

> I accelerate, nowhere and nothing to hide,
> race to preserve on the seat a sackful
> of price-reduced chocolate eggs, in the slaughterhouse
> trunk seven, yes seven legs of post-resurrection lamb
> purchased for a carnivore's song.

—*from* "The Bounty of Easter"

Lamb Curry with Sweet Potatoes & Peas

I can't quantify exactly why this is one of those especially fun to eat dishes, but it is, partly due to the variety of the ingredients, which meld flavorfully together. If you can't find prepackaged ground lamb at the grocer, in my experience most "meat guys" are accommodating about cutting a pound from the shoulder or a leg roast and grinding it for you.

1 Tbs. olive oil

1 Tbs. unsalted butter

1 lb. ground lamb

1 medium white onion

3 large cloves garlic

1 medium sweet potato (or 2 small ones)

1 Tbs. fresh ginger

2 Tbs. curry powder

1 cup low-sodium chicken broth

1 14-oz. can unsweetened coconut milk

½ rounded cup frozen peas

¼ rounded cup fresh cilantro

sea salt & freshly ground black pepper

for serving:

white basmati rice

garlic naan (if possible)

Skin and chop the onion and garlic and skin and mince the ginger. Rinse and skin the sweet potato and slice into ½" cubes. Thaw, rinse, and drain the peas. Rinse, dry, and chop the cilantro. In your favorite large skillet, heat the olive oil and butter until just foaming. Over medium heat, sauté the onion, garlic, and ginger until beginning to soften, around 4 minutes. Add the lamb, breaking it up with a spatula, salt and pepper lightly, and cook for 8 minutes, stirring and turning periodically, until it browns. Add the sweet potato cubes and the curry powder, mix all together well, and cook for 2 more minutes. Turn the heat down to medium-low, add the chicken broth, stirred coconut milk, 8-10 additional turns ground pepper, and a pinch more salt. (Note that as this book progresses I'm generally, gradually less specific regarding the amount and ratio of my beloved sea salt and freshly ground pepper. Rather than my impatience, let's call it part of the initiate's learning curve?) Mix together, partially cover, and cook for 10 minutes, stirring 2-3 times. Remove the lid and cook for 3-5 minutes more, until the potatoes are tender (but not mushy). Stir in the peas and cook until they're just warm, no more than 1 minute. Stir in the chopped cilantro.

Serve in wide bowls over white basmati rice, with Tabasco on the side and, if you can manage, hot garlic naan. To drink: cold, sweating bottles of Kingfisher lager.

CHAPTER 29

·

On Morel Mushroom Farming
& the Agrarian Impulse

I was surprised and delighted several years ago to learn that the prized morel mushroom was native to Tennessee. This was news to me. In our area they seem to all originate from a single county, during a small window of 2-3 weeks during the late spring (duration and dates much dependent upon variables of weather). I know of nowhere to purchase these directly, but our best Murfreesboro restaurant, Five Senses, sends out the e-news when a gatherer knocks on the door with a few pounds. Mitchell and Anna will feature morels on the menu for a brief span of days.

If our moderate climate, and perhaps yours as well, can nurture a harvest of such delectable, delicate, and costly fungi—usually only available to the home chef as a rare treat in precious dried form of perhaps ½ oz.—why not cultivate and farm our own? It's not brain surgery, and it will get us outside *en plein air*. For once, we leave aside our specialty grocers and farmers market for a muscular sojourn to the home improvement box store. Empty out the trunk and backseat of the convertible or borrow your begrudging neighbor's pick-up truck (you can promise him or her some of the morel bounty): You'll be returning with an impressive load of goods. It's an investment, but with the promise of a perennial return. And good lord, have you ever seen what fresh morels cost, *if* you can find any?

for the raised bed:

4 untreated 6' 2x8s

non-toxic wood sealant (to extend the bed's life against rot)

box tenpenny deck nails (galvanized, to resist rusting of the heads)

20 bags 1 sq. ft. garden soil

1 small bag fast-acting lime

for the plants:

1 package morel spore (easily available online; *vide* Food & Literary Sources)

1 five-gallon plastic bucket with tight-fitting lid

collected biodegradable kitchen refuse

4 tomato seedlings + 4 metal cones + baby lettuce seeds + . . . ?

Work backwards on the calendar to determine the best time to begin the project. (The spore, by the way, will last for months in your refrigerator should you need to hold onto it for a while, and of course the unprepossessing square of brown will be extensively displayed at any dinner or social event you host in the meantime.) You should stop composting your raised bed approximately one month before morels would normally be expected in your area. Estimating, say, early May as the beginning of mushroom season, cease composting on April 1. You will have needed to compost for at least three months to get an optimal yield, which has you beginning on January 1. (Yes, yes, this puts you outside in the direst of winter hammering together the bed, but "no cost, no reward." Tell yourself—and your numb hands—that it's merely "brisk.")

Collecting the Biodegradables. Perhaps two weeks before you assemble your bed, the spore alive and strange and slightly unnerving in the back of the fridge, begin saving biodegradables for composting. In as convenient—vis-à-vis carrying dripping scraps from the kitchen—a spot as possible outdoors, place your five-gallon bucket, lid on. You'll be looking at this bucket for the next three months and more, so convenience and discretion are ideal. Save all bread trimmings, vegetable and fruit peelings, coffee grinds, and eggshells. (Nothing, however, that will turn rancid, such as meat scraps.) You may find that collecting the composting materials is actually rather fun and fills you with a sense of environmental and agrarian purpose. (Or you may not, rather regarding the practice as tiresome and slightly odious, but you'll need to cultivate the habit anyway. Keep the lid on firmly to prevent insects and deter critters.)

Building the Raised Bed. Assembling the bed is cake. More important that it's functional than beautiful. Prepare the 2x8s by rubbing them all over with a rag dipped into the shaken and well-stirred sealant. In a cool spot with minimal direct sunlight but within reach of the hose—perhaps behind the garage or shed, or under the (anticipated) heavy shade of a stand of trees—hammer together the four pieces of lumber to form a 6' square. The nailing can get tricky. Use your ingenuity, use your foot as a brace, just persist until a square is standing that's sturdy enough to hold the soil and endure the subsequent turning of compost. Tediously, either in a wheelbarrow or over your sturdy (albeit sagging) shoulders, fill the bed with the bags of soil. 20 square feet should fill it just about perfectly.

Planting the Spore and Composting. This is when the fun begins. On our theoretical date of January 1, your morning's construction complete, retrieve the spore from the refrigerator and break it apart in your hands fairly evenly over the raised bed. Turn it into the soil for a few minutes with a shovel, then dump your kitchen scraps on top of the soil and turn these in as well. (As you work them with the shovel, you must admit that the carrot tops and potato rinds and eggshells look sort of interesting there, as if you're onto something of forgotten, atavistic import.) Lastly, remember that you need to keep the morel habitat "sweet," with the soil at a pH level of about 7.0. The composting should help with this, but to be safe and sure and get the process jump-started, open your lime, attempt to read the indecipherable numbers and strategies—and anything else in English—on the back of the bag, and then go ahead and sprinkle a couple of generous handfuls of tiny pellets over the soil and turn these too with the shovel. Water lightly.

Although it's cold out and getting colder, at 5:00 p.m. bundle up and take your first Martini outside and admire your industry, your reconnection to the earth, in the quickly fading light. Walk around the bed and inspect it from all sides. Before it gets too dark to see, go back inside and insist your enduring companion come out as well and admire the bed, dirt, eggshells, whether he or she wants to or not. You're undertaking this for the greater fungal good of you both, after all, and this initial sharing will mean a lot later, when it's over.

Continue saving kitchen scraps and compost your morels often over the next three months. I recommend once per week. Dump the biodegradables and turn them vigorously and well into the soil. This will not hurt your spore. (N.b.: Keep in mind during all this that mushrooms are odd, alien forms little understood by science. Keep feeding yours those organic, fair trade, shade-grown coffee grounds.) On our theoretical April 1, stop composting and let nature take its proverbial course. You don't have to look at the bucket anymore until next year, thank almighty god. Rinse it out, dry, and store in the shed.

Now, *be patient.* Your morels need time to grow. This is a living organism with its own pace, preferences, and whimsies, and moreover imported spore will likely produce mushrooms later than an indigenous species. Typically, you may see morels coming up from between 30-45 days, but this is widely variable according to matters understood and otherwise, alterable by human invention and not, and remember always, as your spore literature wisely reminds, "'Morel spring' is at a different time of the year in each part of the country," from as early as January to as late as June. (Tennessee is commonly considered in garden zone 7, at this climatic moment; if your climate is dramatically harsher or milder, anticipate this by adapting the theoretical dates offered here.) In either heavy rains or drought, the tiny mushrooms will not mature. You'll never be able to detect any of this with the human eye, and bear in mind that the morel organism lives almost entirely underground. Have faith. Be patient. Stay hungry. Keep the soil moist.

Around June 15—if you took a holiday or busman's honeymoon in May or early June, make sure to hire a desperately poor former student to water the garden and pay special attention to the morel bed—after a month of unusual rain or of drought and great heat, with nothing detectable growing in the bed but a few weeds and a curl of "stiff wild-carrot leaf" (from the scraps, with a nod to William Carlos Williams), you may notice that the spot is sunnier than you'd initially hoped or bartered. Too, it is possible you have mistimed this first season and may have to wait—worst-case scenario—until next year for your mushrooms. (It will, of course, be far, far too late in the season to enjoy the local morels that were on brief offer and beautifully prepared by your local restaurant. [Stuffed with goat cheese, battered, and deed-fried as an appetizer?, followed by a sautéed chicken breast in a morel cream sauce?] No matter. Next year? Next year! You may even sell the chef some of your own excess supply . . .) In the meantime, you might as well exploit your hard work and all that worrisome, unexpected sunlight (all morning and afternoon) by planting tomatoes there, another project you've wanted to undertake in your long-anticipated return to the soil. Down at the garden shop, pick four healthy seedlings: two unimpeachable and invulnerable varieties—say a Better Boy and, for his companionship, an Early Girl—and two types exotic and seductive and risky—White Wonder, Yellow Pear, Brandywine, or dark-skinned Cherokee Purple? To support these glorious young ones, buy four sturdy metal cones that you can reuse for years. Plant the seedlings in the raised bed—recall that turning the soil doesn't hurt the spore—place the cones securely, and between all, for good luck and measure, scatter a package of seeds, microgreens or sweet butter lettuce, to crown mid-summer salads. Water sufficiently but not excessively.

Possibly, in fact quite likely, just as the bed received too much sunlight for morels, it inversely receives far too little to nurture tomatoes. Continue to water periodically until you delegate the job entirely to a student or just quit it "bugger all" and trust the elements. Less and less often will you find necessary bringing an anticipatory Martini out to inspect the bed's progress, although the days now grow long. Maybe too damned long, sweltering and thick with blood-parched mosquitoes.

Sometime around late August or the beginning of September, remove the metal cones, stack them, and store somewhere to be forgotten forever. Pull the straggly, anemic, nearly leafless tomato plants from the soil, including the desiccated and yellow Cherokee Purple, and throw them into the woods (you needn't bother to throw them purposefully—just toss the mothers). A hammer won't be required to break down the feeble raised bed frame: Kick the discolored 2x8s apart with your shoe and gingerly load the nail-sharp boards into the car for the trash collection center. Shovel the stubborn soil—i.e., a mass of root-addled dirt full of rotted vegetables and eggshell fragments, topped with burned and twisted thumbnails of "lettuce"— into any low spots on the property, around any exposed foundation of the house, or just dump the shit in the woods on top of the dead tomatoes. The exposed and remaining 6' x 6' spot where the bed reposed will remain toxic for a while. Expect nothing to grow there for a year or more. You won't have to weed it.

Cartons of button 'shrooms "buy one, get one" at the grocer until Tuesday. We planted on April 1, if you didn't catch the date. True story? What is truth, and what the sorry, comic, cosmic reality?

CHAPTER 30

·

A Native Son's Kentucky Derby Dinner

It seems a lifetime past—
two minutes of destiny, a bugle blast,
that blanket of roses smelling, for one instant,
like heaven caressing the genius of your legs.

—*from* "Apologia to War Emblem, 'Dud as a Stud'"

I dedicate this obligatory chapter to my mother, a woman proud of her Bluegrass heritage. (Mom considers Kentucky Deep South, and after more than 20 years of her youngest son living in Tennessee still reflexively refers to me "driving down" to visit the Commonwealth.) My folks wouldn't endure the chaos of attending the races on Derby Day (or any other day of the meet, for that matter, or Lights Over Louisville or the Great Steamboat Race, et cetera) if you dragged them kicking and screaming *and* rented the limousine *and* paid them handsomely for their time—I don't necessarily disagree with them—but you must admit it's fun to follow the *Courier-Journal*'s celebrity watch for the week and report by phone whether George Clooney's in town, maybe Bill Shatner? And this year's fashion in women's hats? Consider the following aperçu: When my parents lived on Southern Parkway, a mile or so from the track, double-parking cars in the yard for the Oaks and the Derby were days of profitable sport. "One born every minute and two to take him . . ." My father and I on the porch swing with Whiskey Sours (Juleps, *hell*), watching the lemmings shuffle by, dropping money as they go. My Old Kentucky Home, indeed. (Speaking of lemmings: This humble chapter and its meal is also co-dedicated to lovely Churchill Downs, where I invested/donated a fair portion of my University of Louisville undergraduate student loans under the spires' inspiring influence.)

To further irritate my parents with my peculiar and dubious loyalties, by the first Saturday in May I've usually put spring semester to bed and am, if at all possible, already in Europe pondering the beret as a credibly renewed fashion statement. However, if I do happen to be stuck—I mean, uh, have the privilege to be—in the South this year when the gun goes off, here's what we'll be serving:

Sure-Thing, at-the-Post Cocktails:

Mint Juleps

What-Went-Wrong Drinks, Snacks, & Appetizers:

Mint Juleps

Loser's-Ticket Main Course:

Hot Browns

We'll-Have-a-Sure-Damn-Thing-Next-Year Dessert:

Kentucky Derby Nut Pies,* two versions

After-All-They're-Just-Big-Dumb-Animals Post-Prandial Digestifs:

Bourbon (neat)

Since the first two courses are Mint Juleps, let's keep the recipe simple and get it right. Below is for a single drink, so substitute your larger metal shaker to make 2-4 at a time (in which event, you'll have to be careful with the distribution of the muddled mint leaves). You could theoretically substitute simple syrup for the powdered sugar and water, but you shouldn't.

Who gives a damn for the best horse
or best luck? It's 1986, dry clear afternoon
in Louisville and Ferdinand, at 17-1 and locked
behind 15 others, knocks the rail twice
before the first turn. But down the backstretch,
when a sudden magic space appears, man/beast
leaps for the dusty portal of that dream.
Or in the fixed verse of history, "Daylight
and victory. Roses and champagne. The Shoe
54 years old, and his beautiful third wife
shouting she loved him."

—*from* "Apologia to Alan Dugan
and Bill Shoemaker"

The Mint Julep

1 tsp. powdered sugar

2 tsp. spring water

4 oz. bourbon

2-3 sprigs mint

silver cup (optional)

In the bottom of your chilled small metal shaker—or silver cup (*yaas, Colonel* . .)—for 15-20 seconds muddle the blazes out of 10 rinsed mint leaves, the powdered sugar, and the water. Add the bourbon. (*Vide* Chapter 25: Maker's Mark and Jim Beam 7-year spring to mind as fine choices, but feel free to substitute a high-end offering from Evan Williams, Wild Turkey, et cetera, according to taste and budget. Woodford Reserve has had a lot of justified success. Meanwhile, Pappy Van Winkle and his more matured kin—god bless'm—remain out of the poet's price range. If he's within yours, maybe *you* should be hosting the Derby party.) The bourbon is room temperature, so shake vigorously.

Remove lid of shaker and pour contents into a chilled Collins glass filled with ice (chipped if possible). If you like, and dismissing what anyone else thinks, top with chilled soda water and stir. (I don't, but it doesn't seem a bad idea for pacing what could be a long evening. The speed horse always loses.) Garnish with a thick sprig of mint and serve, if preferred, with a straw. (Again, not for me. But.)

Make certain that Mint Juleps are made and served before the horses are at the post at 6:24 p.m. EST (approximate). You don't want to be in the other room muddling and shaking and missing the action when the Greatest Two Minutes In Sports comes out of the gate.

After the race, after the disbelief and recriminations and calls of foul play, and especially after the realization that during the excitement you've all drunk your first Mint Juleps in 2:03.29 (and the party's off and running at a thoroughbred's pace), repeat for the next course, *vide supra*.

Hot Browns

I've no notion of how closely this approximates the original Brown Hotel recipe. (I do recall as a youngster having an interview with Rotary Club officials in that hotel's ornate lobby and being informed after the fact that, inter alia, I wasn't friendly or gregarious enough—I paraphrase after 30 years—to represent or speak for the organization. I'd been sniffing around for some free travel even then, pre-writers colonies by a long gallop.) Further, I've sampled some delicious variations on this famous local dish—one with country ham in place of the turkey; another, a revelation, made with seafood—but here we're sticking to the traditional composition as I see it. To my mind, my main contribution to the evolution of the Hot Brown has been to simplify the "two sauce" method by combining the béchamel and mornay into a single, fluid preparation, meanwhile eliminating superfluous and deleterious steps such as concocting a double boiler (superfluous) and straining out the onions (deleterious).

For the record, I do not condone the inclusion of mushrooms on top of Hot Browns, and the crumbling of the bacon, rather than leaving the strips whole, is anathema. Let's get to business, the way it's supposed to be done.

For two.

1 turkey breast (from freezer, saved from Thanksgiving

for this purpose) 4 strips thick, smoky bacon

1 tomato

4 large slices quality white bread with body

Italian parsley (for finishing, optional)

for the sauce:

⅓ cup + 1 Tbs. unsalted butter

½ medium white onion

⅓ cup all-purpose flour

3 cups hot whole milk

1 tsp. sea salt

12 turns freshly ground black pepper

8 turns freshly ground nutmeg

4 shakes (or generous pinch) cayenne powder

2 farm egg yolks

½ cup coarsely grated Parmesan (+ more for finishing)

¼ cup heavy whipping cream

Fry the bacon in a skillet until cooked through but not crispy (you're putting the strips under the broiler later). Drain on a paper towel and set aside. On a cutting board, with a large, sharp knife, carve the turkey breast into slices of ample thickness. Wrap the slices in aluminum foil and place them in a 200° F oven.

Preparing the Sauce. Heat the milk in a medium pot. In a larger pot, melt ⅓ cup butter and add the finely chopped onion. Cook over medium heat, stirring occasionally, for 5-6 minutes until the onions are translucent and lightly brown. Whisk in the flour to make a paste, then whisk in the heated milk. Add salt, pepper, nutmeg, and cayenne and mix well. Bring sauce briefly to a boil as you stir, then reduce burner heat to medium-low and cook for 20 minutes, whisking frequently. (You don't need to stir continuously, only attentively. Go ahead and slice your tomato, fiddle with the bread and plates, et cetera, but stay close to that pot and don't let the sauce stick or burn. Stir it each minute or so.) Remove the sauce from the heat and let it cool for 2-3 minutes. Whisk in the beautiful, deeply orange yolks from your local eggs, then return the pot to the burner. Add the grated Parmesan cheese and the additional 1 Tbs. butter and stir until melted. Whisk in the cream. The sauce is now complete, thick and wickedly rich. Taste it. Try not to swoon. Keep warm on a low heat until ready to assemble the hot browns.

Cut 4 healthy slices (around ¼") from the center of your tomato. This is your vegetable for the evening. Regarding the bread slices, trim according to preference. If the top crust contains some oats or interesting grains, nuts, herbs, or whatnot, I incline toward leaving it and minimally trimming the side and bottom crusts. Sometimes, if the crust isn't hard and excessive, I'll leave most or all of it. (I have no philosophical problem here with bread crust, per se, and believe it lends the sunken raft of slice—so to speak—a bit of structural support under the weight of what's to be its fate. You may feel differently.) Toast the bread.

Before you begin assembly, make another round of Mint Juleps to pep up the crowd, even if it's a crowd of two. The roses will have long been placed over the beast's glistening neck, the announcers' postmortem of the race and dramatized rematches for the Preakness mostly elaborated. (I'm proceeding again as if you're cooking for two, although a generously proportioned turkey breast can easily make 4 Hot Browns. The sauce recipe also suffices for four, so revise and deviate accordingly. In the case of the sauce, however, I insist you make the full batch, even for two. It's hardly more trouble, and the result is sinfully addictive. You'll want to ladle it all over yourself, or at least dip some asparagus later. Whatever scenario you prefer, I assure none will go to waste.)

Assembling the Hot Browns. These can be cooked on baking sheets, especially if preparing more than 2, but I strongly oppose this ugly industrial model. Use sturdy, colorful plates—so far, my stalwart Fiestaware has served bravely—that won't be bothered by 2-3 minutes under the broiler and prepare the Hot Browns individually. On each plate, place 1 whole slice of toasted bread, trimmed as preferred (*vide supra*), and a second slice, halved diagonally, on either side of the first. Over the bread, arrange 2-3 slices of the warm turkey. Spoon the warm sauce over the turkey. Place 2 tomato slices on top of the sauce, and artfully arrange 2 slices of cooked bacon around the tomato. Sprinkle with a bit of the additional Parmesan, and, if your Mint Julep tells you so, finish with additional twists of pepper and nutmeg.

On an upper position in the oven, put the plates under a high broil for 2-3 minutes, until the bacon is crisping, the Parmesan browning, the tomato softening, and the sauce just beginning to bubble. Lordy, our luck's turning! *Using oven mitts*, remove the plates carefully, optionally top with a toss of chopped parsley, and serve immediately on large oven potholders/trivets. Accompany with steak knifes for cutting the turkey and with a bowl of extra sauce close at hand (in case an angle of toast becomes indecently exposed). To drink, if you want to take a break from the MJs, perhaps iced tea with a sprig of mint (as homage to the Julep). Careful of those hot plates.

·

Kentucky Derby Nut Pie (Two Versions)

*"D____ P__" is a trademarked term of Kern's Kitchen that, story has it, the company has guarded ferociously through an estimated 25 lawsuits (including one involving *Bon Appétit* in the 1980s in which the magazine won a [temporary] victory). This proprietary ferocity is obviously solely to do with profits, as their mediocre boxed product doesn't even contain any bourbon, as I recall. I've never had a slice at the Melrose Inn, in Prospect, Kentucky, where it's been served since 1950, and considering their off-putting position have no great desire to. It's a *pie*, dudes. As a consequence of litigation real and threatened, the score of similar recipes in print and floating in cyberspace must concoct awkward yet resonant variants for titles: Pegasus Pie, Horserace Pie, Kentucky Walnut Race Pie, ad nauseam. I phoned my lawyer, and today we're going to risk baking two versions of "Kentucky Derby Nut Pie." Sound

good? I think you'll find a thick wedge of whichever recipe you decide to embark upon, served warm with whipped cream and a glass of icy milk, just the healthful ticket to settle your stomach after the Hot Brown. (N.b.: The gustatory constitution of the honorable [or otherwise] Kentucky Colonel is long revered, his speed of recovery from an impressive portion of *spiritus frumenti* the stuff of legends. The author should know. *Vide* Chapter 8.)

Kentucky Derby Nut Pie #1

1 uncooked pie crust, floured on both sides (*vide* Chapter 9)

½ cup (1 stick) unsalted butter

1 cup white sugar

3 medium farm eggs

1½ tsp. vanilla

⅓ cup bourbon (mixed with ½ tsp. cornstarch)

⅓ cup all-purpose flour

pinch sea salt

1 rounded cup coarsely chopped walnuts

1 cup semisweet chocolate chips (large Ghirardelli 60% cocoa chips?)

In a medium-large mixing bowl, add the melted butter—not too hot—sugar, eggs, vanilla, bourbon stirred with cornstarch, and pinch of salt. Whisk vigorously until frothy. Add the flour and mix well. Add the walnuts and chocolate chips and combine all with a spoon. Pour into the floured, uncooked pie shell that you've previously arranged in a 9½" glass pie pan and crenellated at the edges a bit for appearance.

Bake at 350° F for about 35 minutes. It will cook quickly, so don't overdo.

Kentucky Derby Nut Pie #2

1 pie crust, *vide ut supra*

½ cup unsalted butter

¾ cup dark brown sugar

½ cup white sugar

½ cup light corn syrup

4 medium farm eggs

1½ tsp. vanilla

⅓ cup bourbon (mixed with ½ tsp. cornstarch)

pinch sea salt

½ rounded cup coarsely chopped walnuts

½ rounded cup coarsely chopped pecans

1 cup semisweet chocolate chips

To prepare, *vide ut supra*. Bake at 350° F for 45 minutes.

As previously advised, serve pies warm with whipped cream and a cold glass of milk, or with homemade vanilla ice cream, or serve cold with whipped cream and coffee.

<u>Notes and Thoughts on the Pies, Plus One Admission</u>. Again, I make no claims about the authority of these pies apropos of the original inspiration, genesis traceable to the afore-maligned Melrose Inn, which has served its pie for generations. Version #1, however, has more of the flavor and consistency that I associate with a traditional D_____ P__—color and texture similar to a blondie brownie, but creamier, and also using only walnuts. (Here's my admission: One reluctance I have about this "Native Son" chapter is that the inclusion of the famous "Kentucky Derby Nut Pie," or whatever, to my mind necessitated the exclusion from the dessert chapters of my own rightly heralded pecan pie, truly a signature dish I've baked scores of times. It was simply too similar and redundant, particularly to KDNP version #2. Some quick tips on pecan pies: use whole pecans, of course, and only dark corn syrup. Add chocolate chips and plenty of bourbon. That's my standard, unsurpassable pie. A second version, highly intriguing, that I appropriated—i.e., again, stole—from a poet-friend, involves, rather than chocolate chips and bourbon, the zest of an orange, a splash of its juice, and rum. Reader, it works. Frankly, I'd prefer a slice of either of these to the pies detailed above—although the pies above are quite good, believe me—but the thematic show must go on.) Version #2, as I've just parenthetically indicated, is more reminiscent of a good pecan pie—dark and rich. I think you and yours will enjoy either version offered here, but you might consider, since those Pillsbury pie crusts come double in packages, anyway, and you've an overabundance of nuts in the freezer (purchased for the secretary's daughter's school fundraiser), well . . .

Bourbon (Neat)

Pappy Van Winkle's Family Reserve, 20 years old (brought by a guest)

rocks glasses (to have plenty of room to swirl, aerate, and get your nose in)

If the Pappy is clearly a "sharing surprise" to be leaving with the foolish guest if any whiskey remains at evening's close, then pour generously of your friend's bottle. If, on the other hand, you perceive Pappy to be more of a "sharing *gift*"—i.e., you've no choice but to open the bottle, but whatever remains stays with you—pour stingily (in shallower glasses?) and after the first round stealthily return to serving Beam. Whoever won the office Derby pool or whatnot, offer him or her an extra finger, so to speak, of Beam, to iterate your giving nature. (Put Pappy in the sideboard and don't mention him again until thanking your benefactor as he/she departs.)

The initial humming by anyone—including the now discredited and maudlin chef—of Dan Fogelberg's "Run for the Roses" signals that the party's over and everyone should go home or, in the case of a party of two, retire to separate corners.

•

Later in the Evening; or, On Ecstasies, Agonies, & Might-Have-Beens

How it was: first seasons, then years,
then decades. I cut the greenest
basil this morning for a final batch
of pesto. As leaves soaked,
spiders and dowsed insects crawled
to highest tips of their sunk ship.
See, this is what I had to tell you.
Mince local garlic, grind Reggiano
and pepper. Pinch of sea salt and steady
drizzle of oil into the pulsing mush—
sexy, easy. Tonight we'll roast chicken,
slice last tomatoes of the year,
even go outside to admire the sharp
border lawn boys carved yesterday.
Then listen again for the owls.
This is what I wanted you to know.
Maybe we'll get lucky. Maybe we were.

—*from* "Field Report"

Our leisure meal complete, the table cleared, and only an ounce, or two, of brandy to close these last late moments together, we need not speak of *cou de canard farci au foie gras* (viz., the can of duck neck stuffed with foie gras I brought back from a previous trip to the Périgord that sat on the shelf like a reproach, and the effort, expense, and lavish ingredients—Madeira, veal stock, a black truffle, more foie gras—all in ruined attempt at a proper *sauce Périgueux* to accompany the neck). Hubris. Nor need we dwell, for example, on lamb tongues bought in the glowing hum of the Mercat de la Boqueria and carried in butcher paper to boil as a surprise for my artist friends—since beef tongue, sliced warm on rye bread spread with spicy mustard, was a family favorite in Kentucky and a tradition I've continued—at Can Serrat, in the village of El Bruc, that summer Ghost haunted me ceaselessly. (The hour on the hot bus from Barcelona did the small, silent tongues no good.)

Moreover, let us not reprimand regarding a haunch of goat, impulsive gift from my wife as she passed the *carnicería* on the way home from the airport, nor lament my two spent days attempting to tenderize and braise the grotesque flesh. (One bite and our shared expression told the tale. The stringy appendage went whole into the bin.) More specifically to this book, many small obstacles, admitted failures: a surprising and incredibly delicious sweet tomato *tatin*, cooked in my championed cast-iron skillet, that I could never get to not stick tenaciously—simply, repeatedly could *not*—so that one's efforts and enjoyment were torn to bits even before the first taste of vanilla-scented Roma tomato and crusted pastry. Or the amusement of "roasting" green coffee beans stovetop in a hot wok, the kitchen filling with smoke and the gentle, floating chaff of the beans.

But what of other, inexplicable omissions? Why no proper chapter on the tagine, its quirky, drooping hat and exotic tastes: no fish stew with white wine, almonds, and sting of fresh tarragon; no chicken infused with lemon and green olives; no lamb with turmeric, dates, and pistachios. What kind of book can it be without a risotto rich with the fall flavors and bright hues of butternut squash, leeks, and sage; no braised leg of spring lamb, young fingerling potatoes roasted in the juices; no stuffed squash blossoms; no red snapper with mussels and chorizo, adapted from M. Jacques Pépin (do not try to scale and clean your own snapper, at risk of injury; that's what the fish lad was hired for); no lemon and pepper fettuccini rolled soft and submissive beneath the hands; no potatoes baked twice in their skins with butter and Roquefort, tops bronzed and bubbling with Parmesan and pale Welsh cheddar; no hot and blood-red borsht with sour cream and dill and heavy black bread our friends served us before beef Stroganoff each Christmas Eve until they couldn't; no chicken breast stuffed with haggis in a heavy cream and whisky sauce, "simple pub food" from Edinburgh still vivid and thrilling in memory after a decade.

How to explain, that is, the absence of grilled duck breasts with reduction of blueberries grown in the garden and harvested throughout July, or anyway whatever berries could be wrested from the beaks of robins and cardinals, who know their own hunger; also no ostrich on the grill, venison loin or chops; no signature coconut shrimp, each plump and enormous on a garnished platter that guests applauded; no roasted marrow bones attacked with a small fork, with hot bread to spread the gelatinous pudding (and also marrow bone butter, that pure white excess of pleasure); no standing roast, ribbed in fat and warm with its own blood, served with airy Yorkshire puddings lathered with lemon and strawberry butters; no squab and far few game birds; no bacon-wrapped scallops or smoked salmon omelets with eggs laid the same morning and whatever herbs smelled sweetest in the garden; no chocolate polenta pudding cake; in fact, not nearly chocolate enough, not enough to solace or to comfort; no yielding swirls of crisp meringue topped with local May strawberries picked down the road.

There should be all of that here, and there should my mother's meat loaf, even better the next day, a thick, cold slab on white bread, lathered with ketchup and heavily salted and peppered; her rich pies from scratch—chocolate and lemon and butterscotch—and banana pudding; my father's chop suey, his breaded and fried salt pork, his dried beef gravy, and most of all his chocolate fudge announced spontaneously and like none ever tasted since (he knew unerringly, from the character and rhythm of the bubbles in the pot, when the confection was ready, a magic he tried and failed to teach me); and other foods of my youth: fried catfish, back bones or pig feet—as reported, Grandma Brewer knew the latter was my favorite—slow-cooked with sauerkraut and halved onions in the Crock Pot; crackling cornbread eaten steaming out of the skillet; sweet tea brewed in the sun; and in the further pleasures of adulthood, there should be my wife's lamb burgers, god yes there should be, wrapped in prosciutto, browned in a skillet and served on a bed of local greens, topped with an spoonful of sun-dried tomatoes oozing olive oil (we keep these burgers in the freezer at all times for emergencies). There should be lofting odes to baked foie gras egg cups with white wine, to the "hot mess" of stout-braised short ribs, to mushroom and cream *vol au vent*, to custard tarts with berries both scavenged and from the summer garden, to grilled lobsters with lemon-basil butter; and speaking again of basil, sweet basil, explain how there can be no pesto, rendered with melancholy from the last good leaves of the year (and almost no mention of pine nuts, their pearls of delicate magic) or else pesto hijacked with cilantro, mint, lime, and cayenne, a heresy that burns the lips with its kiss.

And what of the tastes, tests, and follies remaining? More rudimentary cheesemaking. A sausage attachment for the Cuisinart. A proper smoker. A rotisserie for the next grill. Plans and dreams. Absurd indulgences. Exquisite waste. A proper book would contain all these things, accommodate all our hunger and thirst and desire, those words arrived in our hands and sung in mouths and bodies, contain as well our regret and joy, our gains and losses, our gratitude even as the days, seasons, years pass into darkness. There's more to savor and what remains of our lives to seek it out. Next time, we'll do the rest, do what was missed and neglected, do what was overlooked and do it all better. In our sequel we'll account for what remains and every result will be perfect, just as planned. For now, though, it's late. Relax. Our work is done. The night vibrates behind a cooling breeze. If you will, indulge me with your company for one more sip. We raise our glasses to this moment together that will not return, and cheers to you.

ACKNOWLEDGMENTS

When I hold the sandwich in place
and press the blade, what comes

is a mess. Reader, I took the sandwich
upstairs. Trees undulated, clouds
came and went. The napkin
did no good. That yolk all over me,
I ate it all and licked my fingers clean.

—*from* "More Honored in the Breach:
Food Porn (or, My Sandwich)"

Thanks to John T Edge, Martha Hopkins, and Paulette Licitra, not only for generous endorsement but for their support and enthusiasm for this unorthodox project. I'm also grateful to Paulette for introducing me—through her lovely journal *Alimentum*—to the illustrations of James Dankert. When I contacted the artist about the possibility of sketches to accent the end of each chapter, Jim happily jumped on board and in short order supplied, pro bono, 32 delightful drawings. I owe him drinks and a meal. Another artist and long-time friend, Billy Renkl, helped me think about the cover of the book, what might or might not work, and also caused me, at the 11th hour, to rethink the title. (His adamantly offered alternative of *Meat Pray Love*, however, didn't make the cut. Sorry, Billy. I was tempted.) Thanks to the poet Mark Sanders for suggesting I show the manuscript to Stephen F. Austin State University Press, as they were up for "everything." Thanks to Claudia Barnett for invaluable proofreading assistance, being dragged into the test kitchen more often than she'd probably have liked, and for many splendid meals reciprocated. I'd be remiss not to also thank my parents, Gail and Harvey Brewer, for teaching me more than a few culinary tricks, for fattening up their boy with a lifetime's worth of fine Southern fare, and for many, many enjoyed hours at the table.

As I mentioned in the Foreword, an early version of the recipe and accompanying text of rabbit salmorejo appeared in the *River Styx* 76/77, the journal's "A Readable Feast" issue, edited by Richard Newman, and suggested to me early on the potential of pairing recipes with anecdotal prose. An abbreviated version of my Martini recipe appeared in the multimedia anthology *Language Lessons: Vol. 1* (Nashville: Third Man Records, 2014), edited by Chet Weise. The excerpted poems throughout initially appeared in journals but were subsequently subsumed in the books listed in Food & Literary Sources. Exceptions are the most recent "Breach" poems, written during a summer 2014 stay at ARTErra in rural Portugal. (Delicious *caracóis*—tiny snails served in butter sauce and speared from the shell with a toothpick. Or you can suck them out.) The two excerpted here appeared in the *Atlanta Review* and the *Baltimore Review.*

Finally, I'd like to thank the foie gras flan I mastered after this book was already into page proofs. You made us very happy.

Food & Literary Sources

Then the pillow is hot, your body moans
in odd places and the mind wanders
where it shouldn't. That's the eating that kills.

—*from* "Changing the Way You Eat"

americanfood.about.com

Amis, Kingsley. *Everyday Drinking*. New York: Bloomsbury, 2008.

Aris, Pepita. *Spanish: Over 150 Mouthwatering Step-by-Step Recipes*. London: Hermes House, 2003.

Best of . . . Fine Dining Tables. Food Network. Television.

Boeckmann, Susie, & Natalie Rebeiz-Nielsen. *Caviar: A True Delicacy*. New York: Macmillan, 1995.

Bowen, Dana. Review of Joseph E. Dabney's *The Food, Folklore, and Art of Lowcountry Cooking*. *Saveur* #134, 28-30.

"A Burger with (Homemade) Everything." *Gourmet* June 2009: 38-41.

Butler, Paula. *Standing Stone Farms: Guide to Cheese Making*. Proprietor-published pamphlet.

"Butter'em Up!" *Tennessee Magazine* Dec. 2011: 26-27.

Chelminski, Rudolph. *The Perfectionist: Life and Death in Haute Cuisine*. New York: Gotham, 2005.

Child, Julia. *The Way to Cook*. New York: Knopf, 1989.

Clark, Melissa. "A Good Appetite: Custards that Put Pudding to Shame." *New York Times*, 29 Feb. 2012: D2.

Clemonts, Carole, & Elizabeth Wolf-Cohen. *The Best Ever French Cooking Course*. New York: Hermes House, 1999.

cooks.com

Daguin, André, & Anne De Ravel. *Foie Gras, Magret, and Other Good Foods from Gascony.* New York: Random House, 1998.

Daguin, Ariane, George Faison, & Joanne Pruess. *D'Artagnan's Glorious Game Cookbook.* Boston: Little, Brown, 1999.

Day, Cheryl, & Griffith Day. *The Back in the Day Bakery Cookbook.* New York: Artisan Books, 2012.

Deen, Paula. *It Ain't All about the Cookin'.* New York: Simon & Schuster, 2007.

De Mane, Erica. finecooking.com

Donnelly, Kristin. "Learning to Love Austrian Food." *Food & Wine* May 2011.

Dupree, Nathalie, & Cynthia Graubert. *Mastering the Art of Southern Cooking.* Layton, UT: Gibbs Smith, 2012.

Edge, John T. *Fried Chicken: An American Story.* New York: G. P. Putman's Sons, 2004.

Edmunds, Lowell. *Martini, Straight Up: The Classic American Cocktail.* Baltimore: Johns Hopkins UP, 1981.

Emerson, Brett. inpraiseofsardines.typepad.com

"Every Day Quick Kitchen." *Gourmet* Dec. 2008: 24.

501 Must-Taste Cocktails. London: Bounty, 2007.

Florence, Tyler. "Amazing Artichoke in Lakewood, CO." *Food 911.* Food Network, 2001. Television.

Greenspan, Dorie. *Waffles: From Morning to Midnight.* San Francisco: Weldon Owen, 2001.

Jacobi, Dana. *The Best of Clay Pot Cooking.* San Francisco: Collins, 1995.

Jeffers, Garth. "A Window into the Jeffers Social Life: Recollections." *Robinson Jeffers Newsletter* 100 (Fall 1996): 8-11.

Justus, Jennifer. "From Field to Table." *The Tennessean* 18 March 2012: D1, 5-6.

Kasper, Lynn Rossetto. splendidtable.publicradio.org/

Keller, Thomas. "At Home." *Food & Wine* Oct. 2007.

Knauer, Ian. "Recipe + Menus: Tomato Tatin." *Bon Appétit* Aug. 2010.

Knox, Gerald M., ed. *Better Homes and Gardens New Cookbook*. Des Moines, IA: Meredith, 1989.

Lacalamita, Tom. *Deep Fryer Tips for Dummies*. New York: Hungry Minds, 2001.

Lagasse, Emeril. *The Essence of Emeril*. Television.

Lawson, Nigella. www.nigella.com

Long, Dixon, Ruthanne Long, & David Wakely. *Markets of Provence: A Culinary Tour of Southern France*. San Francisco: Collins Putnam, 1996.

McKee, Gwen, & Barbara Moseley, eds. *Best of the Best from Kentucky: Selected Recipes from Kentucky's Favorite Cookbooks*. Brandon, MS: Quail Ridge Press, 1988.

Mr. Boston Official Bartender's Guide. 50th anniversary edition. New York: Warner Books, 1984.

myrecipes.com

Nathan, Joan. *Quiches, Kugels, and Couscous: My Search for Jewish Cooking in America*. New York: Knopf, 2010.

Parisi, Grace. "Fast Make-Ahead: Quick Coconut Lamb Curry." *Food & Wine* May 2004.

"Party Planner 04. Dessert." *Food & Wine* Dec. 2002.

Pépin, Jacques. "Le Fast Food." *Food & Wine* Sept. 2004: 73-75.

Peterson, James. *The Duck Cookbook*. New York: Stewart, Tabori, and Chang, 2003.

Rabbit: An International Delicacy. Roger, AR: Pel-Freez Rabbit Meats.

recipecircus.com

Romanelli, Leonardo, & Gabriella Ganugi. *Olive Oil: An Italian Pantry.* San Francisco: Wine Appreciation Guild, 2004.

Ronco Food Dehydrator: Instructions & Recipes. Beverly Hills: Ronco Inventions, 1998.

simplyrecipes.com

Stewart, Martha. marthastewart.com/everydayfood

Stryjewski, Stephen. "Slow Food Fast: Panéed Rabbit with Citrus, Sage and Caper-Butter Sauce." *Wall Street Journal* Nov. 5, 2011.

whatscookingamerica.com

"What to Cook Next." *Food & Wine* March 2012: 82.

Ying, Mildred. *The New Good Housekeeping Cookbook.* New York: Hearst Books, 1986.

•

Excerpted verses come randomly from the following books of my poems. (As noted in the Foreword, my comic novella *Octavius the 1ˢᵗ* [Los Angeles: Red Hen Press, 2008] also contains an inordinate amount of obsessive cooking and eating.)

Brewer, Gaylord. *Barbaric Mercies.* Los Angeles: Red Hen, 2003.

_____. *Country of Ghost.* Pasadena: Red Hen, 2015.

_____. *Devilfish.* Los Angeles: Red Hen, 1999.

_____. *Exit Pursued by a Bear.* Cincinnati: Cherry Grove, 2004.

_____. *Four Nails.* Cambridge, NY: Snail's Pace, 2001.

_____. *Give Over, Graymalkin.* Pasadena: Red Hen, 2011.

_____. *Let Me Explain.* Oak Ridge, TN: Iris, 2006.

_____. *The Martini Diet*. Aptos, CA: Dream Horse, 2008.

.

Those interested in further poems on these general subjects might enjoy the wide-ranging peculiarities to be found in:

Washington, Peter, ed. *Eat, Drink, and Be Merry: Poems about Food and Drink*. Everyman's Library Pocket Poets. New York: Alfred A. Knopf, 2003.

.

For an international, multigenre range of the pithy, curmudgeonly, and dubiously profound ("If you think you are a mushroom, jump into the basket."—Russian Proverb), here's a secret weapon I've often turned to, now revealed:

Rowinski, Kate. *The Quotable Cook*. New York: Lyons, 2000.

.

Countless poets have composed fine verses on the inexhaustible topics of food and drink, but no book of mine would be complete without a deferential nod to Pablo Neruda, and no poet's guide to food, drink, and desire worth its sea salt can fail to remind the reader of Neruda's delightful and utterly enchanting odes. Mitchell's selection below includes sure translations of the master's *odas* to the artichoke, the onion, the tomato, wine, salt, the lemon, and the watermelon. It's a good, inviting place to begin, or renew, your exploration of Neruda's vast and various oeuvre.

Neruda, Pablo. *Full Woman, Fleshly Apple, Hot Moon: Selected Poems of Pablo Neruda*. Trans. Stephen Mitchell. New York: Harper Collins, 1997.

.

Penguin has selected and edited a series of quirky, entertaining, and attractive little books in its Great Food series, my favorites including Alexander Dumas' amusing, arrogant expertise in *From Absinthe to Zest: An Alphabet for Food Lovers*; the gossipy revels of Samuel Pepys' *The Joys of Excess* (excerpted from his years of diaries in such a way as to give a wonderfully debouched emphasis on social meals and libations); and Charles Lamb's purposely cheeky *A Dissertation upon Roast Pig and Other Essays*. They're fun books to hold in your hand, to be seen reading at the bus stop or while waiting for an oil change, and volumes generally run 100 pages or less. The whole series is worth reading and looks charming on the bookshelf.

Additional recent reads of note: Bob Shacochis' *Domesticity: A Gastronomic Interpretation of Love* is a 1994 collection of the author's food articles written for *GQ*. Although I didn't discover the volume until after the completion of the book in your hands, the former is—in spirit if not in style—a sort of kissing cousin predecessor to this project. Well, not quite, but you might take a look. Meanwhile, the enthusiastic science—especially regarding yeast and fermentation—in Michael Pollan's touted *Cooked* is impressive, if sometimes daunting. His "fire" recipe for smoking a Boston butt on a gas grill is entertaining to try, with an addictive result, although expect to double (or triple) the suggested slow-cooking time. Just as I was completing the last revisions of this manuscript, I enjoyed Luke Barr's *Provence, 1970*, an engaging and ultimately touching account of M. F. K. Fisher, Julia Child, and others in a historical culinary moment in the South of France; and Dana Goodyear's perverse *Anything That Moves*, regarding renegade chefs and the outré foodies who deify them. I'll try anything in the latter except the insects and the *balut*. (Ms. Goodyear makes a compelling case that insects, ever plentiful, will be the sustainable protein of the future. Luckily, I'll be dead.)

.

Finally, this coffee table recommendation: *The New Intercourses: An Aphrodisiac Cookbook*. Martha Hopkins was kind enough to send me a copy of the 10th anniversary edition of her gorgeous, witty, and sexy book. It's hard to say what's best: the delicious recipes, the racy testimonials, or the sensually eye-popping photographs, which you'll want to linger over. If you find the book unsuitable for your coffee table (because you'll not want anyone else fingering your private copy), you can always hide it under the bed.

Hopkins, Martha, & Randall Lockridge. *The New Intercourses: An Aphrodisiac Cookbook*. Austin: Terrace, 2007.

.

Last note: I went back and forth on the notion of suggestions for product sourcing. My affection for D'Artagnan's raw and prepared foie gras is probably apparent in this book, JR Mushrooms is a good company, La Tienda is excellent for blood sausage and all comestibles Spanish, and variously and anecdotally

I mention a buttermilk dairy, a goat meat producer, a spice shop, et cetera. Otherwise, factoring in the vagaries of businesses coming and going along with the importance of local sourcing, I decided to leave the reader largely to his or her own ingenuity and resources. (I opted differently in the mention of specific restaurants, as these are fixed moments for me, regardless of any establishment's current status.) Obviously, you need to track down your best seasonal farmers market and a reliable source for fresh local eggs, honey, corn meal, and occasionally butter, and to buy the freshest meat and seafood you can afford for special meals, preferably from a reliable butcher or, again, local meat farmer.

Of course, there's one specific company I must report by name: When you're ready for that morel mushroom spore, look no further than GMHP Gourmet and Mushroom Products, Graton, CA. They'll set you right up (and leave you wanting more).

Index of Recipes

About the Author

Gaylord Brewer is a native of Louisville, Kentucky, and earned a Ph.D. from Ohio State University. He is currently a professor at Middle Tennessee State University, where he founded and for more than twenty years edited the journal *Poems & Plays*. The most recent of his nine books of poetry are *Give Over, Graymalkin* (2011) and *Country of Ghost* (2015), both from Red Hen Press. He has published 900 poems in journals and anthologies, including *Best American Poetry* and *The Bedford Introduction to Literature*.